Praise for *How to Get What You Want*

"In *How to Get What You Want*, Joshua Bandoch blends neuroscience and psychology with practical tools to help anyone sharpen their skills of persuasion. It's a terrific guide to communicating with clarity and confidence and, ultimately, making an impact on the world."

—Carmine Gallo, Harvard instructor and bestselling author of *Talk Like TED* and the audio original *Viral Voices*

"Wise philosophers and brilliant investigators have taught us much about persuasion, from Aristotle to social psychology to neuroscience. And Josh Bandoch synthesizes this wisdom and delivers to us a book filled with practical advice. This book is about more than getting what you want; it's about how to lead a more effective life at work and at home. Josh grounds his observations and suggestions in serious scholarship and science in a way that is readily accessible and easily put into practice. *How to Get What You Want* will be enjoyed by people everywhere who would like to hone their abilities to persuade others—ethically, mindfully, and effectively."

—Peter Salovey, president emeritus and Sterling professor of psychology at Yale University

"*How to Get What You Want* is written with heart and humor and reminds us that true influence always starts with empathy—a powerful message for a noisy age."

—Caroline Goyder, author of *Gravitas* and *Find Your Voice*

"*How to Get What You Want* not only offers the reader valuable information, but also practical applications that can be immediately implemented to improve personal and organizational effectiveness. Josh provides easy-to-follow insights on how to leverage the art and science of persuasion to fully understand the human dimensions of decision-making in order to build teams, align efforts, and get things done. I highly recommend this book to leaders at all levels who are interested in unleashing the potential of what is truly our greatest asset—our people!"

—Robert D. Sharp, United States Navy vice admiral (ret.) and former director of the National Geospatial-Intelligence Agency

"Persuasion isn't about winning—it's about creating shared action. Drawing on neuroscience and psychology, using real-world examples and years of practical policy and communications leadership, Joshua Bandoch reveals a transformative approach to getting what you want while building trust, connection, and influence that lasts. *How to Get What You Want* turns everyday conversations into opportunities for impact."

—Joe Ross, chief strategy officer at Ideas on Stage

HOW TO GET WHAT YOU WANT

Mastering the Art and Science of Persuasion

JOSHUA BANDOCH

BENBELLA

BenBella Books, Inc.
Dallas, TX

This book is designed to provide accurate and authoritative information about negotiation and persuasion. Neither the author nor the publisher is engaged in rendering legal, accounting, or other professional services by publishing this book. If any such assistance is required, the services of qualified professionals should be sought. The author and publisher will not be responsible for any liability, loss, or risk incurred as a result of the use and application of any information contained in this book.

BENBELLA

BenBella Books, Inc.
8080 N. Central Expressway
Suite 1700
Dallas, TX 75206
benbellabooks.com
Send feedback to feedback@benbellabooks.com

BenBella is a federally registered trademark.

Printed in the United States of America
10 9 8 7 6 5 4 3 2 1

Library of Congress Control Number: 2025046766
ISBN 9781637748305 (hardcover)
ISBN 9781637748312 (electronic)

Editing by Stephanie Gorton and Claire Schulz
Copyediting by Evan Herrington
Proofreading by Karen Wise and Natalie Roth
Indexing by WordCo Indexing Services
Text design and composition by Jordan Koluch
Cover design by Tom McKeveny
Cover image © Shutterstock / Srgr
Printed by Lake Book Manufacturing

To Kent Lawrence, for always believing in me.

Contents

PART 3: APPLY TESTED TECHNIQUES TO ANY SITUATION

INTRODUCTION

When was the last time you felt like you said all the right things, and you just couldn't persuade someone? Take a moment to remember it. This morning? Last night? It probably hasn't even been 24 hours.

Maybe your boss tuned out your great idea. Your friend is upset with you for sharing a different take on today's headline. Or your spouse wouldn't support the change you know your family needs.

You made all the right arguments with all the right facts. But they just . . . wouldn't . . . listen. It was worse than talking to a brick wall! This happens all the time—at work, in politics, and in our personal lives. And yet we rinse and repeat. One definition of insanity is doing the same thing over and over again expecting a different result. But here we are, all a little crazy.

We're stuck in a weird trap that makes it hard, often impossible, to get what we want. We follow our instincts, and it doesn't yield the desired result. There are a few big reasons for this. Our own perspectives and interests don't always match up with others'. Communication is hard—never mind persuasion.

More than that, persuasion doesn't work the way we think it does, which causes us to make some crucial mistakes. That's because our brains aren't wired to persuade. And society teaches us lots of bad habits that make it even harder to get what we want. We've got a lot working against us.

Let's start with the two most common misconceptions that stop us from persuading others, including our friends, parents, colleagues, and spouses: that persuasion is about winning, and that logic is the key to getting what you want.

A few summers ago, I struck up a conversation with a spunky new intern. I asked him why he was attending law school, and why he was spending his summer with our think tank. His response? "I like winning!"

Hmm. If I win against you in any personal or professional context, what does that make you? A loser! When someone makes you feel like a loser, do you have any desire to work with them? Nope. You just want to pay them back, preferably in spades. If you "win" against your spouse, you even wake up next to a loser—until you're sleeping on the couch, honey. That's the first mistake: that persuasion is about making someone else a loser.

This all-too-common assumption quickly surfaces in the persuasion workshops I teach. I begin by asking participants to define "persuasion." The most popular response is that persuasion is about "convincing" someone to think like you. Well. The word "convince" comes from the Latin *vincere*, meaning to "vanquish" or "conquer." Conquest is barbaric, not persuasive.

The second mistake is that we think persuasion is a battle of reason: Lock and load your logic, aim at your opponent, and fire away. So we launch our logic at people, hoping it'll knock something loose.

Totally unrelated question: Has anyone ever changed your mind this way?

We tend to think persuasion is about defeating wicked people and their bad ideas. Doing our best impression of Buffy the Vampire Slayer, we try to drive a stake right through them.

Sure, some things—on the scale of, say, the Soviet Gulag—need a stake through the heart. Now: Are you *usually* talking to Joseph Stalin? Luckily not! Besides, we're all wrong every day. I sure am. Why try to slay someone just for being human?

Society doesn't just reinforce the idea of conquest—it *teaches* it to us and ingrains it in our daily lives.

Our educational institutions hold up argument and debate as the pathways to persuasion. K-12 teachers and professors instruct students to "prove" they're "right." It starts early. A Miami news station did a segment on an elementary school preparing for a debate competition in Broward County in 2024. Their shirts said, "We talk, you listen."[1]

Once you get to college, the academic peer review process embraced by your professors is viewed as the gold standard. It works like this: Do an abundance of research, gather data and logic, and "prove" your interpretation is right. When I was an academic, I experienced it firsthand, because I published my work and was a journal editor.

I can assure you: Outside science, technology, engineering, and mathematics (STEM) fields, which are about measurable quantities like microbes and energy, this process usually fails to yield consensus. Quite the opposite: Despite the volumes of research that go into each published paper, academics fiercely disagree about what's "right." And reviewers sure let authors know it!

In political discussions, it's now normal to dismiss people who don't think like us as crazy, stupid, evil, or all of the above. Last summer, I played tennis with someone on my tennis team for the first time. After finishing two sets, he asked me what I do. I said that I research poverty. He literally responded, "Then you can't possibly be a Republican." That's toxic, because it flattens everyone involved: myself, my organization, and Republicans. And it'd be equally toxic if he had said "Democrat" instead.

It's no surprise, then, that in a recent study on polarization in twelve countries, including Germany and the UK, since the 1980s, the United States is where polarization increased the most.[2] In a 2023 survey from Pew Research Center, when asked to describe U.S. politics these days, only 2 percent of respondents offered a positive word. Seventy-nine percent responded with a negative one. One of the top responses was actually "dumpster fire."[3] In an environment like this, constructive conversation, let alone agreement and persuasion, feels impossible. Cross-party friendship? Not a chance. So why even bother?

We're forgetting, or never even learning, how to connect with others. Even our own kids. A few months ago, I was on the subway. A dad came in with his little girl—about eighteen months old. He sat down and immediately shoved a screen in her hands to distract her so he could bury his head in his phone. Daddy?

Technology gets better at sucking us in by the day. In 2023, Americans spent an average of four hours and thirty minutes on their smartphones, checking them 144 times per day.[4] That's nine times per hour, assuming you don't sleep with your phone, which 66 percent of Americans admit to doing.[5]

This all leaves us culturally, socially, and personally divided from others. This book offers you an escape hatch from this mess. By understanding what persuasion really is and how it works, you can reconnect with others and get more of what you want and need in your personal and professional lives.

You might want to be able to explain yourself better or communicate your ideas more powerfully. Perhaps you're trying to learn how to interact with your higher-ups more effectively. Maybe you're learning to manage—up with your boss, down to your direct reports, and across with peers—which all have different dynamics. You need to push through your barriers the right way to keep growing. Each level presents new challenges, sometimes quite different from the last one.

You'll learn to navigate these and other situations. You'll help create a more functional society. You'll be happier along the way, too.

So: What *is* persuasion? Persuasion is shared action. Shared, because it's something we voluntarily do together with others. And it's action, because it's about getting things done, not about speaking pretty words.

By embracing this understanding of persuasion, you can become a persuasion genius. A persuasion genius is someone who knows how to get what they want and need the right way in just about any situation, especially when it matters most. Whether the stakes are low, like scoring a free room upgrade at hotel check-in, or high, like negotiating a job offer or promotion, persuasion geniuses adopt Bruce Lee's mantra: "To hell with circumstances; I create opportunities."

What opportunities, exactly? The ones where you can get what you want and need. When an opportunity is in front of you, you'll learn how to seize it rather than missing it. If you're in a meeting with the CEO, you'll be ready to impress everyone in the room by raising your hand and speaking persuasively, instead of being reluctant to put yourself out there. You'll learn to *create* opportunities, too, like when you identify ways to partner with someone you never thought you could work with. You'll also be preparing for the next opportunities before they present themselves.

There's more to it, though. Being a persuasion genius will bring you joy by engaging others authentically, which is a great way to grow relationships. You'll prioritize genuine communication and connection over division and defensiveness. You'll learn to finally make the difference you care about. You'll also learn when persuasion isn't possible. Although it's almost always worth trying to work with someone, sometimes it just won't happen.

Persuasion has three simple steps: First, adopt the "persuader's mindset." Second, use knowledge of how our brains work to your advantage. Third, apply tested techniques to any situation.

It's not easy, though, because in an odd twist of fate, we're not wired to persuade others. Instead, some key parts of our brain that helped our ancestors survive and avoid threats make it hard for you to get what you want. The brain seeks self-preservation and affirmation, which, oddly enough, can prompt us to push other people away. That's why everything in this book is grounded in the best neuroscience and psychology available today. How can you persuade people if you don't know how our minds really work, and how to navigate complex interactions? This isn't a trick question: You can't.

Consider just two of many facts about the brain we'll discuss throughout the book.

We're wired to think primarily about ourselves. What's in it for *me*? While understandable, this often prevents us from thinking about the person we're trying to persuade. Small oversight. So we mostly just end up persuading ourselves more, which we're great at, while leaving the person sitting across from us unmoved.

While we like to launch our "logic" at people to try to persuade them, we're actually wired to *feel* first. That's why we need to put the emotions of others (and ourselves) front and center—before logic—and tend to them carefully.

The trick, as you'll come to learn, is to observe, accept, and work within the contours of these cognitive realities rather than judge or fight them.

A few pages in, you're wondering: What am I going to learn? Does it work? And what makes you the person to teach me?

Short answer: You'll gain a fresh approach to persuasion fusing groundbreaking research and practical experience together to get you what you want and need, especially when it matters most.

I've spent more than a decade understanding the foundational aspects of what persuasion is and how it happens. As a researcher who trained and taught at elite universities, I rigorously surveyed massive amounts of literature. Then I figured out how to make my conclusions actionable. That's a step academics generally neglect to take, which is the biggest reason I left academia. Still, I love the academic peer review process for its rigor, so all these chapters have been peer-reviewed by experts in their fields to ensure accuracy.

Do the recommendations in this book work? Yes, because I've road-tested them. As a speechwriter, I helped craft and communicate Department of Defense policy, brought airmen to tears, and gave senior government leaders the right words to navigate the COVID-19 pandemic successfully. I've helped senior government leaders present persuasively to every audience imaginable, including the president and Congress, business and industry executives, trade associations, top media outlets such as *The Washington Post* and *The Wall Street Journal*, elite universities like Harvard, K-12 and university students, the intelligence community, scientists, and uniformed servicemen and servicewomen.

I test, apply, and enhance these persuasion strategies and techniques on a daily basis as the head of policy at a prominent think tank. My team and I use these techniques to advance the exact same policy recommendations on issues like poverty and housing to conservatives and progressives alike. We don't insist on being "right." Our goal is to make a difference. So we frame issues for our audiences, not for ourselves. This allows us to persuade elected officials, the media, grassroots activists, and anyone else we engage regardless of their politics.

I regularly speak to diverse audiences as a keynote speaker and public policy leader, including TEDx Talks, legislative testimony, panels at national and international events, radio, and podcasts. As a consultant, I teach these tactics to a wide range of professionals in fields like fundraising, journalism, marketing, politics, public policy, and political campaigns through workshops and one-on-one training.

The techniques in this book have not only transformed my life and let me excel at work. They've helped people I care about in their professional and personal lives, too. They've helped my mom and wife overcome their fear of advocating for themselves, find their professional voices, and get the raises and promotions they deserve—the ones their bosses said weren't even on the table.

You'll learn how to get more out of low-stakes situations, too. Here are a few recent examples: On a family trip that involved air travel delays, I got us into a nice airport lounge right away when there was a long line. After stupidly knocking a continuous blood glucose monitor I bought off my arm, I got the company to send me a replacement for free, which otherwise would have cost me fifty dollars. It's fun to get free stuff.

More importantly, these low-stakes situations are also where you train for high-stakes opportunities. As the Greek poet Archilochus said, "We don't rise to the level of our expectations; we fall to the level of our training."

You'll learn what words and deeds make your audience feel good and generate the desired result consistently. Two key elements are the formula for persuasive storytelling and why fighting your neural wiring to be negative will help separate you from the pack.

Persuasion can be learned by anyone who commits to doing so. I've taught fundraisers, students, executives, interns, people working in sales, scientists, doctors, professors, researchers, friends, and family members to become persuasion geniuses. While there's no silver bullet that guarantees you will get what you want all the time, what we do know about the art and science of persuasion is powerful—that's where this book comes in. It requires practice and a growth mindset, too—that's where you come in.

It's true that some people start with a natural leg up. When I was conducting dissertation research in Bordeaux, I lived with a host family. My Parisian (not French, he insisted!) host father, Pascal, was a radio journalist with a majestic voice. Whenever he talked, you just melted from the pleasant experience of hearing his voice. His tone was naturally appealing. Lucky him!

Mostly, though, you master skills through intentional practice. That's true even for elite persuaders; it's what distinguishes them from people content with mediocrity.

Once someone I managed was giving a panel presentation at a big conference and I asked if she wanted to practice. Her response? "No, I don't need to practice. I've done this before." To which I responded, "Ronald Reagan and Barack Obama practiced speeches. It showed. George H. W. Bush didn't. It showed. You pick who you'd like to emulate." This person chose not to practice, and it showed. Steve Jobs started practicing presentations months ahead of time. That showed, too. You pick.

As you practice, treat what follows as a process that you'll need to individualize. It takes time to get good, let alone great, at something. So if things don't go perfectly the first time, don't be too hard on yourself. Perhaps you're already good at some of the things we discuss, like having confident body language or communicating clearly. You'll get even better at them. And you'll learn to pay special attention to areas where you're not as strong.

Here's a bold claim: This book offers a comprehensive treatment of persuasion. Just to make sure I'm not missing anything, I've consulted dozens of executives and elite communications professionals. They agree: This book is comprehensive.

The book's nine chapters are broken into three parts. Part 1 (chapters 1 and 2) lays the foundation for knowing how to get what you want in any situation by training you to frame things properly.

We're wired to focus on ourselves, which is why we tend to talk in terms we find persuasive. The only problem with this me-first mindset is that it's an antipersuasion approach. In chapter 1, you learn to **put them first**. This requires you to do a cognitive 180, since we're wired to focus on ourselves. A them-first mindset maximizes your chances of persuasion because it's the best way to connect with your audience, and because it points the way to sharing action and getting what you want.

A compelling vision that resonates with and motivates an audience is persuasive. You learn to **animate action with vision**. Without a vision, you're rudderless, lacking direction and purpose. With one, you have a target at which to aim and the motivation to hit it. Steve Jobs had vision, and he used it to "put a dent in the universe." You need it, too, if you want to make a difference. In chapter 2, you learn how to craft and enact a persuasive vision that leads to shared action and the achievement of shared goals.

Part 2 (chapters 3, 4, 5, and 6) observes that persuasion requires you to understand how the human mind actually works to be able to navigate it effectively. Neuroscience and psychology reveal that our minds don't work how we assume they do. Initially, you might reject some of these realities. Learning to accept and embrace them is liberating, though, and makes you far more effective in your attempts to persuade anyone but yourself. We focus on the four most important realities of the human mind for getting what you want, and how to use them to your advantage. These realities offer insights on how our brains tend to work in general, not necessarily in every instance.

For most people, the default mode of attempting to persuade is to use "logic" (the more, the better) to "win" an argument with your audience. This approach even *feels* oh so good. There are just two tiny problems with it. It's counterproductive, because it makes your audience feel like a loser. And it ignores the cognitive reality that we feel first, then reason. Which means you need to **start with feelings**, not "logic." Chapter 3 makes these neurological insights actionable for persuasion. You get an innovative step-by-step approach called the Emotionally Intelligent Persuasion Model for *how* to engage anyone and generate feelings that help you get what you want.

Chapter 4 focuses on another complication: Our brains aren't wired to generate persuasive feelings. We're wired to be negative, which is why our media landscape values the dark and outrageous above all else. There's just one problem with negativity: It's counterproductive. Instead, we need to generate positive feelings and **be *for* something** so we can advocate for things the right way.

However, what lifts people up, or brings them down, differs based on their values. That's why chapter 5 focuses on identifying which moral appeals drive shared action. It turns out that morality works a lot like your tongue. Just as your tongue has physical receptors that shape how you experience food (salty, savory, etc.), moral psychology reveals morality has flavors, too. To spice things up further, people of different political ideologies (conservatives, leftists, and libertarians) have distinct moral tastes. You need to learn to **activate their moral tastes**, even if your audience's morals are sharply different from yours.

The human mind is a story processor before it's a logic processor. That's why persuasion geniuses are phenomenal storytellers. What *kinds* of stories, specifically? Chapter 6 reveals a secret persuasion tool more powerful than any other: **Tell emotionally intelligent, morally motivating stories.** You learn how to craft persuasive stories for any audience. To see what this looks like in action, I walk you step-by-step through a case study of a Medal of Honor speech I wrote. The speech was widely lauded across the service as a true Air Force "moment."

Part 3 (chapters 7, 8, and 9) offers practical techniques to *maximize* your chances of success.

High-stakes negotiators are among the most persuasive people because they usually have no-fail missions, whether in law enforcement, business, or diplomacy. Chapter 7 brings proven negotiation techniques to help you **negotiate what you want**. You learn how techniques like focusing on losses and identifying barriers help you navigate situations with enhanced emotional intelligence and increase your chances of securing durable deals. They're applicable throughout your day, including during tense work conversations and when you're talking to a customer service agent.

Many of us harbor the illusion that persuasion is all about finding the "right" words to get what you want. Persuasion geniuses know that words can be the *least* important part, sometimes as little as 7 percent. You need to **go beyond words**. In chapter 8, you learn about key factors impacting your ability to persuade, including tone, likability, and body language. You get techniques to master all of them, and learn what to avoid doing. For example, certain postures or facial expressions convey insecurity or even contempt—eye-rolling is a classic culprit—making them antipersuasion tactics. By contrast, the right tone makes even firm criticism land much softer.

All the fancy techniques in this book are for naught if you can't ace the simplest and toughest test of all: the granny test. What does Granny want? Clarity. That's the simple part. How do you pass it? That's the tough part. You need to present your ideas in a way that's accessible for anyone, including—especially—regular people. Chapter 9 provides techniques to **ace the granny test**. Many of my students at elite universities failed it on a regular basis.

While the principles in these chapters stand alone, the integrated whole really is greater than the sum of the parts. Consider storytelling. If you read only chapter 6, you wouldn't appreciate that the best stories are oriented around the audience (chapter 1), present a vision (chapter 2), tap into the audience's emotions (chapter 3), are *for* something (chapter 4), communicate morals (chapter 5), are a form of negotiation (chapter 7), are much more than mere words (chapter 8), and are clear (chapter 9).

Persuasion geniuses put emotional intelligence (EI) at the heart of everything. EI is the ability to monitor your and others' emotions, understand them, and think and act accordingly.[6] Since we feel first, high EI is necessary for persuasion. Even some people with a high intelligence quotient (IQ) fail to get what they want because they have low EI and don't know how to navigate situations appropriately.

You might be wondering: Can't you use all this persuasion stuff for evil, too? Absolutely. Manipulation is wrong, though. And it'll come back to bite you quickly, and hard. Manipulation is like being a pyromaniac. Playing with fire seems great, until you burn yourself and those you purport to care about.

I close this introduction with an admittedly bold claim: If you embrace the lessons in this book, they'll change you. You'll get way more of what you want and need by learning how to cultivate great relationships. You'll learn a magnetic mindset that attracts people and opportunities to you. You'll get more than you ever imagined.

Let's get started.

Part 1

ADOPT THE PERSUADER'S MINDSET

Persuasion, above everything else, is a mindset. After all, your mindset always frames how you act and how others experience you. With the right mindset, your chances of getting what you want and need skyrocket, because you know how to engage anyone in any situation. With the wrong mindset, well, you can guess what happens.

Here's the rub: In crucial ways, we're not cognitively wired to persuade. We're wired to survive, which can impede our ability to thrive. You need to rewire yourself to become a persuasion genius. While that might make persuasion seem out of reach, the good news is that this rewiring is simple (though not easy) and pleasant once you start tasting success.

What's the right mindset? How do you adopt it?

Part 1 teaches you the persuader's mindset, which is grounded in core realities of the human mind. You learn what those realities are, and how to navigate them effectively to maximize your chances of persuading in any situation.

In chapter 1, you learn that persuasion starts by simply flipping your perspective from *you* to *them*.

In chapter 2, we zoom out to look at the big persuasion picture. Ultimately, what animates action? What motivates us to strive toward big goals and achieve great things? How do you figure that out?

Chapter 1

PUT THEM FIRST

Talk to someone about themselves and they'll listen for hours.
Dale Carnegie, *How to Win Friends and Influence People*

For an hour, I listened intently, sipping my espresso, saying little. Mohammed recounted every detail from his journey to bring a TEDx event to his university. The school had seemed intent on making it impossible, erecting barrier after barrier. There were bureaucratic rules to follow! You can't just host an event! And Mohammed simply refused to take "no" for an answer. He had been determined to will his first TEDx event into existence—and he'd succeeded a few months prior. It was a great story, and I was thoroughly impressed. I kept asking questions, wanting to know more. It took a lot of grit. He just kept smiling the whole time, explaining how he politely toppled all those barriers. He had another goal in his sights: make the next TEDx event even better, with full university support (which he eventually secured).

Then a funny thing happened: Feeling connected to me, he asked about me. What do I work on? So I mentioned I was writing a book on persuasion and gave him a short description of it, focusing on a few big ideas in it. TED events are about "big ideas," after all. And he quickly asked: Would you like to speak at our next TEDx event?

Now, my goal for the meeting was actually to get that invitation. We had connected on LinkedIn. I was struck that someone so interested in and dedicated to technology was also committed to communicating big ideas and giving others a platform. That's not easy, and most tech people aren't interested in taking that next step.

Most people would approach the meeting this way: "Hey Mohammed, I'm writing this book, and I'd love to speak at your TEDx event." That is, they would have made it all about themselves, then hoped to spark some of his interest.

Putting ourselves first aligns with our cognitive wiring, so that approach is understandable. The only problem is that it's ineffective at best, and counterproductive at worst. How come?

Well, how would you feel if you were on the receiving end of it? Would it persuade you if you were in Mohammed's position? Probably not. When we deploy this me-first approach, we mostly just end up persuading ourselves. If I had made my meeting with Mohammed all about me by leading with my desire to be a speaker, the odds of me getting invited to do the TEDx Talk would have been much, much lower. I formed such a good connection with him that he introduced me to his family at the event, and I was the only speaker he took separate photographs with.

Persuasion geniuses flip the script and **put them first**. That's because at the heart of the persuader's mindset is a simple insight: *It's about them, not you*. A them-first approach is actually the best way to get what you want. It shows your audience you're authentically interested in them. You listen, learn about their wants and needs, their concerns and problems, and address them. That's powerful, because it makes them feel connected to you, and motivates them to work with you. The conversation and insights that follow grease the wheels of shared action. You uncover more opportunities than you ever expected, and you both feel excited to pursue them.

This shift can sting a bit at first, because it goes against how we're wired. You need to reorient your frame of reference. Instead of putting yourself front and center, lead with the other person's needs. Once you taste some success, you'll eagerly embrace the persuader's mindset, which is also the foundation for everything else you'll learn in this book.

ME-FIRST VS. THEM-FIRST

When I was a speechwriter for one senior government official, they always asked the same question in our weekly meetings: "What do *we* need to tell *them*?" This question is intuitive. It's also an antipersuasion tactic, because it's exactly backward.

It's intuitive because our brains are wired to think primarily about us. This is adaptive. It helped our ancestors survive and avoid threats. It still helps us survive and prioritize our needs. If we don't think about and tend to ourselves, who will?

Talking about ourselves *feels* good, too, so good that it triggers the same sensations in our brain as money and sex.[1] So we do it. A lot.

It's no surprise, then, that the average person, anytime and anywhere, usually has the same favorite topic of conversation: themself! Doubt it? The data show people talk about themselves about 60 percent of the time, and this number rises to 80 percent on social media.[2]

This wiring leads us to adopt what I call a me-first mindset. We put ourselves at the center of what we say and do. Since it helped our ancestors survive, we assume it helps us thrive.

With some people, "me-first" even becomes "me-only," otherwise referred to as clinically diagnosable narcissism. As psychologist Mark Goulston explains in *Just Listen*, "A narcissist's motto is, 'So . . . enough about you.' (And that's true even if you haven't opened your mouth yet!)."[3] They only care about what's in it for them.

Unrelated question: How would you feel if you were on the receiving end of this approach? Unimportant, neglected, maybe condescended to.

That's why the me-first mindset is an antipersuasion tactic. What makes us think talking about what we want will persuade our audience to do anything but tune out? It doesn't.

It gets worse the longer you do it. While you're thinking and talking about you, your audience is thinking about, and yearns to talk about, themselves. How can you motivate your counterpart to share action by talking about yourself and ignoring their wants and needs? You can't.

The persuader's mindset completely flips this. Here it is: It's about them, not you. Simple, yes. Just put them first. Not easy, because as you've seen, this seismic shift goes against our cognitive wiring. Which means this change will feel odd initially. The good news is that you *can* rewire your brain in this way, especially because it's in your interest to do so. Putting them first is actually the best way to get what *you* want.

Persuasion happens when you meet your audience where they *are*, not where you want them to be, and certainly not where *you* are. Meeting people where they are is powerful because it means you're standing with them, side by side. And when someone stands with you in your corner instead of the one across the ring, you're much more inclined to listen to and be persuaded by them.

Meeting them where they are starts by demonstrating your genuine understanding of their wants and needs as well as their concerns. They need to feel like you understand who they are, what they care about, what they want and need, and what they're facing. Perhaps your spouse needs you to help more with the kids because they're stretched too thin. You need to understand and acknowledge where they are and why, then act accordingly to assist.

Your desire to understand them must be authentic. They'll know if it isn't, which will quickly sour the relationship, or cement it as purely transactional. At which point, when you no longer serve an assigned purpose, they'll move on. It's much harder to cut ties with someone with whom you have an authentic relationship.

Once you get this pulse on your audience (more on how to do that shortly), put it front and center by telling them what you see, and letting them tell you more about it. Fight the strong temptation to insert *your* "how," because it shifts the focus back to you, and it might even demonstrate *mis*understanding. Instead, help them feel like you get what they're facing and how they're experiencing it. Acknowledge your direct report's desire for a raise and hear them out. Understand why your friend is feeling overwhelmed on their terms.

Observe, don't judge. You meet someone where they are by simply observing and understanding their feelings and thoughts. They have them for a reason, and it's not that they've been sent from the underworld. If you insist on judging them, this quickly erects a big barrier to shared action, because invariably there will be something you don't like about their perspective.

Don't confuse understanding with agreement. You can understand someone's view, even on contentious topics like abortion or immigration, without sharing it. This realization is liberating, because you can observe—and, yes, understand—different views without insisting yours is the only tolerable one. It opens up conversation, too. Even if you disagree with how a colleague wants to proceed, start by stating their position as clearly and strongly as you possibly can.

You meet someone where they are, and demonstrate authentic understanding, through words and deeds. As you'll learn in chapter 8, *how* you say something is often more important than what you say. The wrong tone quickly colors the "right" words. And if your words ring hollow because they don't align with your actions, you're far from persuasion. By contrast, when someone feels and sees that you get them, it's powerful. It connects you to them, and this connection greases the wheels of shared action.

Someone will only move from where they are—maybe even to where you want them to be—through two-way conversation. That starts with them feeling heard and understood. It also presumes *they* need to move. Maybe they're in the right spot, and it'd behoove you to move toward them. Recognition of that requires humility.

Demonstrating understanding works in both low- and high-stakes situations. On a recent family vacation, I was checking out of the hotel. By observing her tone and body language, I noticed that the lady at the lobby desk had clearly faced some challenges earlier that day. So I asked about them. Turns out, the hotel was having trouble finding enough employees, which puts more of a strain on her and the rest of the staff. One of the reasons for this was what she saw as bad public policy. My ears perked up even more, since I work in that space. I was genuinely interested, so we chatted some more, and she felt connected to me. Then she saw a kiddo standing behind me. She asked, "Is he yours?" I said, "Yes, that's Thomas. He's two." She said, "Would Thomas like a toy?" I said, "He sure would!" And Thomas went home with a fancy plush seal. Connection yields unexpected benefits.

This works when the stakes are higher, too. One of my direct reports was visibly anxious in our weekly meeting. He hesitated, then asked for a raise. At first, it felt like he wanted a promotion, too, which would have been more complicated. I heard him out. He wasn't just being greedy; he was an entry-level employee. He was feeling the pinch of inflation. So I asked him, "If you could pick between a raise and a promotion, which one would it be?" He quickly said, a raise. Since he works hard, I worked hard and got him one. His anxiety in our meetings evaporated. And since I delivered, I was able to come to him a few months later and ask him to step up with something important. And he delivered.

When the audience is more than one person, demonstrating understanding is trickier. The individuals in the audience have different wants and needs; sometimes a little different, sometimes a lot. In these cases, the best strategy is to address the most important people and issues in the group. When possible, figure out how the wants and needs of everyone overlap. Here's what all this looks like in practice.

I was a speechwriter for the director of an intelligence agency when the COVID-19 pandemic started. The director needed his audience, the workforce, to remain engaged and productive, because our national security was at stake. What's more, prior to the pandemic all employees had to work in person in a facility requiring a security clearance.

What did they care about? What did they want and need? What were their concerns? They needed to know the director cared about their safety and understood the difficult situation (global pandemic) and negative emotions (fear and anxiety) they were experiencing, and be given a plan for them to continue contributing to the agency's mission. Many of them had never worked remotely a single day while at the agency, because it wasn't possible given the nature of the work. They were worried about being able to work effectively. They'd remain motivated to work only if they felt supported; otherwise, many would check out mentally.

We achieved shared action through regular interactions that demonstrated understanding. We addressed the workforce directly multiple times each week: in a Monday morning speech, then in a Thursday town hall where the director fielded questions from the workforce. Much of our messaging focused on making sure they knew the director understood their feelings and concerns. Rather than ignoring or discounting their concerns, we acknowledged them directly with empathy. We discussed ways the agency would address and help alleviate them. The director told stories about the good remote work people were doing to celebrate these colleagues. We emphasized that their individual contributions were keeping America safe.

Did it work? Employee satisfaction skyrocketed during the pandemic, as measured by numerous surveys. And it stayed high. That's even more remarkable because it had been on the decline under the previous director.

So yes, our words helped persuade people to happily stay productive and boosted workforce morale.

So how should the senior government official mentioned at the start of this section have shifted their thinking? Instead of asking "What do *we* need to tell *them*?," a much better question would be: "What do *they* need to hear from *us*?" Which is exactly what the director and I did during the pandemic.

There are missionary and mercenary reasons for putting the other person first. The missionary reason is that it's the right thing to do. You need to have genuine interest in your counterpart. Otherwise, you'll just use them to get what you want, which is manipulative. We all deserve better.

The mercenary reason is that adopting a them-first mindset is actually the best me-first strategy. You generate credibility, goodwill, and trust, which significantly increases the likelihood that they will want to work with you. This mindset also allows you to learn about their interests, some of which will invariably overlap with yours. That overlap, as we will discuss later, is consistently a path to shared action.

BECOME THE ULTIMATE LISTENER

The unsung hero of persuasion isn't talking. Everyone knows how to do that, especially about themselves. It's listening. How *else* would you learn about and address their wants and needs? How else would you even know what to *say*?

We face three immediate challenges, though. The first is our impulse to talk. We have it for many reasons, some of which are undoubtedly well intentioned. Ambitious young professionals often view talking first as a way to showcase the value they can add. They want to prove to their boss that they're smart, that they have solutions to the problems the team or organization is facing. That could even be their ticket to a promotion and raise. They also don't get too many opportunities to do this, so whenever they see one, they often feel the pressure to seize it (often too quickly) and make something of it. My interns do this a lot, because they're so eager to prove themselves.

The second challenge, as communications expert Matt Abrahams highlighted to me, is that people are never taught listening skills. It's hard to do something well that you've never learned. You'll learn it here.

The third challenge is that listening is hard. It's different from simply not talking. *Not talking* just means words aren't coming out of your mouth. What your audience says can still go in one ear and right out the other as you wait for a chance to start talking again. *Listening* requires you to focus fully on your audience, connect with them by demonstrating understanding, and figure out how to share action. How?

By becoming the ultimate listener. The ultimate listener embraces listening as foundational to persuasion. Everyone yearns to feel and be heard. The ultimate listener lets them share what's on their mind, then demonstrates an understanding of it. This earns you moments when the audience feels they have an identical, in-the-moment experience with you. That's called "I-sharing." It helps us feel connected to people, determines how much we like someone, and leads to prosocial outcomes like giving and helping,[4] and, ultimately, to shared action.

The ultimate listener listens to learn, because there's always more to learn, both from your counterpart and about the world at large. They don't listen "in order to," because that puts the focus on trying to get something from someone, such as listening to find an opening "in order to" make your point.[5]

Doubt listening truly is foundational? How do you feel when someone *isn't* listening to you? Especially someone who's supposed to listen, like a spouse, parent, or friend? Annoyed, rejected, and unimportant. And consider the opposite, when you know someone is locked in on you and what you're saying. You feel connected, heard, and important. That's transformative.

Listening is hard because our me-first default compels us to talk—a lot—either about what we think or just about ourselves. A talk-first mindset makes listening challenging, often impossible. It's also counterproductive, because the other person usually won't listen until they feel heard. Until then, you're talking to a brick wall.

Listening requires you to be present, locked in on the person, the conversation, and the moment. Recall a conversation when someone was present with you. That was powerful and felt good. It's hard, too. Being present requires focus, which requires intentionality, because there's so much that can bring us out of focus. You have to shift your attention away from what was on your mind and over to your counterpart.

Think of a time when you were talking to someone about something important and felt they were somewhere else. "Oh, can you repeat that?" Ouch. Distraction is normal, but it makes listening impossible, and it can be hurtful to your counterpart.

There's a politician whose mastery of being present helped propel him to the presidency. He makes the person he's talking to feel like they're the only person in the world. As one article explains, he "built a career on doing what most politicians can't or won't do: connect with ordinary people, look them in the eye and listen to what they have to say. His ability to listen was instrumental in his ability to win people over."[6] He used this superpower in a presidential debate. While his opponent famously looked at his watch to check the time (is this almost over?), he confidently walked closer to the town hall audience members to connect with them by listening, then knowing what to say. His name is Bill Clinton.

My listen-first approach helped me boost a mentee's confidence and feeling of belonging. He reached out to me to meet for coffee, and hinted in a text that he was eager to discuss some shared professional interests. So rather than diving into mentor mode at the start of the conversation (I have a tendency to do this), I said, "Let's set aside mentoring for today. We'll do that another time. Let's talk shop." Then we were off to the races. At the end, he told me how much he appreciated being treated like a colleague.

This will seem terribly counterintuitive: The listener, not the speaker, controls the conversation. Most people think that when they're talking, they're in control, making their points, shaping the agenda. Not really. First, you don't know if you're even saying what your audience needs to hear. Second, you're actually sharing lots of potentially valuable information—often more than you intended—your counterpart can use to get what *they* want. Let your audience overshare instead.

When I was a nonprofit fundraiser, people overshared all the time because I listened. They shared highly personal financial information like bank account balances, will beneficiaries, and how much they gave other organizations. All this information helped me learn about them, and about the prospects of growing their relationship with my organization. This usually led to them increasing their financial support.

Listening provides you time to reflect, process information, figure out how your wants and needs overlap with your counterpart's, and develop a strategy to proceed. You can be more intentional with what you say and do. That's particularly important in difficult, high-stakes situations, which is also when it's often most challenging to just listen. You have to learn to push through this discomfort and trust the listening process.

Are leaders an exception to the listen-first approach? Aren't they supposed to be prepared to talk first and give direction? This impulse is understandable, and it's what motivates a lot of mid-level professionals to talk too much. To the contrary! The best leaders spend a disproportionate amount of their time listening—learning what's working, what isn't, and how their team feels about things—before speaking up. They also know that if they talk too quickly, they'll stifle conversation and creativity on their team. That's why I also start by asking my team for their perspective and recommendations. Sometimes I'm even intentionally vague because I want to give them as much space as possible to share their insights. Invariably, they have lots of good ideas.

It's in your interest to have genuine interest in your audience. People can usually sense if you're disingenuous, and it causes them to clam up, even avoid you altogether. They might feel like you're using them. (Are you?) This feeling destroys trust and makes shared action nearly impossible. *With* genuine interest, you'll learn what they really care about, and how you can collaborate most effectively. As Harvard Law School professors Douglas Stone, Bruce Patton, and Sheila Heen note in *Difficult Conversations*, "If your intentions are false, no amount of careful wording or good posture will help. If your intentions are good, even clumsy language won't hinder you."[7]

How can you generate genuine interest? Instead of treating conversation as a tennis match where you focus on hitting the ball back over the net (at or away from them) to win a point, psychologist Mark Goulston recommends treating it as a "detective game, in which your goal is to learn as much about the other person as you can."[8] Don't make communication transactional, like going to the ATM.[9] Without a connection, they'll stop transacting with you when it suits them.

Curiosity is great fuel for your listening fire. As Stone, Patton, and Heen explain, being curious is the "only way to come to understand the other person's story," to understand who they *are*.[10] And as the authors of *The Go-Giver* (a great sales book) explain, when we're curious, "*everyone* becomes fascinating."[11] By adopting the mindset that we have a lot to learn from people and situations, we realize we might even learn from *this* person and *this* situation. Which even has the virtue of being true. This growth mindset will take you far.

Be especially curious about your counterpart's pain points. As negotiation coach Jim Camp explains, pain brings people "in every negotiation to the table." And pain is "whatever the negotiator sees as *the current or future problem*. People make decisions in order to alleviate and take away this current or future problem—this pain."[12] You need to understand what's causing your counterpart trouble and how to make it better (or at least less bad).

Research shows we can actually learn to become more curious. One way to do this is through mindful activity (such as mindful walking) and behavioral changes likes using a "when-then" framework. For example, "When I am on my lunch break, then I will listen to a new podcast."[13] The simplest and most effective way to be curious is to ask questions about the other person: their wants, needs, and concerns.

Now, let's be a little more specific. The ultimate listener masters three kinds of listening: passive, active, and proactive.

The most basic form of listening is passive. It's simple: Just listen. No more, no less. After all, if you rearrange the letters in LISTEN, it spells SILENT. Invite your counterpart to share what's on their mind (like by asking an open-ended question). Then? Close your mouth and open your eyes, ears, heart, and mind to them. After all, you have two ears, and one mouth, for a reason.

The only thing you "do" in passive listening is use a "minimal encourager," an intervention like nodding your head or saying "mmhmm," that lets your counterpart know you're hearing them, and encourages them to keep talking.[14]

Passive listening is hard work, because you have to actually listen. That means truly absorbing, processing, and understanding their words as deeply as necessary. It's worth it, because it helps your counterpart feel connected to you.

Next, master active listening. Active doesn't mean actively inserting your feelings and thoughts into the conversation, however well intentioned those insertions are. Quite the opposite! It's active because you look for important issues and moments requiring further exploration. For example, you might observe they're excited and anxious, or scared and uncertain. Then, you motivate your counterpart to share more information about themselves so your understanding is richer. Once you notice this dynamic, investigate it. Maybe their anxiety is coming from a big decision ahead of them. When you give them space to explore an important issue, and hear them out, it strengthens your relationship with them. They feel noticed and seen. When they share information that relates specifically to a potential opportunity to share action (as opposed to simply growing the relationship), it helps you figure out how to move forward, including by identifying shared goals or removing barriers to action.

As an active listener, your goal is to gain a fuller understanding of your counterpart and what they're dealing with, and how working with you can benefit them. Ask questions, make observations about how you think they're feeling and what you're seeing, and notice where your counterpart goes with them.

Open-ended questions are a potent active-listening technique that strategically encourages your counterpart to share. An open-ended question is a "how" or "what" question that can't be answered with a "yes" or "no" and encourages your counterpart to share information. For example, "What's your assessment of the situation?" Any of the above information is important for sharing action.

The goal of proactive listening is to step back and figure out where the conversation needs to go to share action. Then, you adopt emotionally intelligent tactics to get it there.

Proactive listening explores what's important, urgent, or otherwise concerning for your counterpart. What problems is he facing? What barriers to shared action exist? How can you overcome them? The listening is proactive because you're navigating toward shared action. At the beginning, it often isn't evident how to proceed. Open-ended questions will help bring clarity.

What does proactive listening look like in practice? Pose questions that show you genuinely value the relationship and have a vision for continued shared action. For example, "What would it take to achieve your vision for your team within three years?" "What does a successful partnership between us look like in five years?" "What about this decision gives you heartburn?" "What are the biggest barriers to us partnering?"

Once you ask a proactive question, fight the urge to keep talking. Instead, stop, listen, and wait for an opportunity to probe more deeply. Don't rush. People need time to work through things.

Proactive listening is difficult. It can easily turn into forcefully nudging, pushing, or coercing your interlocutor to go somewhere they aren't comfortable going (yet or ever). That never ends well. Questions like "So you're good with this, right?" are pushy, not proactive. We can also easily forget that the "proactive" part of the phrase simply modifies the core word: listening. Proactive listening still requires you to spend the bulk of your time listening.

Here's an example to distinguish the three kinds of listening. Suppose your friend is having problems with her difficult boss. To engage in passive listening, ask her, "What's wrong?" Then let her share, and see where that goes. With active listening, press on certain things that seem important. Maybe she says, "The worst is when she treats me like I'm stupid." You might ask, "How so?" She'll tell you, and might see it's better or worse than she initially thought. With proactive listening, aim at next steps to address the situation. Ask, "How do you want to move forward?" or "What would it take for you to be happy at work?" Such queries start a conversation that'll improve your friend's situation, perhaps by changing jobs or moving internally to another division.

You need to be able to toggle among all kinds of listening in one conversation depending on how it flows and what your counterpart needs. For example, you might go in planning to do lots of proactive listening to arrive at shared action. Your counterpart might have other ideas! You might start by asking, "What are our next steps?" They might then start discussing something else, which may or may not seem related. You'll need to pivot to passive listening to see what's on their mind, then decide how to proceed.

The ultimate listener notices what someone *doesn't* say, because that's frequently more important than what they do. Someone might be reluctant to share what's on their mind, or might not know in the first place. The ultimate listener learns to sense what's missing from the conversation, and helps their counterpart feel comfortable enough to share, such as by asking good questions.

The ultimate listener generally avoids interruptions, because they stifle conversation. We interrupt because we feel compelled to say something now, usually with good intentions. One of my interns was an eager beaver who compulsively interrupted me because he wanted to be helpful and offer an answer or solution to whatever we were facing. He would literally cut me off mid-sentence to share his thoughts, because he wanted to prove himself.

When someone does this to you, how does it make you feel? Not good, and probably that they're uninterested in what you're saying. I had to gently tell him this wasn't a good practice to embrace. And not everyone will be gentle when you interrupt them. In fact, this is one of my weak points: If someone interrupts me too much, I get irritated.

The trouble with interrupting is that it's antithetical to listening. You rob yourself of the opportunity to learn from your counterpart and figure out what to say by talking too quickly. That's not in your interest!

Interruptions are only appropriate to clarify misunderstandings or stop unproductive talking. Suppose your friend misunderstood something you said and is angry. Rather than letting him fume, interject and clarify. "I'm sorry, that's not what I meant. What I meant was . . ." If your counterpart is talking unproductively, you might need to short-circuit that talking with an interruption; otherwise, you might waste lots of time. Try to redirect them in a more productive direction. "You're making a lot of important points here. Do you mind if we focus on this one [insert key issue]?"

Learn to listen justly, which means hearing and engaging your audience for the right reasons, in the right way, on their terms, in their context. Your default needs to be to treat them with respect, empathy, and an assumption of reasonable motives, until proven otherwise. Understand what they truly intend or mean to say. If they cannot articulate it clearly, help them do so, or probe more deeply to gain understanding. Show some compassion. Try to find something you like about them, because as we'll see in chapter 8, likability facilitates persuasion.

Perhaps you're wondering: Why listen justly to someone who's unjust? It depends on what you seek to accomplish. Are you trying to tell them they're stupid, evil, crazy, or some combination thereof? Then fire away with self-righteousness. Or is your goal to persuade them of something? Then open your eyes, ears, heart, and mind to them to create space for conversation. You're thinking: That's cute, and hopelessly naive. Fortunately, no.

Daryl Davis is a Black blues musician who has persuaded over 200 KKK members to leave and denounce the KKK by directly engaging them. His inspiring TEDx Talk, viewed over 12 million times, shares his story.[15] In an interview, Davis said, "If I can sit down and talk to KKK members and neo-Nazis and get them to give me their robes and hoods and swastika flags and all that kind of crazy stuff . . . there's no reason why somebody can't sit down at a dinner table and talk to their family member."[16]

How does Davis do this, even with Roger Kelly, who was a grand dragon of the KKK? Simple: respectful conversation. In the TEDx Talk, Davis explains that he was driven by a question: "How can you hate me when you don't even know me?" So he asked Kelly. Davis wasn't there to fight Kelly. He "was there to learn from him. Where does this ideology come from? . . . Once you learn where it comes from, you can then try to figure out how to address it and where it's going."

Then a strange thing started to happen: They grew a relationship. Davis had Kelly over to his house for dinner. Then Davis invited other Black people. Then some Jews. Eventually, Kelly invited Davis to his house for dinner. Then Kelly invited Davis to Klan rallies. And Davis went backstage. Kelly started going to see Davis's concerts. Any guesses how this story ends? Kelly left the Klan.

The driving force of all these encounters was respect. Kelly explained, "At least he respects me, to sit down and listen to me, and I respect him to sit down and listen to him."

The best part? The data support Davis. A meta-analysis of 500 studies reveals that "intergroup contact typically reduces intergroup prejudice."[17] If you want to promote justice, and even persuade, listen justly.

Throughout the listening process, make sure you have a method for capturing all the information you gather. Don't rely on your memory, because you won't remember everything. Research has shown the best way to take notes to capture and retain information is by hand in a notebook.[18] It's a sign of respect to someone when you value what they say enough to write it down. And you now have a record to rely on as you work to share action with them. Just be sure it's situationally appropriate. Taking notes while having dinner with a friend would be weird.

Listening differs in important ways across various mediums. The best way to listen is in-person, because you can connect with someone most effectively, see their body language, and even feel how they're feeling (for example, are they sweating because they're nervous?). As a society, though, in-person is not really the default anymore. This makes it harder to maintain a listen-first approach, because you aren't as connected with your counterpart.

Video calls are next best, because you can at least see facial reactions. Pay attention to the person's body language when it's available to you. Phone calls allow you to gauge their tone, so listen to it carefully. Are they calm or anxious? When you're only listening through the written word, like an email or text, listening is much harder because you don't have access to information that helps you interpret their words. We're inclined to interpret written words ungenerously, especially when they seem or are negative. When reading someone else's written words, be as generous as you can when interpreting them. And when you're responding, assume your counterpart will not be generous in their interpretation; which means you need to be extra careful to not prompt an undesirable response.

To avoid these problems, make in-person your default so you can listen first.

WHAT ABOUT *ME*?

You're thinking: Listening to others sounds all well and good. But what about ME? After all, didn't this chapter highlight that I'm wired to think and talk about ME most of the time? I need people to listen to and think about ME. Is that wrong? Not at all.

Reciprocity is foundational in relationships. Even in close relationships—spouse, friend, parent, child—if things are too one-sided, we start to feel and think they're not interested in us (sadly, sometimes they aren't). This strains relationships over time. Persuasion is a two-way street, which requires both parties to be authentically interested in each other. Them-first is different from them-only.

How do we make things about the person across from us enough to facilitate persuasion, without things being *only* about them?

Start by placing them at the center. Then, note how much interest, if any, they take in you. If you try to share your feelings and thoughts and they're dismissive or uninterested, that's a red or yellow flag. Stop, or at least proceed with caution. There might be a good reason why they aren't listening to you. Maybe they're distracted or having a bad day. Persuasion might still be possible.

Sometimes, it's necessary to put your wants and needs at the center of the conversation. You might need to do so assertively. Perhaps you're dealing with something significant, and you need your counterpart to listen. Do this with emotional intelligence.

This happened to me at dinner with a friend. I was facing some difficulties at work and was eager to discuss them with him. And for the first two hours, he just kept rambling about a wide range of things. I kept looking for opportunities to make the conversation about me, because that's what I needed. I felt myself getting annoyed internally (though luckily not externally). Then I just had to literally say, "I'm sorry. Do you mind if we shift gears? I have something I need your advice on." And he quickly said, "Of course not!" We discussed my issues for another two hours, then a few times after that, and his insights were valuable as I figured out how to proceed.

You can shift the attention to you directly, like I did, or indirectly, by saying something like, "I'm just exhausted from everything that's on my plate." Or connect your issue to something they bring up: "That's rough, and I'm struggling with something similar on my team . . ." Hopefully, they'll give you an opening to share what's on your mind. If they don't, either now isn't the right time for them, or it might be a sign of a deeper gap in the relationship.

I still struggle with this. I excel at putting my counterpart first, so much that I can talk for hours about them. Countless times, I've done this, and my counterpart asks not a single thing about me. It makes me feel unimportant and unseen.

I've come to realize my them-only approach is counterproductive, because their lack of knowledge about me is a missed opportunity to form a connection. I've learned to gently insert myself when appropriate to establish more of a relationship with them. I do this especially by noting I've experienced something similar to what they're discussing, then talking about it and seeing how they respond. Are they interested? Or do their eyes glaze over? This helps let me know whether they're truly interested in sharing action with me.

If your counterpart makes it only about them, and demonstrates no interest in you, maybe persuasion isn't possible with them, and you need to look elsewhere.

USE A STAKEHOLDER ANALYSIS TO IDENTIFY YOUR AUDIENCE

You can allocate your time more effectively by identifying the right people to engage through a tool called a stakeholder analysis.

A "stakeholder" is someone interested in or concerned about an issue. Let's use a public school principal as an example. Their stakeholders include:

students, parents, teachers, administrators, staff, local politicians (who allocate funding), and taxpayers.

In a stakeholder analysis, you consider people who can impact an issue and their different views on it, then you decide how to engage them. This process has five steps.

Stakeholder Analysis Steps

Step 1: Identify your goals.
Step 2: Consider key people interested in the issue.
Step 3: Prioritize and rank stakeholders.
Step 4: Determine where interests overlap.
Step 5: Develop a stakeholder persuasion plan.

The first step is to identify your goals. This focuses your attention on your wants and needs, since they motivate you to act.

The second step is to consider key people interested in the issue. Who cares about, works on, is impacted by, or advocates for a particular issue?

Assess how much power, interest, and alignment stakeholders have. Power is a product of someone's influence or impact. Executives usually have a lot of power in their organization. Sometimes their gatekeepers (otherwise known as executive assistants) have even more power, because they decide who gets some of the executive's time. Interest is about how much attention stakeholders are prepared to devote to an issue. Activists have a high degree of interest in particular issues. Alignment is an assessment of how close their views are to yours. People on opposite ends of the political spectrum often appear to have minimal alignment on most issues.

The third step ranks and prioritizes people based on their power, interest, and alignment. Issues like education usually have more stakeholders than building a park. Rankings help allocate your time effectively. If someone is powerful yet uninterested, or highly interested without any influence, interacting with them usually isn't a good time investment.

Alignment is more complicated, even though it seems simple: Do they agree with you? If not, move on. However, there's often more alignment than you realize, if you know where to look. Also, if someone is high in both power and interest, and not aligned, your goal in engaging them could be to reduce how strong their opposition is, so they don't act as a barrier to you persuading others.

Here's what all this looks like visually:

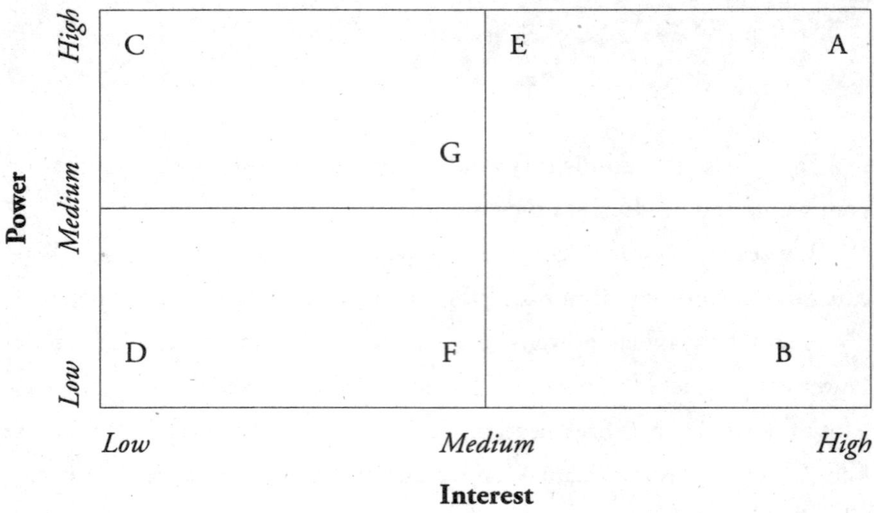

Interest is on the horizontal axis, and power (or influence) is on the vertical axis. You measure both from low to high (or somewhere in between). Based on the best information available, assign each stakeholder a point in the matrix. Then, assess their alignment with your views.

The most important stakeholders are those with high power/influence and high interest (A). If they're aligned with you, they can be effective advocates, because they want to advance the same goals. If they're not aligned, decide whether you can engage them to address their concerns, or at least reduce their opposition.

While stakeholders with significant interest but low power (B) can be nice cheerleaders if they agree with you, they won't really impact your success. Stakeholders with high power and low interest (C) don't care enough to engage. If they agree with you, it's tempting to court them. Unfortunately, this often wastes time. If they disagree with you, at least they're unlikely to actively work against your initiative.

Stakeholders with low power and low interest (D) who agree with you are worth keeping informed only if it takes minimal effort. Individuals E, F, and G show people can fall anywhere in the matrix. Locating a stakeholder in the matrix gives you a better sense of how many resources to invest in interacting with them.

Consider a business deciding a new direction: Should the company focus on international expansion or research and development? Who are the stakeholders? The CEO and board of directors, sure. Who else? Other employees, especially those who would work in those divisions. And many others, including potential and current customers, vendors, product managers, developers, and others working on the issue. Assess their interest, power, and alignment.

When possible, do background research to better understand stakeholders before engaging. Search the internet. Read what they've written. Talk to people who know them. Check their LinkedIn profiles. Ask directly what they want and need, and how they want to achieve it.

The fourth step is determining where your and your audience's interests overlap. This intersection is ripe for sharing action. Even if you only agree with someone on 10 percent of an issue, focus there and work together. You'll often find more areas of agreement later.

What's more, sharing action with someone for the first time helps you form a fruitful working relationship.

The fifth step is developing a stakeholder persuasion plan. Focus on the people closest to the top right of the matrix. Put the quality of stakeholders over quantity. Then ask: What's the best way to interact with your stakeholders to maximize the chances of sharing action? Note well that sharing action *does not* mean only trying to get what you want. That's a recipe for failure, because it makes things all about you. Persuasion requires identifying a process and an outcome all parties are eager to embrace. That might mean taking a course of action different from the one you originally preferred.

Unrelated question: If you're unwilling to adjust your original position, how can you expect your stakeholders to do so?

LET'S GET SPECIFIC

You might be thinking: A them-first approach seems nice. Is it actually persuasive? During my time as a nonprofit fundraiser (basically a salesman), the answer was a resounding "yes, better than you could ever imagine, and better than any other approach."

A lot of people think fundraising (and sales) is about being a great talker, which is why they try to sell their organization or product to the prospective donor. They tell the donor how great the organization is so he or she writes a check. As you now know, this approach is backward, suboptimal at best, and counterproductive at worst.

Fundraising is really about listening. That's why the best fundraisers and salespeople use this simple formula: It's 99 percent about the investor, 1 percent about the organization, and zero percent about the fundraiser or salesperson. Only through listening can you understand their goals and explain how your organization can help meet them. Most salespeople flip this: 99

percent about the salesperson, 1 percent about the organization, zero percent about the investor.

I once met with a gentleman in Wisconsin who had supported my former organization for the first time a few months prior, upon receiving a generic fundraising letter. We sat in his office for about ninety minutes, and he talked for about eighty of them. New to fundraising, I felt disappointed I didn't share more information about how great we were. And at the end of the meeting, he said, "Boy, I have such a better idea of what you all do." I thought to myself: No, you don't!

Then it dawned on me: I was wrong, and he was right. He *felt* like he did because I sat there, listened, and chimed in when appropriate, enabling him to feel connected to me and my organization. That's what really mattered. If I had started rattling off all the amazing things we do, it would have been a short meeting, because it wouldn't have been about him.

This has you wondering: OK, fine, but does it actually bring in money? Well. The 99-1-0 formula routinely persuaded people to significantly increase their investments in my organization by five- or tenfold.

I met with another gentleman who also sent a check after receiving a fundraising letter. All he wanted to talk about was how his alma mater was suppressing free speech, since my organization worked on this issue in the university space. Sitting on his porch, I locked in, listened, understood his concerns, and went to work. I needed to earn his trust and help him make a difference. His next investment was bigger—three thousand dollars for a reading group at the school. Then we secured a meeting with the provost and some deans to discuss his concerns about free speech. With trust soaring, I made a big ask: Would he invest thirty-five thousand dollars in a blockbuster free speech event with two famous professors? He quickly said yes. Which meant my mistake was not asking for more. So next time, I did. And he invested one hundred thousand dollars. And that wasn't the last big investment he made, either.

LET'S REFLECT

The guy was shocked. Speechless, in fact. He stared, then blinked. "No one has ever asked me that before." How could I stop an experienced, influential gentleman in his early seventies dead in his tracks?

First, the context. Alongside two lobbyists, I was attending an event of over thirty elected officials, mostly mayors. The lobbyists' goal was to get people to partner with us based only on our policy initiatives (alert: that's backward!).

The lobbyists always adopt a me-first mentality in these encounters. Their MO is to walk up to everyone there, tell them about a great idea they have, shove a folder into their hand explaining this great idea, then move on. Would that persuade you to adopt their idea? Hardly.

The persuader's mindset puts *them* first. So that's what I did when I walked over to the guy running the show, the one with more influence than anyone else.

After he brushed off the lobbyists, I walked up to him and said, "I'm going to ask you a really stupid question." He said, "There aren't any stupid questions." I said, "Oh, no, here comes one." He looked at me. Then I said, "How can *we* be helpful to *you*?" He paused, dumbfounded. Then finally responded, "No one has ever asked me that before." I thought: Really?! I doubled down: "We're here to help *you*." He said, "OK, let me think about it. Let's meet after the holidays." An offer the lobbyists would never have gotten, because I put him first.

It's in your interest to make it all about them, because this is how you learn whether you can partner fruitfully together. If there's no space to work together, it's best to learn that early. If there is, dive in and figure out what's in the interest of all parties involved, how those interests overlap, and what sharing action could look like. This gets you more of what you want and need.

And yet if you approach your audience exclusively with this mercenary mindset, your successes will be smaller and less frequent, since your interest in your audience will be inauthentic. When you're not fully invested in listening, you'll miss crucial information and misunderstand people and situations. You'll veer off course more than you'd expect. Your audience will often sense you're not really listening, or that you're not genuinely interested in them. You might be tempted to say and do things just to get your way. When they realize that, it'll damage or destroy the relationship, and your chances of getting what you want will plummet.

The ultimate listener invests resources, especially time and energy, into demonstrating understanding of their audience because they're genuinely interested in them. They're curious about what motivates the audience. They want to know how the audience feels and thinks—in general, and in this specific context. They listen—passively, actively, or proactively—so the audience feels heard. They're present. They learn the audience's wants and needs.

A magical thing happens next: The audience feels connected to you. This connection opens space for conversation and collaboration. That conversation yields invaluable insights—about them, you, and the issues at hand—that allow you to move forward more productively than you ever imagined. The collaboration that follows will be rewarding and durable. That's how you persuade regularly.

With as many fibers of your being as possible, make it about them, not you. You'll begin a journey uncovering exciting paths that otherwise would've remained hidden, and reach destinations that would've been inconceivable without putting your audience first.

Imagine both you and your counterpart committing to being ultimate listeners. You both make it about the other person. You listen, understand each other's wants and needs, and find areas ripe for collaboration to meet them. This approach yields enormous returns on your investment of time and energy. It's satisfying. And it's how you reap the biggest rewards from your persuasive endeavors.

Key Takeaways for Putting Them First

1. Put your audience and their wants, needs, and concerns first. It makes them feel good, forms an authentic relationship, and shows you the best path forward for working together.
2. Leverage listening as the best way to understand your audience, connect with them, and identify overlapping interests and goals. Make listening rather than talking your default whenever possible to acquire this valuable information.
3. When you make it about them, especially through listening, observe and seek to demonstrate understanding. Resist the urge to judge your audience's wants and needs, because those judgments will become a barrier to shared action. Instead, meet your audience where they are, not where you want them to be, and certainly not where you are.
4. Focus your efforts on how your and your audience's goals overlap, because that's the ripest area for shared action.
5. Identify and prioritize your audience through stakeholder analysis. Your time is limited, and not everyone has equal interest in and say on any given issue.
6. Make sure interactions aren't *only* about them. If your counterpart has no interest at all in you, the chances of achieving your goals are much lower. Some reciprocity is necessary.

Them-first Focusing Question: What is the ONE Thing (a concept we discuss in chapter 9) you can do to put your audience first that will move you toward shared action?

Chapter 2

ANIMATE ACTION WITH VISION

The only thing worse than being blind is having sight but no vision.
attributed to Helen Keller

I once interviewed for a speechwriter job with a Senate-confirmed government official. At the end of the interview, I got to pose questions. I asked, "What's your vision for your organization ten or twenty-five years out?" The official meandered for a few minutes, then literally said, "Well, that doesn't really answer your question. I don't really think in those terms."

I was flabbergasted. I wondered: How could someone lead an organization without knowing where it's going, where it *needs* to go, or even where they want it to go? But I thought: Maybe it was a fluke. So I persuaded them to offer me the job, and I accepted it.

A few months later I was traveling with them. They asked me how their remarks were, and how they might improve them. I thought to myself, maybe I can ask about that whole vision thing again. So I did. Another nonanswer followed, and they glared at me. Message received: Never ask about that again! Unsurprisingly, this person didn't last in the position long, because you can't lead if you don't know where you need to go.

Now consider visionary leaders. Henry Ford had a vision for transforming the way production operates. Steve Jobs had a vision for Apple to create world-changing products. Elon Musk's vision for SpaceX is to make mankind multiplanetary. Those visions drive tremendous progress at their organizations, and in society as a whole, through the shared actions they inspire.

Isaac Newton's first law of motion states that a body at rest will remain at rest unless an outside force acts on it. In persuasion, one powerful force that sets shared action in motion is vision. You need to **animate action with vision**. That's why persuasion geniuses spend lots of time crafting compelling ones.

Vision gets us excited about the great things we can achieve by reaching our goals, and it motivates us to pursue them. Vision gives our actions purpose; otherwise, it's just the daily grind. Same stuff, different day. Work without vision brings in a paycheck, but nothing more. By contrast, work *with* vision gives us meaning and satisfaction. Vision gives us focus by directing our attention and efforts. Crucially, vision imbues confidence. You know what you stand *for*, and you're actively moving toward it. Without a vision, you're rudderless. *With* vision, everyone rows in the right direction and moves toward your shared goals.

WHAT VISION IS

Biological vision is about your sight. How well do you see? 20/20? 20/10? 20/200? Are you nearsighted or farsighted? Do you need glasses? How well can you see when it's dark? Are you colorblind? Without clear biological vision, it's much harder to reach your destination. So, too, with your intellectual vision.

Your vision is how things will look once you achieve your professional or personal goals. That makes vision future-oriented; it's about a better tomorrow, and what you have to do today to get there.

Sometimes, your goals are big, like transforming your life or the industry you work in. Sometimes they're narrower, like your athletic goals. Vision requires imagination, because you're trying to create something new that doesn't exist today. You need creativity and imagination to craft a vision. At the same time, a vision has to be practical enough to be realistic and achievable. My personal and professional vision is to help create a world where as many people as possible have the opportunity to unleash their potential.

Ideally, vision is guided by your North Star. That's the thing way up high that points the way to where you need to go to achieve your goal. Your North Star guides all the big, important things you do to achieve your vision. It shines bright, even—especially—when it's dark, and keeps you on track. Your North Star is like the seed, and your vision is the tree or flower that blossoms and grows from it. My personal and professional North Star that guides my vision is the knowledge that we are all bundles of potential and can be more than we are.

Vision is different from mission. An organization's mission focuses on what it's doing today. Vision focuses on tomorrow, on what you want to become. Mission is more about "what" and "how," whereas vision is about the underlying "why," or the purpose and meaning of what you're doing.

Think about some business and organizational visions. Southwest Airlines's vision is "to become the world's Most Loved, Most Flown, and Most Profitable Airline." Teach for America offers a vision centered on children getting the education they need to unleash their unique potential: "One day, all children in this nation will have the opportunity to attain an excellent education." eBay has a vision for being the best marketplace: "to be the world's favorite destination for discovering great value and unique selection." These pithy statements drive these organizations' success by framing what they stand for, what they hope to achieve, and where they want to take people.

Contrast these with how the Ford Motor Company presented itself as of 2023: "We are here for one purpose, to help build a better world, where every person is free to move and pursue their dreams."[1] That sounds like a vision for a nonprofit or politician, not a car company. Suppose Ford turned to Southwest for guidance: "Our purpose is to become the world's most loved, most driven, and most profitable car company." Which vision would get Ford farther?

You certainly don't have to look at grand political or business visions from leaders and important historical figures.

I'm a total sucker for mentoring, so I do a lot (maybe too much!) of it. And I speak to students often. When those talks are about professional development, I start by asking them to close their eyes, and imagine they're near the end of their life, old and gray. I ask them to look in the mirror. What would it take for them to honestly be able to say to themselves, "That—my life—was worth it." Rarely does it take more than a minute for them to have a clear picture of how they want their professional and personal lives to look. So I tell them, "Great. That's your current vision for your entire life. Now let's reverse engineer how you get there." This is a great exercise for anyone, so consider stopping and trying it.

All visions start by zooming out and looking at the big picture. This provides greater context and clarity, and a broader perspective on what's most important. Without the ability to zoom out, you risk losing the forest in the trees, branches, leaves, and the bugs on them. You miss the broader landscape.

The most effective visions are driven by ONE Thing, a concept we discuss in chapter 9. If your vision is driven by two, five, or ten things, it usually points in too many directions and can lack focus, which makes it harder to achieve. Ask this focusing question: What is the ONE Thing driving your vision that, if you unite around it, will motivate shared action and success?

For example, my ONE Thing driving my life's vision is to empower people to unleash their unique potential. That starts with my children, Thomas and Elizabeth. And it's why I'm a poverty researcher. In the richest nation in the history of the world, far too few people are empowered to live their version of the American Dream. I work to change that by removing unfair barriers to work and making housing more affordable. That vision is also why I wrote this book. If I added other things to it, like expanding scientific knowledge, it would dilute the power of my ONE Thing by making it two.

The best visions strike a balance between dreams and reality. Dreaming and thinking big motivates people to share action. Aiming too low is much more dangerous than aiming too high. If you aim too high, and your vision is too lofty, and you don't quite get there, you've probably still made a lot of progress and achieved something important. If you aim too low, even if you achieve it, you won't really have accomplished much at all, and you'll always know you could have given more. People who aim high create and capitalize on far more opportunities than those who don't.

At the same time, if your vision isn't tethered to reality, you can quickly become delusional. You'll put yourself on flimsy footing, and probably fall. The Cleveland Clinic describes delusional disorder as "a type of mental health condition in which a person can't tell what's real from imagined. There are many types, including persecutory, jealous, and grandiose types."[2] Delusional people don't see things clearly. They see things that aren't there. It veers them off the path of shared action quickly. And it usually leads to bad decisions.

The risks of being delusional are enormous. You might mistake a far-fetched mirage for a real opportunity. If you point yourself, an organization, or a small or large group in a direction that's unrealistic—maybe wildly so—then the best-case scenario is that you waste lots of time, energy, and other resources, while not capitalizing on real opportunities. The worst-case scenario is complete failure, hurting the people who followed your delusional impulses. For example, if a CEO has a "big idea" to take a company in an entirely new space because he sees it as a growth opportunity, and they either aren't equipped to do it, or going into that space is a bad idea, his inability to clearly assess the situation will harm the company and its employees.

HOW VISION ANIMATES ACTION

Vision animates shared action both by serving as a motivating spark and by fueling continued action. It gets us excited about where we can go if we work together and reach our goals. Life without vision is just hopping from one thing to the next with little if any purpose. Without vision, it's just one day, one thing, after another. Something needs to inspire you.

A big vision, or complete lack thereof, can transform any activity. Suppose you walk up to three guys at the end of their shift and ask, "What are you doing?" The first guy says, "I'm a bricklayer." He's employed. The second guy responds, "I'm a builder. I'm building a wall." He has a profession. The third responds, "I'm building a cathedral for God." *That's* a vision.

Vision gives us focus, concentrating our attention by clarifying where we're going. Once we know that, we avoid doing things that won't get us there quickly or at all. For example, if your vision for your café is to be widely recognized as offering the best espresso-based drinks in town, then you need to focus on perfecting your cappuccinos, not your smoothies.

Vision unites people around shared goals. People come together and coalesce around something they're eager to implement. As an old proverb says,

"If you want to go fast, go it alone. If you want to go far, go as a team." Visions drive teams farther than anything else.

Persuasive visions arise through conversation with relevant stakeholders. How else would a vision be shared? People need to mutually decide on a destination. This occurs through conversation, which is the best means of generating good ideas. Otherwise, it's imposed from above and likely will be resisted, or at least not embraced.

Homeowner associations are a great example. One buddy of mine was a part of your stereotypically crazy HOA: Everything had to 100 percent exactly conform to the HOA's rules and regulations. Even the tiniest deviation drove some people mad, and they'd go after any violators (including my buddy, who's a defiant dude). The stories were funny mainly because I didn't live there. I was much luckier with my HOA. We all operated through happy consensus and created absolute minimum friction for the community. Which is why I was happy to join the board.

A vision appeals to someone only if they have a good answer to the question: What's in it for me? It needs to be in their interest. Why else would they embrace it? So you need to know who they are and what they care about. After all, it's about them, not you.

Moral visions animate action most vigorously. As you'll see in chapter 5, human beings are driven by an array of moral values and concerns. People are significantly more likely to share action with you if your vision has a moral thrust with which they agree. You'll learn the best ways to make moral appeals to any audience.

Good visions seek to make people better off. Gutenberg sought to make the printed word widely accessible. He manifested this vision in his printing press, possibly the single most important invention ever. The Wright Brothers had a vision for a new form of transportation—up in the sky, like a bird—that has given us access to more destinations, more quickly, than we ever imagined possible before they took flight. Henry Ford had visions for transportation and production that resulted in Ford Motor Company. His production lines revolutionized how we make things, while his automobiles were at the forefront of allowing individuals to traverse hundreds, even thousands, of miles a week.

We also need to be prepared to tear down flawed visions and replace them with strong ones. Some visions are simply immoral. Think about the apartheid regime's vision of racial inequality in South Africa. When a vision crosses a moral red line, we need to be prepared to explain why it's bad, and animate action against it, in favor of a better alternative.

HOW TO CRAFT A VISION

To craft a vision that animates, start by pausing and writing down your answers to these questions:

- Thinking big picture and longer-term, where do you want or need to go in your personal and professional life? Be specific about your goals.
- What are the underlying desires driving you to pursue these goals? Be specific. Ambitious young professionals especially have to be intentional about including personal goals in their life vision; otherwise life becomes work, work, work.
- Are your personal and professional goals aligned, or do they point in different directions? If they're not aligned, can you bring them into alignment? If not, what's more important to you?
- What medium- and short-term goals do you need to accomplish to achieve this vision?
- Whose help do you need as you undertake your journey?

Once you know where you want to go, consider what would inspire others to join you in working to make this vision a reality. Unless you give them good reason to do so, you'll walk down that path by yourself, which usually is a lonely and less effective way to proceed.

Craft an aspirational vision. Aim high, as high as you can, higher than you thought possible. Setting your sights too low puts a ceiling on your accomplishments. Better to try to scale Mount Everest and fall a few thousand feet short of the summit than to triumphantly plant your flag on a molehill. At the same time, make sure your vision is realistic, something a better-trained, more persuasive version of your current self could potentially achieve.

In part 2 you'll get a research-based psychological approach to crafting an animating vision. The short answer is that you need to elicit the right feelings (chapters 3 and 4), make motivating moral appeals (chapter 5), and tell powerful stories (chapter 6).

The actual business of crafting a vision must be methodical. Rarely do we have true "Eureka!" moments whereby a vision descends upon us in a moment of clarity. We usually arrive at a vision through lots of little steps that take us a great distance. Even world-historical moments of insight were made possible only after years or decades of work. For example, Isaac Newton published his *Philosophiæ Naturalis Principia Mathematica* in 1687, when he was in his forties, after twenty years as a fellow at Trinity College.

You need to consider the past, present, and future when crafting a vision. Knowledge of the past lets us look back, see what happened, and understand why. What has and hasn't worked? The present is about what's happening and why. We need to see the present clearly because it's our launchpad for shared action. That's more difficult than it sounds, because we often don't see many things. Sometimes, that's simply because our vision is limited, since there's so much we can't see. Sometimes, our vision isn't clear, or it might even be blurry. That's why conversation is important. Ultimately, vision is about building a better future. You paint a picture of where you want or need to go, and how you intend to do that.

VISIONS CENTER ON WHAT'S IMPORTANT AND MEANINGFUL

It has almost become a commonplace that, in an age of constant distractions from things like devices, social media, and streaming, audiences only want brief communications that are barely surface level. We're told we're lucky to get someone's attention for more than a few seconds, and it'll wane quickly. So the common advice is to share your information quickly in bite-sized chunks.

If it's impossible to keep someone's attention for any real length of time, how can so many multihour podcasts garner millions of viewers? Consider Joe Rogan. His number of monthly listeners has been estimated at around 14 million in 2025 just on Spotify,[3] and in 2021 (just after moving to Spotify) had 190 million monthly downloads.[4] His longest podcast is over five hours long. There's also Jordan Peterson, who has delivered hundreds of up to two-hour lectures around the world, to silent audiences hanging on every word. How can we square these realities with the alleged inability of people to keep their attention on something for a long time?

Audiences are eager to hear about topics they find meaningful and important. Key examples include love, family, friendship, faith, and work. It's therefore best to tie your vision to these things, so they'll naturally gravitate to it. That forms an authentic connection.

As you craft your vision, be sure it will resonate with your audience at this deeper level. It needs to form a stronger and more durable connection, which will serve as a better foundation for sustained shared action.

HOW TO TURN YOUR VISION INTO REALITY: STRATEGY, OPERATIONS, AND TACTICS

Unless you turn your vision into a reality, it will remain a dream, or even a fantasy. Military strategy provides surprisingly helpful guidance for implementing a vision. You need to work at three levels: strategy, operations, and tactics.

Strategy puts the big pieces in place by setting priorities and mobilizing resources to achieve your vision. The word comes from the ancient Greek *stratēgia*, which is the overarching means by which a war is won. A general sets direction and identifies, attains, and mobilizes the resources required to achieve his goals. Any effort must define how victory looks (the vision) and the means by which you'll achieve it (the strategy). A strategy establishes (generally higher-level) plans for enacting a vision. These plans consider the strengths and weaknesses of the specific group that will enable or inhibit them from reaching any goal. Strategy tends to focus on the longer term and is wide in scope.

For example, the U.S. Department of Defense releases its National Defense Strategy periodically. It sets broad, overarching goals that guide key efforts to meet America's defense needs. The most recent one, released in 2022, identifies four top-level strategic priorities to secure the nation, including "Defending the homeland, paced to the growing multi-domain threat posed by China" and "Building a resilient joint force and defense ecosystem."[5] These priorities set strategic direction for the department's primary efforts.

Here are some questions to help you craft your strategy: What do you do? For whom do you do it? How do you excel at it? What resources do you need to do it? Boil your strategy down to just a few core items—ideally one, maybe two—that guide all your efforts. That's why the National Defense Strategy has four, which is at the upper end of workable.

Operations implement a strategy. Operations set clear objectives and goals for your work. You identify the activities you need to do, and the resources you need to do them. Then you develop processes for monitoring progress toward your goals, like monthly, quarterly, or annual assessments.[6]

Operational planning decides when, where, and how to undertake tactics in service of the team's strategy. It decides which tactics will advance the strategy and, ultimately, the vision.

To orient your operations, ask questions like: Where are you now? Where do you want to be? How do you actually get there? How do you measure your progress? What are your staffing requirements to implement the strategy? What's your timetable for the work? How will you judge the quality of your work?

Tactics are the specific actions taken to execute your strategy and implement your vision. They're the outputs or products you generate for your audience to make progress in your persuasive endeavors. For example, you could meet with a client to understand their needs more clearly, drop the price on a service, or offer a new product. Tactics tend to focus on shorter-term goals (days, weeks, months) rather than longer-term ones (years and decades), which are the realm of operations and especially strategy. Tactics tend to be directive in nature since they're about doing specific things. This makes their scope narrower than operations or strategy.

At the tactical level, ask: What specific things do you need to do to achieve your vision? Be as detailed and expansive as you can, especially in identifying potential tactics. Then whittle down your list.

It's rare that any one person is great, or even good, at working at all these levels. For example, people who excel at operations tend to be more focused on processes, benchmarks, and metrics, and generally aren't as good at strategy. Even if they are, they won't have the time to do all of them well. That's why it's so important whenever possible to work with a team of good performers with diverse and complementary strengths.

How is persuasion a team effort? Almost all professional and personal contexts involve many people who either work with and support you, or who are your counterparts. Suppose you're trying to persuade a potential client to sign with your company. While you might be making the pitch, your team helped you craft and practice it, and even more people will be responsible for implementing the deal once signed.

LET'S GET SPECIFIC

Let's make this tangible and relevant to persuasion with an example. Suppose you're advising a political campaign on crafting and implementing a vision through tactics, operations, and strategy. Your candidate must first discern their vision for the community they seek to serve. If they're more progressive, the vision might center on care for the dispossessed. They then need to identify strategies for realizing that care. This could come through policies like welfare programs or income redistribution.

Operations focus on how to manage the day-to-day work of the campaign. How should the candidate allocate their time? What do the different parts of their team need to do to help the candidate advance their goals and get elected, or get a policy implemented once elected? Successful operations require clarity on where the candidate wants the campaign to go, and will have to devise a plan for getting there. What does the day-to-day need to look like to win the election?

The tactics of the campaign are the specific things the candidate can do to advance their candidacy. These include speeches and remarks, town halls, constituent meetings, campaign events, panels, interviews, traditional media, social media, other news and media, press releases, visuals (graphics), printed items (pamphlets, memos, letters, reports, books, articles, etc.), interpersonal (meetings, visits), op-eds, campaign ads, and websites.

To give another example, I mentioned I'm a poverty researcher. My vision for my work in this space is simple: I want to empower as many people as possible to unleash their unique potential and live their version of the American Dream.

Poverty is a tough issue to discuss, though, because it quickly triggers negative emotions and accusations. My strategy is different. I focus on positive common-ground solutions to poverty that the Left and Right actually agree on, because these areas are ripest for shared action.

I'm happy to report that my research shows seven substantial areas of overlap on issues like removing unfair barriers to work. I found overlap because I looked for it. And I'm even happier to report that people are slowly recognizing this overlap. Operationally, I work to identify and advance agreed-upon solutions on these issues. Tactically, this means I do things like publish research, appear in media, and meet with stakeholders.

Indeed, my vision for poverty alleviation is viable precisely because it's a common-ground and common-sense vision. That's also why it's persuasive.

LET'S REFLECT

Vision drives decision—if you let it. When you see clearly how things will look when you share action, you can orient your short-, medium-, and long-term efforts around putting the pieces together.

You'll be able to communicate your vision up to your managers, across to your peers, down to your direct reports, and out to the world.

As you develop the ability to craft a vision, something spectacular will happen. You'll start to see more opportunities, more clearly, over greater distances. Your horizons will broaden. Opportunities you never knew existed will appear. You'll turn dreams into realities.

At the same time, don't confuse being a visionary with being a delusion-ary. Visionaries dream big. Delusional people have pipe dreams. Visionaries are tethered to reality and work within it, while eventually transforming it. Delusional people are untethered from reality and veer into fantasy. They see things that aren't there. They have no idea how to make their vision real. Ultimately, delusional people can't persuade.

Apple founder Steve Jobs said, "We're here to put a dent in the universe. Otherwise, why else even be here?" You'll never make a dent without a vision. That's why persuasion geniuses have a clear vision. What's yours?

Key Takeaways for Animating Shared Action With Vision

1. You need vision to animate shared action, especially on important initiatives and over time. An effective vision excites people both about where you're going, and about the work you need to do to get there. This requires clarity of purpose. Without a clear vision, you're rudderless. With one, everyone rows in the right direction and moves toward your shared goals.
2. A vision needs to focus on the future. It's about where you want to go, and how good things will look when you get there.
3. Crafting a vision starts with zooming out and looking at the big picture. It's the proverbial forest, and even the broader landscape, not the trees. These three questions will help you craft a persuasive vision: Where do you want or need to go? How come? What would inspire others to join you in working to make this vision a reality?
4. Your vision has to be at once aspirational and realistic. You need to be able to dream and think big to do exciting, novel things. Even if you don't quite get there, you'll often achieve a lot more than you expected. If your vision isn't realistic, though, you risk becoming delusional, seeing things that aren't there, and pursuing things that are highly unlikely or impossible. You'll end up pointing yourself and others in a direction that's unlikely to bear fruit and might even derail an entire organization.
5. To implement your vision, you need to work effectively at three levels: strategy, operations, and tactics. Strategy sets priorities and mobilizes the required resources. Operations implement your vision by setting clear objectives and goals for your work. Tactics are the particular actions needed to implement your vision. You need to work, preferably on a team, to successfully execute at all these levels,

because it's rare that one person is great at all of them; and even if they are, they won't have the time to do all of them well. So build a strong team with diverse talents.

Vision Focusing Question: What is the ONE Thing driving your vision that, if you unite around it, will motivate shared action and success?

Part 2

USE KNOWLEDGE OF HOW OUR BRAINS WORK TO YOUR ADVANTAGE

We operate under reasonable yet flawed assumptions about how our brains work. These assumptions make it hard to persuade others. Too often, they're actually counterproductive.

Part 2 is centered on the questions: How are our brains wired with respect to persuasion? How can you navigate this wiring and use it to your advantage? We answer those questions with the best neuroscience and psychology research available. Then, you learn how to *apply* that knowledge to get what you want and need. Most academic researchers don't take this step, because they focus more on understanding mechanics than on implementing knowledge practically. To become a persuasion genius, you need to know how to act on what you know.

Initially, these realities will be difficult to encounter, because they throw your understanding of reason, emotions, and morality (among other things) for a real loop. You'll question them, maybe even reject them, which is a reasonable response. It will feel like they don't conform to your lived experience. These realities will disrupt how you understand yourself, and how you understand others. That's sure how I experienced them. Nonetheless: Is ignoring reality a recipe for success? Not exactly.

Here's the good news: While it isn't easy to accept or navigate these scientifically established realities, it is simple to rewire yourself to become a persuasion genius. You'll get lots of simple techniques to get what you want.

To prepare you for the discomfort you're going to experience, here's an example. We're wired to be negative. We think that's the pathway to persuasion. It even *feels* good! So we do it all the time. Now, remember a time when someone unleashed a deluge of negativity on you. Did it increase your desire to share action with them? Hardly.

A lot of the advice in these chapters simply requires you to flip your frame of reference and ask: How would I feel if I were on the receiving end of these practices? Then, since it's about them, not you, just apply this to your audience.

Chapter 3

START WITH FEELINGS

People will forget what you said, people will forget what you did, but people will never forget how you made them feel.

attributed to Maya Angelou

For a decade, the gold standard of persuasion seemed clear to me: academic peer review. When I was earning my PhD at Notre Dame, and working as a researcher at Brown University and the University of Wisconsin–Madison, everyone's work pointed at the same process: Do an abundance of research, gather data and logic, and prove your interpretation is right. When done properly, consensus would emerge behind your carefully researched and reasoned position.

This approach is so pervasive that all our educational institutions celebrate it. Professors and teachers show students how to "prove" they're "right." It's *the* pathway to success.

So I published articles and a book with a university press. I even saw the inner workings of the process as an editor for one of the top journals in my field.

Something was off, though. And it wasn't just that 90 percent of papers published in academic journals are never cited, and 50 percent are only read by the peer reviewers and journal editors.[1]

Sure, in STEM fields, things seemed to more or less work this way, since they're generally focused on black-and-white scientific data. But elsewhere, in the social sciences and humanities, that didn't seem to be panning out.

Despite decades of searching for the correct understanding of issues, a remarkably large number of academic issues remain hotly contested, especially in the humanities and soft social sciences, including political science. In fact, disagreements are fierce. And when hidden behind "double-blind peer review," meaning neither the author nor the reviewer know each other's identity, disagreements can turn downright nasty. Reviewers often delight in showing how "wrong" an interpretation is when they disagree with it. Their reviews are often peppered with spicy language. And after the reviewer hits the author over the head with their logic, any guesses what happens? Anything but persuasion.

Unrelated question: How would you respond if someone treated you this way? Would you start to think like them? No.

When academics receive peer reviews that tell them they're dead wrong, almost invariably they just send that paper, with little if any revision, to another journal, hoping to find a reviewer who agrees with them.

This educational training aligns with our intuitions about how persuasion happens, too. We know persuasion is about logic, data, and reason. What would the alternative even be—irrationality? That doesn't sound persuasive. The idea that persuasion is about logic is aligned with our enlightened sensibilities. So we hold "logic" up as the ideal.

There's just one minor problem with viewing "persuasion" as primarily "logical": All the neuroscience and psychology literature show it's not how our brains work. This logic-first approach is actually illogical.

Now, a big part of me *hates* what I'm about to share with you. It threw me for a loop for years. It goes against everything we know. It sure goes against all my professional training, as a former academic and as someone who works at a "think" tank and leads a team of "thinkers."

Well, here's how our brains are really wired: We feel first, then reason. Sometimes it goes feel-boom-reason, sometimes it's feeeeeel . . . then reason, and sometimes we feel and never get to reasoning. We've all been there—I sure have. Feelings, emotions, or intuitions always come first, for everyone. That's why neuroscientist Antonio Damasio calls humans "feeling machines that think,"[2] not thinking machines that feel.

Here's the upshot you'll really hate: Since logic doesn't come first in our cognitive sequence, persuasion can't start with logic. It starts with feelings or emotions. So *you* need to **start with feelings**.

Let's be clear: We do need good reasons for what we say. They just come second.

I know this feels wrong, so much so that you might be tempted to set this book aside. My highly analytical research assistant admitted that before working with me, that's probably what he would have done.

After all, no one really says, "Yeah, man, I just follow my feelings and stop there." Everyone's personal story centers on the assumption that logic drives our decisions. So when most people encounter this core cognitive reality, they just ignore it—to their detriment. That's especially true of high performers who thrive on their intellectual abilities. They know they're logical, and they find the idea of starting with feelings highly aversive.

I once attended a policy workshop with someone who led a federal regulatory agency. He insisted we hit regulators over the head with our logic. When I suggested this wasn't in accordance with how our minds actually work, he blinked, ignored me, then continued telling us how to "win." Rather than rejecting this core cognitive reality, learn to navigate it.

Since we feel first, you need to rewire your brain to focus on generating persuasive feelings that will lead to shared action. For that you need the

Emotionally Intelligent Persuasion Model (EIPM). Emotional intelligence (EI), according to psychologists John Mayer and Peter Salovey, who coined the term, is "a type of social intelligence that involves the ability to monitor one's own and others' emotions, to discriminate among them, and to use the information to guide one's thinking and actions," principally toward problem-solving.[3] EI is about our ability to perceive, understand, navigate, and manage our emotions and the emotions of others. Crucially, whereas IQ is measured with standardized tests and is largely fixed,[4] EI can be learned and therefore increased. Indeed, Mayer, Salovey, and David Caruso have shown with their EI measurement test that EI increases with age.[5] The EIPM shows you how with a simple process and tested techniques.

But first, some evidence-based background on how and why we feel first.

BEWARE THE LOGIC TSUNAMI

Over 2,400 years ago, a wise man from Greece gleaned some foundational insights into persuasion. Aristotle identified three mechanisms of persuasion: ethos, logos, and pathos. Ethos is our status, defined by things like character (are they honest or not) and position (like professor of medicine at Johns Hopkins University). Logos is logic or reason, through which we attempt to show "the truth or the apparent truth from whatever is persuasive in each case."[6] Pathos is emotion. Aristotle saw that persuasion requires all three.

Since then, research has shown that people are actually much more receptive to what you're saying when they perceive intellectual humility in you.[7] We're all wrong every day. I know I am! That's part of being human. When we don't insist that ours is the only right opinion, and admit that we might have something to learn, it's persuasive.

And yet Mr. Spock's annoyance in the *Star Trek* episode "Day of the

Dove" resonates: "May I say that I have not thoroughly enjoyed serving with humans? I find their illogic and foolish emotions a constant irritant."

Logic's allure is undeniable: Do your homework, collect good data, make logical arguments, prove you're right, convince your counterpart, then win the debate. Voilà—persuasion! There's a certain virtue to that. It even feels good.

Logical "persuasion" is cumulative: The more logic, the better. You stack on however much logic necessary (or more!) to break the will of your counterpart.

The only impediment to this process is your opponent's "illogic and foolish emotions." Their inability or unwillingness to see the truth is their failure, not yours. You let yourself off the hook, and dismiss your audience by the same token.

Frustrated, we double down on our logic. Its momentum grows, getting bigger, rumbling over open waters, until it forms a logic tsunami. Your goal, your desire, is for your logic to overwhelm your audience so that they have no choice but to succumb to its power. Maybe it'll wash away their bad or mistaken thoughts, cleansing them so they think like you? Is that how someone persuades you? Hardly.

Tsunamis are dangerous and destructive. When a logic tsunami crashes into you, you initially feel helpless and under siege. Once the threat passes, you feel irritated and usually become defiant and hurl *your* logic at *them*. Perhaps the only thing you don't feel is persuaded.

"Experts" are particularly adept at launching logic tsunamis. They think they remove opinion, bias, and bad judgment from their thought processes, and instead deliver "facts," plain and simple. However, "expert" judgment is flawed, just like everyone else's. Psychologist Daniel Kahneman explains that "humans are incorrigibly inconsistent in making summary judgments of complex information . . . When asked to evaluate the same information twice, they frequently give different answers," even if asked only a few minutes later.[8]

Psychologist Philip Tetlock has shown experts resist admitting mistakes, too. When compelled to admit error, they provide a long list of excuses: Their timing was off, something unforeseen happened, or they were wrong but for the right reasons.[9] And yet "expert logic" remains unimpeachable.

Logic tsunamis are actually more akin to counterproductive emotional deluges hiding under the guise of reason. Even the hyperlogical Mr. Spock admits irritation! "Proving" our points in an emotionally righteous manner *feels* good. It also feels good to defeat our opponents and their ideas. A logic tsunami is often an emotional appeal masquerading as a "logical" one.

WHOSE LOGIC?

We operate under the reasonable yet mistaken assumption that we all reason the same way. The trouble begins with the complicated nature of facts themselves. Sure, some scientific facts are indisputable, like the chemical makeup of water being H_2O. Political, economic, and social facts are more complicated, though. They're difficult to measure. And even if we can measure them, opinions about them differ. Consider income inequality. How do we measure it? Only by actual income? Or do we include government and private assistance? How much inequality is acceptable, and what kinds of inequality are acceptable? All up for debate.

Facts are shaped by experience, too. It wouldn't be surprising if someone who grows up poor might be more sensitive to extreme income inequality than someone who grows up rich.

We tend to disregard facts that don't conform to our beliefs. As Kahneman explains, "even compelling causal statistics will not change long-held beliefs or beliefs rooted in personal experience."[10] We know what we know, factual or not.

When we encounter "facts" that challenge our worldview, we feel under attack. So we adopt a warlike mentality, digging in our heels and fighting back, not giving an inch.

WE'RE NOT EVEN THAT LOGICAL

For a belief to be logical, it needs to be sound and stable. It can't change haphazardly over time. A seminal study shows that by these basic standards, most people's "logic" is badly impaired, making "logical" persuasion extremely difficult.

In 1964, political scientist Philip Converse studied the coherence of people's beliefs. He looked at whether beliefs are "constrained," meaning you understand a term, and that understanding predicts what you think about other issues.[11] Converse measured constraint with questions like "Would you say that either one of the parties is more *conservative* or more *liberal* than the other?" If respondents said yes, the interviewer then asked, "What do you have in mind when you say that the Republicans (or Democrats) are more conservative than the Democrats (or Republicans)?" Generally, Republicans are more conservative, Democrats more liberal. If someone said something like, "Democrats are more conservative because they oppose abortion and reject a large role for government," this person would have failed the test. So, how did people do?

Poorly. Only about one in thirty Americans had truly coherent political beliefs, demonstrating a sound understanding of the terms.[12] One in ten people mentioned the liberal-conservative continuum and seemed to have a shallow understanding of it. The rest, about seven in eight, fell into one of three groups, including one called "no issue content."[13] For them, "little constraint is felt, even, quite often, in instances of sheer logical constraint." The vast majority of people didn't have coherent political beliefs, "even on issues that have formed the basis for intense political controversy among elites for substantial periods of time."[14]

People's beliefs also fluctuate over time, often with little obvious cause. When Converse interviewed the same people four years later, only 65 percent of them located themselves on the same *side* of an issue. Fifty percent could have done so just by flipping a coin.[15] Other researchers have reached the same findings.[16]

You might wonder: Is this only true in America, and better elsewhere? Nope. Converse and Roy Pierce reached the same conclusion about France.[17] *Incroyable!*

You might also wonder: Since we have more access to information and technology, aren't our beliefs more constrained today? Unfortunately, no. In 2000, Converse showed the vast majority of other researchers continue to arrive at the same conclusions.[18]

How can we persuade people principally through "logic" when most people don't define terms or understand concepts the same way? That's not a trick question. It's decidedly difficult.

HUMAN JUDGMENT IS DEEPLY BIASED AND NOISY

"Logical" persuasion is even harder because our brains are full of bias and "noise." Bias is "systematic deviation," which is "the average error in a set of judgments."[19] Noise, by contrast, is "random scatter."[20] Imagine you're shooting at a target. If your shots are scattered around the board, then your aim is noisy. If they're clustered together—say, in the bottom left—your aim is biased. Cognitive psychology and behavioral economics show both are pervasive and shape how we feel, think, and act. And it's hard, though not impossible, to avoid these barriers to shared action.

Extensive research shows our brains are full of "cognitive bias." Cognitive bias occurs when our brain attempts to simplify information to make life easier. We create rules of thumb that help us understand the world and make decisions more quickly. Without these rules, we'd experience decision paralysis. With them, we develop systematic yet flawed thinking patterns. We have processing errors in our judgment resulting from imperfections with our memory, attention, focus, and attribution, as well as other cognitive errors. Researchers have discovered at least 188 of these systematic biases.[21] That's a lot of bias! Let's consider how some prominent biases impede our ability to persuade through logic.

Confirmation bias is our tendency to confirm what we already feel and think. We select information supporting our views, and disregard information that counters them. For example, if we try to persuade someone by showing them a news article to support our view and disprove theirs, they'll just ignore it and look for another article aligned with their views. We're wired to justify ourselves. Skeptical? Driven by their ideological outlook, partisan brains react instantly, *within a half second.* As psychologist Jonathan Haidt explains, "We are dreadful at seeking out evidence that might disconfirm our initial judgments."[22] And research shows even training interventions only reduce confirmation bias modestly, by 19 percent.[23]

Hindsight bias is the I-knew-it-all-along effect. It describes our tendency to look at past events and overestimate how well we predicted the outcome, and how predictable the outcome was in the first place. We look back at an event like the 2008 financial collapse and persuade ourselves that we saw it coming, even though in reality we didn't.

The halo effect describes our "tendency to like (or dislike) everything about a person—including things you have not observed," based on how we perceive them.[24] We put a halo on this person's head and judge them to be beyond reproach. You might place a halo over someone's head at work because they graduated from a prestigious university or came highly recommended from someone you trust. Even if they do something that logically deserves reproach, the halo we see hanging over their head makes it hard to persuade us of negative things about them. By contrast, the horn effect motivates us to judge people we dislike more harshly. That makes it hard to persuade us that they're better than we think, even if they're doing a great job.

The anchoring effect occurs when one piece of information, however irrelevant to the matter at hand, shapes our thought process. In one experiment, researchers rigged a wheel to land on either ten or sixty-five, then asked participants to guess the percentage of countries in the United Nations that are African. Participants who saw a ten on the wheel guessed 25 percent, whereas those who saw sixty-five guessed 45 percent.[25] (The actual answer is 28 percent). It's obviously "illogical" for a number on a wheel to impact this belief . . . and yet it does. People are easily persuaded by irrelevant information.

Far from being simply maladaptive, many of these biases evolved due to our ancestors' need to process information quickly. Was that the wind, or a vicious predator? If I eat this plant, will it kill me? We often *need* to act quickly, especially in dangerous situations. If we tried to "logically" process every decision based on all available information, we'd make few decisions and get nothing done.

Our brains are noisy, too. Noise is unexplained randomness and variability in our judgments, when we would expect those judgments to be similar or identical. Kahneman and coauthors Olivier Sibony and Cass Sunstein explain that noise is pervasive: "*Wherever there is judgment, there is noise—and more of it than you think.*"[26] *Everyone* has some degree of noise in their judgment process; many people have lots. When our brains are noisy, "logical" persuasion is much more difficult.

There are different kinds of noise. "System noise" occurs when people vary undesirably in their judgment of a case. For example, different judges might issue quite dissimilar sentencing decisions for the same defendant.

System noise "can create rampant injustice, high economic costs, and errors of many kinds."[27] "Level noise" arises when a judge is either harsher or more lenient than the average judge. "Pattern noise" occurs when someone deviates from their own average. We'd expect them to arrive at one judgment based on their past, and they don't.[28] "Occasion noise" refers to the randomness that is the occasion when we judge. Lots of factors, including mood, tiredness, the sequence of events, and even the weather create noise.[29] They all impact our ability to persuade someone.

The cognitive wiring underlying bias and noise makes purely "logical" persuasion nearly impossible (though some researchers are more optimistic).[30] Our best chance to reduce bias and noise is to develop policies and practices that help identify and address it. For example, to avoid confirmation bias, a team could have a policy of reviewing a certain number of articles that present views divergent from the team's.

Ultimately, we need strategies that don't rely purely on "logic" to bypass bias and noise to share action. One of the top strategies is at the heart of this chapter and chapter 4: Generate persuasive feelings. The second is at the heart of chapter 6: Tell persuasive stories. For example, to overcome the "horn effect," someone needs to have more positive feelings about the person with horns. One good technique to achieve that is to tell stories about good things they've done. That will push back against the preexisting, negative narrative.

PAUSE AND BREATHE

Let's take a moment to pause, breathe, and assess where we are. The ideal that reason and logic ought to guide thought and action is noble. It's also a mirage. Logic is not the primary driver of human decision-making. Since we pride ourselves on our ability to logically think through problems both large and small, that's a tough pill to swallow.

WE FEEL FIRST

What are we, if not mere logic processors? Feeling,[31] emotion,[32] or intuition processors.[33] Neuroscientists and psychologists have shown that we feel first. Neuroscientist Antonio Damasio explains feelings "come first in development and retain a primacy that subtly pervades our mental life."[34] As Haidt has put it, "*Intuitions come first, strategic reasoning second.*"[35] This doesn't mean that we don't reason. It just means that it doesn't come first in our cognition.

What exactly do we feel? Psychologists generally offer between five and eight basic emotions. Fear, anger, and sadness make all the lists. Other candidates include disgust, enjoyment/happiness/joy, surprise, anticipation, love, and trust.[36] Intuitions are preceded by, and closely connected to, emotions and feelings.[37] Researchers generally define intuition as an automatic, rapid form of cognition that recognizes patterns and is related to emotion and interaction.[38] Through this rapid cognitive process, "we come to a particular conclusion without being aware of all the immediate logical steps."[39]

Kahneman provides the best explanation of the feel-first dynamic by separating our thinking into two "systems." Most of what we see, say, and do is guided by "System 1," our default system. It generates "impressions, intuitions, intentions, and feelings" automatically, quickly, and involuntarily.[40] These feelings are strong, and we use them to construct coherent narratives about everything.

"System 2," by contrast, engages in effortful mental activities like complex computations. It's capable of reasoning and doubt, and is cautious (whereas System 1 suppresses doubt in favor of action). When our spontaneous search for intuitive (System 1) solutions fails, then we switch to slower, more deliberate, reasoned (System 2) thinking.[41] An example of System 1 thinking is driving a car. An example of System 2 thinking is writing an essay.

System 1 generally dominates our thinking. While we like to identify mainly with logical System 2,[42] and System 2 *can* overrule System 1, we usually just adopt System 1's suggestions with little if any modification.[43] System 2 is inactive for most people most of the time because reasoning takes much effort, while intuiting doesn't.

Data and logic don't change System 1's assessments. The quality and quantity of information have little impact on System 1's impressions and intuitions.[44]

While we intuitively think it's bad for System 1 to rule the roost, it's actually good and adaptive. Kahneman explains System 1 is "the origin of much that we do wrong, but it is also the origin of most of what we do right—which is most of what we do. Our thoughts and actions are routinely guided by System 1 and generally are on the mark."[45] We don't even have the time, resources, or inclination to engage System 2 with everything. Consider driving a car. Using System 1, once we're trained, we just do it—stop and go, turn left or right. If we primarily engaged System 2, we'd question each action and be slow or paralyzed, unable to drive. Cognitive traffic jam.

Intuition, not reason, drives judgment. Reason is neither unimportant nor nonexistent. We aren't irrational creatures. Reason just doesn't come first. But reason *can* help guide our intuitions—if we let it.

Perhaps most surprising to people who remain committed to reason's supremacy, emotions actually *enhance* and *improve* our reasoning processes. Emotionless processes result in irrational behavior.[46] Without emotions, our reasoning simply breaks down.

Emotions tell us quickly when we do and don't like something, which is crucial for sharing action. When we have a positive or negative reaction to something, that's in part our mind's way of telling us we do or don't like something, or that it does or doesn't work for us. Our emotions often know what we're thinking before we do. For example, if someone shares news they think is good for you, and your response is muted, you both immediately get access to important information.

To get what we want, we need to observe, accept, embrace, and work within the psychological and neurological reality of the human mind. Here's how you do that.

HOW TO START WITH FEELINGS

A proven process for persuading through emotions is the Emotionally Intelligent Persuasion Model. It has four steps:

Emotionally Intelligent Persuasion Model

Step 1: Observe how you and your audience feel.
Step 2: Identify shared goals.
Step 3: Facilitate feelings necessary to share action.
Step 4: Share action.

Start with step 1. Simply observe—don't judge!—feelings, yours and theirs. How do you both feel in general? About each other? About the potential collaboration? That'll let you know whether and how you can engage.

Start with your feelings, since you have direct access to them, and they color everything you see, say, and do. Assess them honestly and accurately. That's hard. We won't, don't, or can't always recognize how we're feeling.

Before engaging with someone, literally pause and ask yourself: How am I feeling (positive or negative)? What's causing me to feel that way? You might need to write your answer down. If you're having trouble accessing your feelings, talk to someone who can help you get clarity, like a close friend. Either share what's on your mind with them, or ask them how they're experiencing you. Maybe you seem sad to them. If clarity still isn't forthcoming, now is probably not the time to engage.

Being in the right emotional state is crucial to sharing action for many reasons. When you're experiencing negative emotions, it's hard to have and maintain a them-first approach, because you're focused on your feelings. It's also highly unlikely that you'll engage someone fruitfully when you're experiencing too many negative emotions, especially if they're about your counterpart. You might need to pause or even step away from engaging with them until you're emotionally ready. Below and in later chapters, we'll discuss some techniques for getting into a better emotional state sooner.

Observe your audience's emotions, too. Otherwise, how can you engage them with emotional intelligence? Focus on correctly *observing* their feelings, not whether you *agree* with or like them. If you start judging them, this usually creates barriers to sharing action, because you quickly find something about their feelings you don't like.

Here's a stealthy, proven technique that works like magic: Ask them! Literally, ask them, "How do you feel about X?," like a decision or issue. Or just ask more generally, "How are you feeling?" I use this technique to manage up with my bosses, and down with my direct reports. They give remarkably honest answers, much different than if I asked, "What do you think?"

Whenever I need to make a request of a direct report, I ask, "How would you feel about doing X?" Any negative emotions are quickly apparent, both because they share them directly, and because their body language and tone reveal a lot. When they share their negative feelings, I address them directly so they don't become barriers to shared action.

If one or both of you are angry or anxious, now might not be the right time to press them on something. Or it might be the perfect time, because a particular concern might be stopping them from working with you.

A few weeks into my job as a fundraiser, I was subjected to a deluge of negative emotions from an unhappy supporter, who had given us over

$1 million, and his adviser. They could not have been more direct. For forty-five minutes they expressed their dissatisfaction with a program they supported. Rather than using my "logic" to fight theirs, I sat there and absorbed the blows. They had stuff they needed to get off their chest. After I took a lot of proverbial bullets for my organization, they were visibly relieved. They even acknowledged they were being harsh, and it wasn't my fault. Finally, a tiny opening.

Understanding their concerns, I went back to my organization and worked to address them. Which I did through sustained follow-up and reporting. My next meeting, with the adviser, was remarkably friendly because I had successfully alleviated their negative emotions. And they continued giving us money.

You can also observe your audience's feelings indirectly. Talk to people who know them, preferably with knowledge of their feelings on the specific issue. Do your own research, too. Check if they post their feelings and thoughts somewhere, like social media. Many people share a lot (often too much) about themselves there. Search the internet for relevant information. For example, if you're meeting with a community organizer who has been outspoken about poverty to discuss housing affordability, her online content might reveal how she feels about it.

Pay attention to their nonverbal behavior. As psychologist Daniel Goleman explains, "One rule of thumb used in communications research is that 90 percent or more of an emotional message is nonverbal."[47] Observe tone and body language (we consider both in chapter 8). Listen to *how* they say things. Are they excited? Defensive? Nervous? For body language, are they slumped over in their chair, visibly sullen? Or bright and perky?

Try to observe how you feel about each other, too. Negative feelings create barriers to shared action. Positive feelings grease the wheels of collaboration. It's often hard to honestly observe how others feel about you, because we generally have positive images of ourselves. We often aren't attuned to how people experience us. If you're bold, ask them. Or ask others how your counterpart feels about you. You may or may not be the right person to try to engage in shared action, or now might not be the right time. Better to know that sooner rather than later.

I once met with an elected official for the first time. He had worked extensively with my organization. Unprompted, he told me other elected officials didn't like my organization's lobbyist. Clearly, that lobbyist was not the right messenger. Instead, I should meet with them separately to build better relationships. He then offered to introduce me to key players, which he did. So I started building better relationships, building trust and influence with them.

The second step of the EIPM is to identify shared goals with your counterpart. This overlap represents the best opportunity for shared action. When you focus mainly or entirely on what *you* want, it usually results in focusing on things that don't interest your counterpart. That's not a recipe for persuasion.

How do you identify shared goals? Gather as much relevant information as possible to find overlap with your goals and theirs. Ask your counterpart directly what they want and need. Research them. Ask others. Look online for things they've said and done.

The biggest sticking point in this step is a rascally little critter called "WHY?!" *WHY?!* do you have that goal? So often, people share observations about a situation (like a problem and its causes) and on solutions to improve it. But *why* are you concerned about that? *WHY?!* do you support this goal? When someone sees their "why" is different from someone else's, that often becomes a huge barrier to working with them, even if they have the same goal. Here's an example of what this looks like in the policy world.

America faces a housing affordability crisis driven by insufficient supply. The best way to make housing more affordable is to make it easier to build homes of all shapes and sizes to meet diverse needs.[48] Experts actually agree on this! So why don't we take necessary steps to make this better? Because of *WHY?!*

Folks on the left, as you'll learn in chapter 5, are driven by concerns about inequality and how policies hurt the poor. Current housing policy in most places impacts both negatively. Folks on the right are driven by concerns about freedom and proportionality (among other things). Current housing policies infringe on both. Rather than setting "why" aside and sharing action, most policy professionals let *WHY?!* become a barrier.

There's a technical term to describe this approach: silly. It's silly.

I don't let *WHY?!* become a barrier. I set aside "why" and focus on our shared understanding (low supply, higher prices) and shared goal (more supply, lower prices). Turns out, this resonates across the political spectrum, as evidenced by op-eds I've published and policies I've successfully proposed.

In step 3, you facilitate feelings necessary to share action, and diffuse the ones preventing it. The next three chapters walk you through how to do this. Here's a quick preview. First, be *for* something, and be a happy warrior focused on generating positive feelings like joy, happiness, love, or anticipation, because they lead to the best outcomes. You will see how this works in the next chapter. Second, generate persuasive feelings by appealing to your audience's values. More on that in chapter 5. Third, tell powerful stories, since stories are the single most powerful persuasive tool that exists. You get a formula for doing that in chapter 6.

How your audience feels about you is in many ways more important for persuasion than what you say. Chapter 8 explores in depth why persuasion is more than mere words. If you get the words "right" and other things wrong, the words don't really matter.

The most important thing you can do is to communicate at the level of feelings. We'll come back to that shortly.

Here are some other key ways to generate positive feelings toward you, many of which we dive into more deeply in chapter 8. Make yourself someone with whom your audience wants to work. Be likable, because it greases the wheels of cooperation; and being unlikable is a huge barrier to shared action. Which means be calm and patient, not annoyed and rushed. Be welcoming and warm, not closed and cold. Demonstrate genuine interest in your audience, because it's the right thing to do, and it points the way to shared action. Listen first, talk last. Demonstrate understanding of what they want and need so they feel like you get them. Adopt a warm, calm tone. A harsh or annoyed tone makes the "right" words toxic. Adopt confident body language and avoid body language that shows contempt for your audience. Build trust, and avoid words and deeds that breed distrust, since it rarely goes away.

You also need to defuse or remove negative feelings acting as barriers to shared action, regardless of whether they have anything to do with you directly. Observe and identify your counterpart's negative feelings, then address them directly. (We discuss this more in chapter 7.) Both of these are hard to do, especially if any negativity is directed toward you, fairly or not. That generates negative emotions in you, which erects another barrier.

Whatever the case, address barriers head-on. If someone is being cold or is clearly agitated, for example, don't overlook it. Intuitively, you probably have a good idea what's causing it. If not, ask them; they'll usually tell you. Try a label: "It feels like something's bothering you." Then see what they say. Once you correctly identify the negative feelings, you need to at least neutralize—and, ideally, remove—them. Often, simply acknowledging and discussing them goes a long way to removing them. That's what happened with the upset millionaire I mentioned above. If you're itching for a promotion, you can say to your boss, "It feels like there are more things I need to do before I'm ready to advance here." They're likely to either name them, or tell you otherwise what's stopping you. If your spouse refuses to talk to you, say, "It looks like I did something really stupid that upset you." They'll probably say, "Yes, you did!" then tell you.

And they'll usually need to see real actions, from you or someone else, to feel better. Without actions, words alone are rarely enough for persuasion.

Consider also what reasons your audience needs to have the feelings necessary for shared action. Since strategic reasoning comes second, you need to ensure your audience has reasons to feel good so they can share action with you. Have those reasons ready at the appropriate time.

Throughout step 3, it's important to control your feelings as much as possible, especially if they're negative, because they can derail any persuasive endeavor. One simple and remarkably effective strategy for managing negative emotions is the "physiological sigh." The practice has been showcased by Andrew Huberman, a professor of neurobiology at Stanford University. It's simple: Inhale once through your nose just about all the way, then inhale a second time through your nose, filling your lungs completely, then exhale through your mouth.[49] It has the powerful effect of physiologically lowering your stress. Do this at least once, and up to twenty-five times, when you're feeling stressed. It'll help get you back on track.

If you want to prevent feeling too negative, avoid venting, either from you or your counterpart. As negotiation professors Roger Fisher and Daniel Shapiro explain, venting can often make a bad situation worse.[50] Reason being, we just make ourselves feel more agitated by complaining, without thinking about solutions to the problem.

Feelings that produce tension are a big barrier to sharing action. Psychology offers at least two tangible approaches to facilitating collaboration when tension is present. The first is Graduated Reciprocation in Tension reduction (GRIT). The idea is you make a gesture, a first move, toward reducing or resolving your counterpart's concern, without agreeing with their concern. This first step can go a long way, and often they'll reciprocate with a step of their own, because they feel like you get them. This rachets down tension and opens up space for persuasion. Former Egyptian President Anwar Sadat used GRIT to establish trust between Egypt and Israel, eventually leading to a peace agreement in 1978.[51]

The second approach is the contact hypothesis. As long as people share big-picture goals, they can end up on the same page and work together toward those goals, even if they hate each other. By letting shared goals drive your interactions with them, positive emotions can overcome the negative emotions of interacting with you.

And step 4 is to share action. This is when you and your counterpart actually work toward your shared goals. That's the best part. And the EIPM is how you get there consistently. Here's an example that shows the EIPM in action.

I initially started writing this book after work at night and on weekends. While a necessary way to start, it was far from optimal. I needed to work on this full-time. And I needed someone to pay me to do that. Once I had four or five chapters drafted, I started shopping my book proposal around to think tanks in Washington, DC. One of them stood out as potentially the perfect fit. So I went all in. I used my connections to get my proposal in the hands of the right people there. Then I used the EIPM to land a research fellowship.

Step 1 was to observe feelings. Everyone I met with felt that our policy movement had a persuasion deficit, and that it was a problem. Step 2 was to identify shared goals. This one was simple, because the organization's founder had been deeply committed to what he called "values-based communications." He knew you had to communicate at the level of someone's values; otherwise persuasion is impossible. We all knew our movement was coming up woefully short on this front. We shared a commitment to changing that.

Step 3 was to facilitate the feelings necessary to share action, namely producing work to address this. They had to feel good about me, and I was an unknown quantity. So I overprepared as much as I could for the interviews with the vice presidents and eventually the president. During each interview, I emphasized my alignment with their values, as well as their mission, with specificity. I shared my book proposal to give them clarity on how I would execute the project. And I identified additional work I could do that would advance their mission.

After meeting for an hour, the president turned to his colleague and said in front of me, "Well, what do you think? Should we bring him on?" Then he smiled, and said, "Let me show you around your new office."

COMMUNICATE AT THE LEVEL OF FEELINGS

The best way, by far, to use the EIPM and generate persuasive feelings is for you to communicate at the level of feelings. That means you need to express yourself verbally and visually in a manner that authentically showcases the feelings you want your audience to feel. How can you expect them to share your passion for or interest in something if they don't feel and see it? You can't.

To communicate at the level of feelings, begin by exploring what makes you passionate about whatever it is you're trying to convey to your audience. Be as specific as you can so you know where to focus your mind when you're communicating.

Passion either shows up or it doesn't. It's the deep-seated conviction that your idea, product, or plan, for example, will make the world a better place. Your passion must be authentic; it can't be faked. We all have a gut instinct that tells us when people really aren't into what they're saying. Passion shines through. Fake emotions fall flat.[52]

Once you know the source of your passion, you need to let it shine through to your audience. Feel what you want your audience to feel in your heart and your gut, not in your head. Which means you need to speak from those places. Literally put your hand on your gut and feel yourself speaking from there. To compare, put your hand on your throat or cheek and try speaking from there. It's a lot different.

Communicating at the level of feelings requires training. Practice every chance you get, starting in low-stakes situations, like talking to a friend. It will gradually become more natural and more authentic, which will help your audience experience it how you want them to.

Another great way to practice is to take improv classes. That's what I did in multiple courses at The Second City in Chicago, one of the best improv training programs in the country. Improv is about working, playing, and performing without a script. You don't have time to pause, think, analyze, then speak carefully. You have to react; otherwise, you pause awkwardly and the scene goes nowhere.

The best and most authentic reactions in improv are emotional. Emotions drive scenes forward and help you connect with your scene partner(s) and audience. As you learn to stop judging and start releasing yourself, you find flow with your scene partner(s). Some of what you will do is silly. Possibly the most absurd thing I've ever done is an improv game called "Bunny Bunny." In games like that, communicating at the level of feelings is the only thing that makes any sense at all—so you just do it.

ON MOUNTAINS AND MOLEHILLS

Even if you master the entire EIPM and navigate a difficult situation as carefully as you can, emotions can nonetheless explode, sending everything off the rails. When someone is overwhelmed by emotion, molehills can become mountains, even lava-spewing volcanoes, in an instant. Someone says or does something, and it provokes an extreme reaction in you, them, or both and . . . boom—eruption!

How should you proceed if a molehill becomes a mountain, or an erupting emotional volcano, with lava rushing at you? Our instinct is to tell the person that what happened isn't a big deal, their emotions aren't reasonable, and you didn't do anything wrong. DO. NOT. DO. THIS! It's like trying to put out a fire with gasoline. Anyone who's tried these phrases on an angry toddler will know how counterproductive they are; the same goes for adults. Inferno.

Even if you don't think you've done anything wrong (and maybe you haven't), you need to understand and openly acknowledge your counterpart's feelings because they're real. This isn't tantamount to agreement, genuine or fake. It just means that you demonstrate understanding of their concerns. One helpful tactic is to address their concern directly (we discuss this in chapter 7). For example, if someone thinks you violated their trust, you can lean in and say, "You think I've violated your trust."

If you did do something wrong, then the high-EI move is—wait for it—to apologize. This is hard, because pretty much no one likes apologizing. And keep in mind, an apology must include real ownership and accountability. "I'm sorry *you think* I misled you" or "I'm sorry *you feel* that way" implicitly blames your counterpart. The phrasing "I'm sorry, *I should have* communicated better," by contrast, actually owns up to something. A thoughtful apology can go a long way toward solidifying your counterpart's trust in you.

When emotions run high, it's important to give everyone involved, including you, time to calm down. That might require an hour, a day, a week, or longer. Just because you want to engage now doesn't mean it's the right time. Lava needs to stop flowing first, then cool down.

I once infuriated a client by delivering exactly what I thought he asked for. He wanted metrics for his division. I delivered him phase 1. He was beyond thrilled, so much so that he sent it to the head of the entire organization. I outlined exactly what I planned to do in phase 2, which included interviewing people who worked there. He approved it. Then I did it and delivered a report on it. Luckily, my boss had read and approved the report.

Because thirty seconds into the meeting, the guy exploded. Reason being, the interviews identified some adjustments his division needed to make—based entirely on what his employees said—to implement the metrics he wanted. Which he took as criticism of his management. For thirty minutes, he screamed at us. My boss, having a sense of humor, said to me right after the meeting, "That went well!"

It took the guy a few months before he would talk to me again. Every time he walked by my desk, I felt uncomfortable. Eventually he started talking to me. And slowly we were able to interact fruitfully again. If I had approached him soon thereafter, it would have been counterproductive because the lava hadn't stopped flowing out of his brain and mouth.

LOGIC RETURNS

After launching what could look like an extended assault on logic, and holding up feelings as central to persuasion, it might seem like we're saying there's little if any place for logic, data, reason, and rationality. Maybe we should set logic aside and focus on eliciting whatever feelings will help our cause? Not at all.

When I say we feel first, that doesn't mean we *only* feel. Rather, it emphasizes the order of how our brain processes and responds to information. Strategic reasoning certainly happens; it just always comes *after* feelings. If you ignore this crucial first step, you decrease or destroy your chances of getting where you want or need to go. While you need to start with feelings, you don't stop there. What, then, is logic's role in persuasion?

Our feelings, words, and deeds undoubtedly need a firm logical foundation. Otherwise, we're building on unstable ground, and our effort will likely collapse. *Only* feeling, then acting on those feelings, rarely results in anything resembling success. We need to get the data and logic right.

Let's take public policy advocacy as an example. Most of the advocacy is rigorous and "logical," and doesn't persuade anyone. How come? Because policy advocates launch their logic at people. They present it in lifeless terms. They focus on "winning" and conquering, er, "convincing" people. They write research papers, wave them around, and think that's the way to make a difference. No! Lots of good ideas stay on the shelf and collect dust. Here's a better process.

Make logic and data exciting. Advocates like to flash numbers, graphs, charts, and slides. Riveting? Nope. Snooze. Snore. Ignored. Happily, we *can* make data exciting, and we can make logic come alive.

For starters, don't lead with data. By themselves, they're boring. Instead, lead with high-EI tactics. Consider how your data will make your audience feel. Good or bad? Nervous or excited? Happy or sad? If you're presenting a quarterly report to the executive team at your company, numbers that are higher or lower than expected will elicit different reactions. Anticipate them. If you expect a negative reaction, preempt it with tactics like addressing their concern directly. "You aren't going to like our results from the last quarter." They'll brace for bad news.

Consider how you'd like your audience to feel when they encounter your data. Suppose you have great financial results to share. Your company was aiming for 5 percent growth last quarter, and you actually grew at 9 percent. When you report the results to the executive team, highlight and praise things they did to make the success possible. That'll make them feel good. Talk about how you're going to sustain it. Paint a positive vision for the next quarter and beyond so they feel excited.

The best emotionally intelligent tactic for sharing data is to tell stories. Rather than merely saying, "We grew 9 percent last quarter, much higher than the 5 percent we targeted," tell a story about how that happened. Tell stories with details about great work among teammates and satisfied customers. That'll make them *feel* good.

Beware neglecting to do this. I once met with a colleague who works in fundraising. She was furious because after finding a billionaire and securing a meeting with him that led to a huge investment, she was completely cut out of the success story. The head fundraiser celebrated getting the investment without so much as mentioning my colleague's great work. It was all about *him*. She was severely demotivated, remained bitter, and quit a few months later, getting a promotion and pay raise somewhere else. It cost the organization a lot of money in the future. Giving her the praise she deserved would have made her feel great and would have been an example of good leadership and team building. How much would praise have cost her boss? Nothing. Giving her a bonus to thank her for her hard work would have motivated her to work harder. Instead, he lost a great prospector and eager employee. Radical selfishness is expensive.

There are specific strategies for making your data more impactful. Chip Heath and Karla Starr, in *Making Numbers Count*, provide lots of good advice: Favor user-friendly numbers; help people understand through simple, familiar comparisons; convert abstract numbers to concrete objects; and recast your number in different dimensions: Try time, space, distance, and money.[53] If you communicate numbers regularly, peruse their book.

It might still seem that STEM fields lend themselves primarily or exclusively to logical or data-driven presentations. After all, the ideas themselves are often hard enough to explain. Even in STEM, the most persuasive visionaries powerfully brought their discoveries to life.

Apple cofounder Steve Jobs was the best corporate storyteller and one of the most effective proselytizers for technology, period. Under his leadership, Apple didn't just release new products and hope they'd sell. Time after time, Jobs gave phenomenal talks that revolutionized public presentations. Communications expert Carmine Gallo has studied Jobs's presentation tactics extensively. Among his most persuasive tools were: answering the one question that matters most, drawing a road map, revealing a conquering hero, and mastering stage presence.[54] Every presentation told a powerful story with a compelling vision for how the product would make people's lives better, and maybe even change the world. The iPhone undoubtedly has.

Jobs's 2007 iPhone launch presentation was a master class. He said, "Today, Apple is going to reinvent the phone." And: "iPhone is a revolutionary and magical product that is literally five years ahead of any other mobile phone." Imagine if, instead, Apple had sent out a press release about a new product. Or if Jobs had said, "Our new phone is 2.4 times faster than the leading competitor, with three times the memory and processing power." Not so impactful.

Jobs's persuasive prowess catapulted Apple to the top of the tech world by making technology exciting. Think more like Jobs when presenting data and logic. How? When I asked Gallo, he highlighted that Jobs didn't come from the tech space originally.[55] Jobs came to technology through beauty. That's why his slides looked great. So focus more on aesthetic elements for all presentations, especially STEM ones.

LET'S GET SPECIFIC

It should have been one of the best days of my life. I had just defended my dissertation, earning a PhD from a top-ten program. I was off to what was widely recognized as the most prestigious postdoctoral fellowship in my field. As I walked to my adviser's office to debrief from the previous day's dissertation defense, with a bottle of my favorite Bordeaux wine in my hand as a tiny token of my appreciation to her, I was on cloud nine.

I sat down in her office, smiling ear to ear. Then she drew her sword and attacked, nearly striking a fatal blow to my professional ambitions.

She literally said, "If you didn't have that postdoc at Brown, I'd have made you rewrite your dissertation." Then she tore into me, making it clear my dissertation needed work. She told me everything that was wrong with it, from her lofty perspective.

At some level, this is always and obviously true: Every dissertation needs to be revised to be published as a book. But having feedback delivered with obvious animosity changed everything. It took six months before I could even look at the dissertation again. Precious time wasted.

Turns out, she was wrong. I revised the dissertation and turned it into a book manuscript. At my book workshop, two premium scholars praised the manuscript. I published it with a university press. During the peer review process, two professor reviewers also praised the work. I asked the two best-known professors from the four if they'd endorse the book on the book jacket for all the world to see. They happily did so.

I learned from this epic assault that it's necessary to put feelings first when you deliver feedback to anyone, in professional and personal situations. I use the approach in this chapter every day when managing my policy team. I put their feelings first and craft my feedback in a way that's constructive, supportive, and actionable. Instead of telling them how inadequate they are, I highlight their strengths. If there are growth areas, I frame them as such rather than discussing them as failings and insufficiencies. Which is why our team maintains a great dynamic and embraces a growth mindset that enhances all our skills much more quickly.

LET'S REFLECT

I was once talking to a state senator. I asked, "What are your legislative priorities?" He outlined them. I then asked, "What appetite is there among the other party for them?" He actually said, "I don't know. That would require me to have conversations with them." He was only interested in being "right," not in making a difference. Which meant he didn't have to even engage people who didn't think like him. Not persuasive.

When you focus only on being "right," you kill your chances of becoming a persuasion genius. You adopt the "crusader's mindset" and insist on proving your points and "convincing" your counterpart to acquiesce and adopt your viewpoint by driving your logic down their throat. That's impossible for them to swallow. So they don't. They spit it out, or maybe even back at you. When you attempt to crusade to victory, you'll never persuade anyone of anything.

Persuasion geniuses focus instead on making a difference. That requires lots of EI. As communications professor Sally Planalp explains, "To *move* people, we must study e-motion."[56] That's why every chapter in this book is centered around emotionally intelligent strategies and techniques. EI needs to permeate all parts of your persuasive endeavors.

Persuasion geniuses always give the right answer to the question: Do you want to be right, or do you want to make a difference? The choice is yours.

Key Takeaways for Persuading at the Level of Feelings

1. We're all wired to feel first, then reason. Which means that persuasion starts with feelings, emotions, or intuitions, not with logic. So start with feelings in all your persuasive endeavors. As wrong as this undoubtedly feels, it's corroborated by neuroscience and psychology. Accept this cognitive reality and learn to navigate it.
2. Being "right" feels good. So our default usually is to launch our "logic" at people until they stop arguing with us. While the allure of "proving" you're right with data, logic, and reason is undeniable, does someone persuade you this way? Nope. It usually makes us *less* likely to work with them.
3. Researchers have found an abundance of ways in which our logic is compromised. Our beliefs are often incoherent and unstable over time. Our judgment is compromised by "cognitive bias" and "noise." We're not nearly as logical as we think we are.
4. The Emotionally Intelligent Persuasion Model (EIPM) is a proven method for sharing action. Start by observing how you and your audience are feeling. Then identify shared goals. Next, facilitate the feelings necessary to share action. Finally, share action.
5. As masterful as you will become at identifying and navigating feelings (yours and theirs), emotions can nonetheless erupt, derailing shared action. When your counterpart is overwhelmed with emotion, try to remove or directly address the source of concern. If it's you, apologize authentically. Or give them time to cool off. These same things work if you're the one erupting, too.
6. Logic is not irrelevant to persuasion. We reason, so we need good reasons for what we say. Otherwise, we risk proceeding on faulty information. Reason just doesn't come first. Have your reasons ready, especially when they ask for them.

7. Persuasion isn't about being "right." It's about making a difference. When you insist on being "right," it's often impossible to make a difference because you turn your counterpart into an adversary.

EIPM Focusing Question: What is the ONE Thing you need your audience to feel to promote shared action?

Chapter 4

BE *FOR* SOMETHING

Who is the happy Warrior? . . .
It is the generous Spirit . . .
Whose high endeavours are an inward light
That makes the path before him always bright.

William Wordsworth, "Character of the Happy Warrior"

What kinds of feelings are persuasive? Take a quick look around social media, cable news, or most anywhere else, and the answer seems pretty obvious: negative ones.

Here's a snapshot of what I saw a few days ago on the homepages of Fox News and MSNBC, two partisan news organizations. Out of literally hundreds of articles, I found one—about school choice—that was clearly positive; unless you count stories about a dog identifying breast cancer in his owner, or Ivanka Trump in a bikini.

Mostly, though, I saw words like "calamitous," "disgusting," "insane," "sabotage," and "toxic." So-called professionals model negativity for us all the time. Once they warm up, the negativity often turns into rage. It's as if they think they help people see by poking them in the eye. Heartening, all of it.

This isn't surprising either, because our cognitive wiring inclines us to be negative. And it's not just big things like spicy political issues that trigger it. Small things like whose turn it is to take out the trash do, too. Worse still, negativity can consume us quickly, in an instant. That's a lot working against us.

Unrelated question: How do you feel when you're on the receiving end of someone's negativity? If someone's angry, embattled, or straight-up panicked, does it increase your desire to work with them? Nope.

While it feels good to unleash negativity on someone, there's just one minor problem with it: It's completely counterproductive. The rage machine doesn't work. Rather than bringing people closer, it pushes them away.

So, what kinds of feelings are persuasive? Positive ones. In order to generate them, you need to **be *for* something** and adopt a happy warrior's mindset. Since we're not wired to be positive, this means you'll need to rewire your brain.

That might sound really fluffy. So perhaps you're skeptical.

Consider three of the most persuasive Americans in the twentieth century: John F. Kennedy said, "Ask not." Martin Luther King Jr. had a dream. And Ronald Reagan saw America as a beacon of hope. Positivity *is* persuasive, much more so than negativity.

Positivity is also key to being a charismatic leader. One research study found that "charismatic leaders express more positive emotions than do less charismatic leaders and that leaders' positive emotional expressions have a direct effect on follower mood."[1]

It's so important to facilitate the right feelings, because emotions are contagious. Literally. Psychologists have discovered something called "emotional contagion," which is our tendency to mimic verbal, physiological, and/or behavioral aspects of someone's emotional experience, such that we actually express the same emotion as them.[2]

Generating persuasive feelings has two parts: reducing negativity and increasing positivity. Let's see how to get less of the former and more of the latter.

RAGE IS INFECTIOUS

In *1984*, George Orwell's dystopian masterpiece, the state (Oceania) uses a tactic called the "Two Minutes Hate" to help citizens unleash their fury on its enemies, above all archenemy Goldstein. It starts with a "hideous, grinding screech." Then, Goldstein's face flashes onto the screen, which elicits hisses and squeaks of "fear and disgust." After just thirty seconds, "uncontrollable exclamations of rage" break out "from half the people in the room." People soon are "leaping up and down in their places and shouting at the tops of their voices in an effort to drown the maddening bleating voice that came from the screen." The rage is infectious:

> The horrible thing about the Two Minutes Hate was . . . that it was impossible to avoid joining in . . . A hideous ecstasy of fear and vindictiveness, a desire to kill, to torture, to smash faces in with a sledge hammer, seemed to flow through the whole group of people like an electric current, turning one even against one's will into a grimacing, screaming lunatic.[3]

Who needs coffee when you can start your day with *that*?

Today, our very own Two Minutes Hate is just one click (or tap) away. Whether it's your favorite partisan news outlet or YouTube channel, there are so many sources of negativity and rage. The media industry stokes rage with its stories and clickbait headlines. Social media allows anyone to launch an assault on a person, thing, event, or anything else. Politicians use rage to showcase their authentic frustration (and for fundraising and marketing). When we feel frustrated, it's easy to seek out negative content to fuel what can quickly become rage.

WE ARE BIASED TOWARD NEGATIVITY

We're wired with "negativity bias." As one psychologist explains, negativity bias is our proclivity to "attend to, learn from, and use negative information far more than positive information."[4] According to another psychologist, our brains are programmed to "give priority to bad news," such that "negative events elicit more rapid and more prominent responses."[5] This evolved mechanism makes sense, since, historically, identifying threats and repelling or avoiding them helped us survive.[6]

Our brains have a pair of almond-shaped clusters of interconnected structures called the amygdala. The amygdala helps us regulate emotions, memory, anxiety, aggression, fear, and social cognition (among other functions).[7] The amygdala also functions as a threat detector.[8] When we sense a threat, the amygdala activates our fight-or-flight response. The amygdala is more responsive to negative stimuli.[9]

When we experience extreme (usually negative) things, an emotional event referred to as a neural or amygdala hijacking can occur. During these hijackings, psychologist Daniel Goleman explains, "a center in the limbic brain proclaims an emergency, recruiting the rest of the brain to its urgent agenda. The hijacking occurs in an instant . . . before the neocortex, the thinking brain, has had a chance to fully glimpse what is happening, let alone decide if it is a good idea."[10] Certain emotional states, like being stressed, increase the chances of these hijackings. When they happen, the amygdala interferes with our ability to respond rationally to a threat to such a degree that we react "in an intense, emotional way that may be out of proportion to the situation."[11]

Scientists think negativity bias is an adaptive evolutionary function.[12] Cavemen who weren't sufficiently sensitive to threats removed their genes from the pool by being eaten by predators, being killed by adversaries, or starving to death on unwise missions. While we generally don't experience that level of threat today, our wiring hasn't changed. Our negativity bias makes us attentive to risk in potentially threatening situations.

We tend to focus on, and thus talk lots about, negative things. Consider how much people love complaining and venting. We're remarkably good at identifying one negative thing, however small, and presenting it as epically bad to anyone who'll listen. In the moment, it feels oh so good to complain, even if it unleashes an avalanche of negative emotions.

Negativity feeds on itself: The more negativity you bring to a situation, the more likely you'll maintain or increase negativity.[13] It grows quickly, even exponentially. It takes over your mind, leading to a downward spiral in your feelings and thoughts.

It gets progressively worse. Over time, your baseline for what you see as negative drops. More things, even little, tiny things, annoy and offend you.

Negativity can easily spiral into rumination, which has many bad consequences. Clinical research defines rumination as "a form of perseverative cognition that focuses on negative content, generally past and present, and results in emotional distress."[14] Other medical research explains that rumination leads us to "repetitively and passively" focus "on the distress as well as its possible causes and consequences," which can lead to depression.[15] Negativity can *cause* rumination,[16] which means we need to avoid or reduce negativity when possible.

It doesn't even take much to trigger negativity. We all get annoyed at little things all the time. Sometimes the annoyance passes quickly. Other times, it spirals out of control.

NEGATIVITY MAKES US DUMBER

Negativity and its elusive cousin, positivity, impact brain function. Harvard-trained psychologist Shawn Achor has shown your brain functions significantly better when you have a positive mindset. "Your intelligence rises, your creativity rises, your energy level rises." How much? Thirty-one percent. Our brains are 31 percent more productive when we're not "negative, neutral, or stressed."[17] That significantly improves results.

A negative state of mind effectively makes you dumber, less creative, and more lethargic. It shackles you, casting you as a grumpy underperformer.

This performance gap helps determine whether you persuade successfully. Most competitions—such as for a job, or in sports—are won at the margins. Especially in the final stages of a competition, the competitors tend to be closely matched. Victory or defeat is usually decided in a few key moments. Consider a job interview. You're one of three finalists. If you're negative, and only operating at 69 percent of your potential, your odds of persuading them that you're the best candidate evaporate.

Negativity impacts groups by feeding off itself and spreading. When enough people underperform, it can threaten the team's or organization's very existence. Negativity can easily become embedded in a culture, breeding toxicity. Good luck cleaning that up.

REJECT THE RAGE MACHINE

You might be thinking: But negativity works, right? We all know a bully who seems to use bad behavior to get what he wants. Cable news stations like Fox, MSNBC, and CNN harness negativity for financial profit. Which is why it's not surprising that research shows negativity is actually getting worse (hard as that is to imagine), in left- *and* right-wing media.[18]

Young kids scream, pout, and engage in all sorts of endearing behaviors to try to get what they want. At least they have an excuse: They can't communicate their feelings and thoughts properly. They're learning to regulate their emotions. Unfortunately, many people continue this behavior, and it evolves into barking orders, venting, and other charming behaviors.

Aggressive tactics like negativity and offensive behavior are antipersuasion tactics. They can only conquer or vanquish through force. When you use force to get someone to do something, they drag their feet and comply slowly if at all. Usually, they undermine you as much as they can. And any apparent gains are reversed at the earliest possible moment, because you didn't persuade people.

A former consulting client of mine was an Army colonel before moving into a civilian role. As a commanding officer, he enjoyed barking orders at people, and they were required to listen to him. They had also signed up for that authority structure, so they had at least consented to it. After all, that structure is required for our armed forces to function properly.

He approached his civilian role the same way: by barking orders at civilian government employees and expecting them to eagerly implement those orders. Did it work? Hardly. He would issue an order, leave, people would roll their eyes, and they'd get around to it when they got around to it, which often was never. They learned to dodge and weave around his requests. He would have been far better off using the EIPM and persuading them to share action with him.

Negativity burns bridges and erects obstacles (both seen and unseen) to persuasion. Rather than opening doors for you, people will slam them shut, sometimes right in your face, just to spite you and your rage. More often, they'll just hide opportunities from you. Negative emotions like anger often drive away people who *agree* with you. People will dislike being in your presence and won't want to work with you.

Too much negativity can push people away, even if it's never extreme.

We all know someone who loves to complain. When it's persistent, it's annoying. It gets old fast. Our desire to hang out with that person decreases.

My wife and I used to be friends with someone. Every time we saw her, she quickly made it all about her and immediately started complaining about something—work (oh, her boss!), finances (no money yet lots of expensive tastes), whatever. We finally reached our tipping point and stopped hanging out with her.

All that said, negativity is a part of the human experience. The only part we control is how we react to it and how much space we allow it to take up in our relationships. Here's the key question: Will you learn to control your negativity? Or will it control you? When your negativity controls you, your chances of getting what you want decline, by a little or a lot. When you learn to control it, they skyrocket.

Now here's a far better path to feeling better and getting what you want.

BEGIN BY ASSUMING GOOD INTENTIONS

Every morning, I walk my two dogs—Pascal (the dad) and Pierre (his son, seriously)—and my two-year-old son, Thomas. Few things give Pascal and Pierre more pleasure than marking their territory. Which means they like to pull to my left when they identify their target so they can fire away. All while I push a stroller. Fun. Realizing we already take up a sizable portion of the sidewalk, made worse when the pups' leashes are taut, I usually walk on the left side of the sidewalk to make sure we don't block the whole thing.

One day, a guy we see on almost every walk started screaming at me out of nowhere. He said, "You always walk on the wrong side of the sidewalk, right in front of me!" I tried to explain that we were trying to be courteous and not block the whole thing. Certain we were out to get him, he started cursing at us. He *knew* we had bad intentions. And apparently the idea of taking one step to the side to pass us without incident was offensive to him.

Far too many people assume someone who doesn't think like them or doesn't do the "right" thing is crazy, stupid, evil, or some combination thereof. This mindset is toxic. (And misunderstands our moral minds, as we'll see in chapter 5.)

Stop assuming your counterpart has bad intentions. Most people try to do what they think is right. When someone is wrong, they usually didn't intend to make an error or do harm. Having different goals, perspectives, and information isn't bad, either. And maybe they're actually right.

Start by assuming your counterpart has good intentions. This increases your chances of persuasion. You see your counterpart in a more positive (or at least less negative) light, which helps prevent negativity from capturing your mind and makes it easier to work with them. You can speak more openly and honestly with people whose intentions you respect. You might even learn from their different perspective.

What does it look like to assume good intentions? Start by understanding their motivations and purpose. Be generous in your interpretation. What good thing are they trying to accomplish? You don't have to agree with their intentions or stance.

Assuming good intentions is not equivalent to naivete. First, people can have good intentions, do what they *think* is right, and nonetheless *cause* harm. Whoops. Second, there are bad people out there who want to harm others. Overlooking this sets you up for trouble. You need to be able to identify when someone poses a true threat, malign or not.

How do you protect yourself without erecting unnecessary barriers? Trust and verify. Assume good intentions until someone gives you sufficient evidence to prove otherwise. Be on the lookout for evidence without being paranoid. Focus more on what they do than what they say, because actions speak far louder than words. If you get an uncomfortable feeling, don't ignore it. Intuitions are powerful. Observe and investigate.

I once assumed a former boss had good intentions, then slowly saw that wasn't the case. He talked a big game in the interview, making lots of promises. The company—Booz Allen Hamilton—is a top consulting firm. The opportunity to work there was exciting. He promised lots of professional growth.

The first day on the job was weird. Rather than meeting me once my orientation was finished, my boss left it to me to navigate a new (and initially confusing) building. After I eventually found my destination, he was nowhere in sight.

A few weeks in, a colleague who used to run the team pulled me aside and asked about my salary. When I told her, she immediately told me I was underpaid—by a lot. She then told me what had been going on with the client over the past 10 months since this guy took over. He cleaned house and brought in new, inexperienced people to save money. The client was furious that he got rid of all the people they liked, which was a big reason they had renewed the contract for five more years just before he arrived. Turns out the only thing he cared about was cutting costs. If you asked for a raise, he threatened to kick you off the contract and move you somewhere else, which might have added one to two hours to your daily commute.

Knowing he had bad intentions, I kept my head low until he left, at which point the whole team collectively exhaled. His departure opened up space for me to persuade the new team leader to give me more responsibility, including managing more people, and a raise.

One obvious way to verify someone's intentions is to ask them directly. Ask open-ended questions like "What's motivating you?" Or "What do you seek to accomplish?" Or "What does a good outcome look like for you?"

When you discover someone has questionable intentions, figure out what's motivating them. If their intentions are bad, like my former boss's were, persuasion might not be possible, and you'll have to wait until you're in a different situation. You also could be misunderstanding them, and shared action actually is possible.

Suppose you have to work closely with a colleague on a new project. You dislike him because you two tend to have drastically different opinions. You could begin by assuming bad intentions, which will quickly put you into conflict with him. That won't end well.

Alternatively, you could assume good intentions. What's driving him to always contradict you? Maybe he has different training—he's an engineer, you're a marketer. Maybe he worries more (or less) than you, or is less (or more) comfortable with risk. Observe his intentions rather than judging them. If you can find a good reason (even if you don't agree with it) for his behavior, conversation and eventually persuasion become possible.

BUILD STEEL MEN

Imagine the following encounter:

> "That's outrageous! I'm gonna rip you and your argument to shreds!"
> "That's not at all what I said. It seems like you're not listening."
> "Look, if I need to oversimplify, generalize, misquote, take what you said out of context, and argue against extreme opinions that barely relate to what you said, I'll bite that bullet."

Straw men are weak, partially or entirely fabricated versions of what your counterpart says or means. You employ these misrepresentations to more easily defeat your opponents *and* make them look bad. Why stand up against the strongest version of their position when you can attack the weakest?

There are just a few minor problems with "straw-manning" someone's position. First, this behavior builds ill will between you and the person whose views you're misrepresenting. That makes shared action hard or impossible. Second, you "defeat" something that doesn't exist, like fighting a ghost. (Boo!) Is *that* success? Nope. It's just intellectually lazy. Building straw men is a sign of weakness, not strength.

To persuade, build steel men. A steel man is the strongest version of your counterpart's view. Begin by listening—openly, honestly, and intently. It takes work (sometimes a lot) to get to the heart of your counterpart's views. Then, demonstrate you understand them through conversation. Be generous and build up the strongest possible version of their claim, even stronger than the one they offer.

Building steel men strengthens your relationship with your audience. They'll judge you as honest and fair. Your generosity will build goodwill. They'll like you more and will be significantly more inclined to *want* to work with you. They might even return your generosity. If you disagree with them, you'll be in a better position to share your concerns with them.

Suppose you're in a heated political discussion about immigration with a friend. You're on the left politically, and she's on the right. You favor allowing significantly more immigrants to move to America legally. Your friend is concerned there are already too many immigrants—especially illegal ones. She thinks the country can't properly care for its own citizens, so she opposes letting more people in. She's uneasy about what she sees as a porous border. If you wanted to build a straw man from her argument, you might say, "Well, it seems like you want immigrants to keep suffering, and that you don't care if they die on their journey." How ungenerous. Don't expect a kind, calm response.

What if you said instead, "It looks like you have some real concerns about the current level of immigration. You think that we're not doing a good job caring for our own citizens as it is, and that that we can't possibly bear supporting anyone else. You're uneasy about thousands of people illegally crossing the border every day. You think it's a dangerous situation for everyone involved." If you build up a steel man, she'll ideally respond, "That's right." That approach is persuasive, because it opens up space for conversation and shared understanding.

BE FOR SOMETHING

Persuasion requires you to be *for* something. You need to present a way forward to improve an undesirable status quo, or to maintain a good one. Otherwise, you only know how to tear things down, not how to build them up.

It's true that before you can build your vision, you might need to clear space for it first. It's not like building a house, though, where bulldozers, chainsaws, and other destructive tools clear the trees, bushes, and other obstacles to make construction possible.

The process of clearing space by clearing other peoples' ideas is usually a negative experience for them, because you're disregarding *their* vision. Be as gentle as you possibly can. No, even gentler! Use conversation and understanding to help them feel understood. See if they can verbalize some of the problems with their approach. You can ask them questions like "What are some of your concerns about your approach?" Or "What's stopping you from moving forward?" The problems might be bigger than they thought.

Ultimately, you have to build a house people actually want to live in, and for which they'd invest resources (time, money, etc.). Otherwise, it'll sit there unoccupied. The house must be architecturally sound, lest it collapse—that's where reason comes in. How do you make that home welcoming?

Be *for* people, values, and beliefs. Ask yourself these questions: What do I care about most? What are my core values? What's my North Star, the thing that guides me?

Then, share that with others to persuade them to work with you. As you think through your answer, be sure it's authentic, otherwise you can't advocate for it effectively. And be sure the values you express resonate with others, since you're trying to persuade people to work with you.

For example, I mentioned my North Star in all I do is the knowledge that we are all bundles of potential and can be more than we are. That starts with my children, Thomas and Elizabeth—both bundles of potential. Every time they learn to do something new, I'm so proud of them. So what am I *for*? Empowering people to unleash their unique potential.

This positive vision is why I'm a poverty researcher.

Whenever I present my work, I know the first thing people are thinking is: Why does *he* care about poverty? Especially if I'm in a suit, not exactly a down-to-earth look. Here's what I say.

Poverty is personal, because it's seared into my family's story. My mom grew up dirt poor. My grandmother raised five kids by herself when her husband left. They were so poor that my grandmother literally had to count pennies. Every year, my mom and her brothers and sister wondered if there'd be presents around the Christmas tree—because most years, there weren't. My mom and her siblings bear the psychological scars of poverty to this day in so much of their behavior.

I don't want other people to suffer the way she did. That's why I care about poverty, and that's why I'm researching solutions for how to expand opportunity so as many individuals as possible can rise out of poverty and unleash their potential. My poverty advocacy is about empowering people like my mom and my granny. They're the heroes. Crucially, it's not about *me*.

It's necessary to advocate *for* something, because without that driving force, your persuasion efforts will be feeble. It's insufficient to simply be a negative Nancy, criticizing others. When you only stand against things, you're purely reactive. That's unpersuasive. We'll look at some great examples of how to be *for* something below when we get specific.

When you put yourself and your ideas out there, you're opening yourself up to criticism. How do you want others to respond? Probably not by being negative. A variation of the Golden Rule is helpful: Do unto others' ideas as you would have others do unto yours.

OFFER A POSITIVE, UPLIFTING VISION

Suppose you want to advocate to address poverty. You could craft a negative vision that seeks to pull people down. You could say, "The rich have too much, stolen from the rest of us. They exploit the poor and working class for their ill-gotten gains. It's time to cut them down to size." Resentment, negativity, and pessimism fuel this vision. How could it lead anywhere good? Historically, it hasn't.

Here's an alternative, positive vision. You might say, "Human dignity is grounded in your ability to unleash your unique potential, to create and do great things for yourself and others. Everyone deserves that opportunity. And the poor and disadvantaged don't have it. We need to work toward a society where they do. It's not just better for them. It makes everyone better off. Let's start a conversation about how to accomplish that."

In poverty advocacy, we can look up and be motivated by love for the poor, or be pulled down by hatred of the rich. The latter salts the soil, making persuasion impossible. The former creates fertile ground for shared action.

Focus on lifting people up, not pulling them down. Rather than poking people in the eye, use genuine conversation to help others see. Paint a picture of an achievable reality that appeals to you and your audience. That reality needs to offer a better tomorrow, centered on growth: of opportunity, of the individual, and of the community.

Positivity facilitates persuasion by tapping into what Achor calls the "happiness advantage." He explains the psychology: "If we can find a way of becoming positive in the present, then our brains work even more successfully as we're able to work harder, faster, and more intelligently."[19] These are crucial ingredients for shared action and success.

A positive vision is unifying in word and deed. People can rally around, advocate for, and enact it. How does this work? Get your substance and style right. Your substance needs to bring together and motivate a critical mass of people to share action toward a shared goal. Your style shows whether you really believe your substance. For example, the wrong tone turns people off to you no matter how "good" your ideas are.

Your positive vision can't unify everyone. People have legitimate disagreements based on different beliefs, values, and priorities. Happily, genuine conversation is possible without agreement. Eschew divisive words and deeds that promote bad will. Unless you're trying to rally the troops for a crusade, which inevitably results in bloodshed, not persuasion.

Avoid presenting your vision as definitive and final, lest you close off conversation. Adopt the mindset that you just might have something to learn, especially since you expect that from your counterpart. The ideas you end up proposing will have a much higher chance of getting you where you want and need to go.

Your positive vision needs to be centered on what will persuade your audience, not you. Your offense will be effective only if you advocate for *shared* values or beliefs, which you do by showing your audience you're on the same page as them. Identify and focus on overlap in values while avoiding issues that might offend them as much as possible.

ON GETTING PUNCHED IN THE MOUTH

There is a saying attributed to intellectual heavyweight Michael Gerard Tyson (aka former boxing champion "Iron Mike"): "Everyone has a plan until they get punched in the mouth." People inevitably are going to attack you, and punch you in the mouth. It's going to hurt. How do you respond?

When someone punches us, the natural reaction is to get angry, defend ourselves, and punch back. We take a swing—physical, verbal, or both. While understandable, rarely is it productive.

The best way to respond when someone goes after you is directly and calmly, with minimal aggression. The goal is to deescalate conflict. Admittedly, easier said than done. Decide first if the offense even warrants a response. Perhaps you can let it blow over without addressing it. Not everything requires a reaction.

When you do need to respond, be direct, calm, and respectful. If you aren't direct, there's a good chance it'll linger. If you aren't calm or respectful, things will likely escalate.

It's necessary to assess, understand, and address what prompted them to become negative in the first place. Look at things from their perspective, and assume there's something real (at least to them) prompting their offense. Respond as you'd hope someone would respond to you when you're offensive. Everyone says things that weren't well formulated or thought out. Clarify and, when necessary, apologize. Sometimes simply stating your opposing view will offend someone. And sometimes someone will actually be a jerk. We all are sometimes. When it happens, you hope someone will respond with grace and kindness.

What if your default when responding to negativity from others was to respond how you want them to respond to you when *you're* negative? It sure beats punching them back.

NEGATIVITY CAN PROMOTE PERSUASION

Are negative feelings *always* counterproductive or unpersuasive? After reading this chapter, you might think the answer is "yes." It's not. Negative feelings help you get what you want in at least two crucial ways.

First, negative feelings are natural and adaptive. They're natural because they're wired into us. And for good reason. When we experience them, it's usually our mind's way of telling us something doesn't work for us. We know that we don't want to proceed under those circumstances, meaning shared action would need to take another form. For example, if someone makes a request and we feel uncomfortable, there's a reason underlying that feeling. Maybe we think it's a bad idea, or we just don't want to do it.

How do you use the reality of negative feelings to get what you want? When someone has a negative response to something you say, rather than ignoring it, or telling them to feel otherwise, observe and figure out how to navigate it. The negativity is arising from some sort of barrier to shared action. If you don't identify and overcome it, you can't get what you want.

Second, negativity plain and simple can be persuasive every now and again. When someone does something you dislike, and you respond with negativity, it sends a signal that they should stop doing it. And sometimes you need to be more pronounced in your negativity. Righteous indignation occurs when a potent blend of emotions and thoughts arising from a perceived moral wrong causes us to be overcome with negative emotions, and then express those emotions strongly.

Imagine a guy is hitting on a woman at work. She has politely made clear that she isn't interested. He keeps doing it, so much that she feels deeply uncomfortable and dreads going into the office. In order to make him feel how inappropriate his behavior is, she might exhibit some righteous indignation over his borderline harassing behavior. Subtler methods are great when they work, but sometimes stronger messaging is required to shut down an unacceptable situation.

While we should default to being *for* things and focusing on positivity, that's not always possible, and it's not even always desirable. And if negativity becomes our default instead, that causes all the problems we've discussed in this chapter.

LET'S GET SPECIFIC: MODEL HAPPY WARRIORS

Perhaps you're thinking, sure, good theory: Be *for* something, be positive, and offer an uplifting vision, then share action. But does it *work*? It worked for three great American presidents: Abraham Lincoln, Franklin D. Roosevelt, and Ronald Reagan. Which makes this the best model for anyone who wants to make a difference.

In his first inaugural address, Lincoln insisted, "We are not enemies, but friends. We must not be enemies. Though passion may have strained it must not break our bonds of affection."[20] Imagine if, as his nation was on the cusp of plunging into the hell of the Civil War, he had dragged it deeper into the inferno with fiery rhetoric, saying, "We are not friends, but enemies. The bonds of our affection have been destroyed, and so must our enemies be destroyed, too."

FDR brought optimism and leadership to myriad challenges, including the Great Depression. Responding to an economic situation that warranted unbounded pessimism and bitterness, in his first inaugural FDR delivered his most iconic line: "The only thing we have to fear is fear itself."[21] He easily could have sounded tone-deaf to the suffering of his countrymen, insisting things weren't that bad. He could have looked down and used the malaise to his advantage by blaming someone. Instead, he insisted on confronting fear head-on. FDR then looked up, insisting the only way forward was together, moving "as a trained and loyal army willing to sacrifice for the good of a common discipline."

Reagan earned the nickname the "Great Communicator" with his sunny demeanor. Consider the uplifting portrayal of America as a "shining city" in his farewell address:

> a tall, proud city built on rocks stronger than oceans, wind-swept, God-blessed, and teeming with people of all kinds living in harmony and peace;

> a city with free ports that hummed with commerce and creativity. And if there had to be city walls, the walls had doors and the doors were open to anyone with the will and the heart to get here.[22]

Whatever your politics, it's hard to not find that positive vision appealing.

This approach has worked for many other presidents, too. Hope and change helped move Barack Obama from Springfield, Illinois, to the White House in four short years. Donald Trump promises to "Make America Great Again." Even if you dislike one or both of them, these positive visions inspired many to support them.

Maybe an optimistic, uplifting approach could work for you, too.

LET'S REFLECT

Being for something requires care and nuance. You can't use a one-size-fits-all approach, because what one person experiences as negative, another might see as positive. That happens in politics, at work, and at home all the time. That's why you have to work hard to understand your audience. Otherwise, you might say or do something you think they'll see as positive, only to upset them unintentionally. If you insist on a one-size-fits-all approach, your successes will be narrow and much less frequent.

Indeed, there's a big complication with our attempts to share action: What lifts people up, or brings them down, differs based on their values. We turn our attention there now.

Key Takeaways for Generating Persuasive Feelings

1. Our bias toward negativity is strong. We're cognitively wired to notice, focus on, and learn from negative information and experiences more than positive ones. Our brains give priority to bad news. This evolved mechanism makes sense, since negative things often present threats. What's more, society reinforces negativity, particularly in media. The trouble is that negativity isn't persuasive, because it pushes people away and isn't a recipe for sharing action in the medium or long term.
2. Positive feelings are persuasive. To generate them in yourself and your audience, you need to be *for* something and adopt a happy warrior's mindset. You need a positive vision people are eager to pursue with you. While this might seem hopelessly naive to some, the most persuasive Americans persuaded with positivity, including Lincoln, FDR, JFK, Martin Luther King Jr., and Reagan.
3. Be generous to your counterparts; otherwise, you'll often develop negative feelings toward them, which makes shared action hard or impossible. Stop assuming your counterpart has bad intentions. Most people try to do what's right. Instead, assume they have good intentions until they prove otherwise. Steel-man their perspective by making the best case possible for it. They'll appreciate this generosity, and it'll make working together much easier.
4. When someone unleashes their negativity on you (which is inevitable), remember the goal is to share action. That requires you to deescalate rather than fanning the flames with your own negativity toward them. Do your best to stay calm. Give them time to calm down.
5. Negative feelings can sometimes facilitate persuasion. First, they're natural and adaptive. It's our mind's way of telling us something

doesn't work for us. That's a barrier to shared action that needs to be addressed and removed to work with someone. Second, sometimes negativity itself is persuasive, like when someone does something inappropriate and you respond negatively to let them know it's not OK.

Positivity Focusing Question: What is the ONE Thing you can communicate to advocate *for* your ideas inspirationally and aspirationally?

Chapter 5

ACTIVATE THEIR MORAL TASTES

So far, about morals, I know only that what is moral is what you feel good after and what is immoral is what you feel bad after.

Ernest Hemingway, *Death in the Afternoon*

What's your favorite food? Mine's peanut butter—salty *and* savory! Maybe yours is ice cream or beef or bacon, or beef wrapped in bacon.

Our tongues have six physical taste receptors that shape how we experience food: sweet, salty, sour, bitter, umami, and fat.[1] The instant tasty foods hit your tongue, they activate one or more of these receptors.

Not everyone has the same tastes. My wife adores mushrooms. Me? I'll pass. Even siblings growing up in the same home develop different tastes despite sharing genes and the same upbringing. That's why I always ask someone what dishes they enjoy and dislike before having them over for dinner.

What if morality worked this way, too? Fun fact: It does! We tend to think morality is about logically crafting your principles. But that's not how morality actually works.

Hundreds of thousands of survey responses across many diverse countries have confirmed that morality has flavors, too, wired into our hearts and minds, that shape how we feel and think about everything. We have moral tastes for care, equality, proportionality, loyalty, purity, authority, and possibly liberty.[2] Examples of factors that trigger these tastes include income inequality, patriotic claims, and religious texts.

We know morality persuades people. In fact, it fires them up! Philosophers love to theorize about how our moral minds ought to work (which coincidentally just corresponds to how the author's mind works). That's unhelpful. Persuasion requires us to know how our moral minds actually work. For that, we need psychology.

A psychological account of morality called moral foundations theory (MFT) is based on the idea that humans have the seven moral tastes above. As social and moral psychologist Jonathan Haidt explains, these receptors "draw people's attention" to certain things "and trigger *instant intuitive* reactions, perhaps even specific emotions (such as sympathy or anger)."[3] We reach different conclusions about right and wrong based on our sensitivity to these receptors. Crucially, not everyone is sensitive to the same moral tastes. That's especially true of people with different political views (conservative, libertarian, and leftist).

Oh, it gets better. We don't really choose which values to embrace. Studies of twins show that 30 to 60 percent of our morality is genetically wired into us, just like our height or hair color.[4] Since identical twins share all their genes, we can determine the environment's impact. Results showing our political ideology is substantially genetic and heritable have been replicated in different countries.[5]

What does genetics have to do with persuasion? Well, should you criticize someone for being tall or short, or having red or blond hair? Of course not, because those traits are genetic. Since our "choice" about our morality is limited, we don't have to hate people because they don't share our moral tastes. In such polarized times, that's liberating.

Here's the trouble, though. We're wired to try and transfer our values onto others. It's like force-feeding someone a dish they find disgusting. "Hey vegetarian, have some veal." "I know you keep kosher . . . but try this bacon." That's offensive, not persuasive.

Persuasion geniuses **activate their moral tastes** by appealing to their audience's values and cooking up tasty moral dishes the audience likes. Chefs do this all the time because they want customers. So become a persuasive moral chef. That means advocating for what you want in ways your audience finds palatable.

Skeptical already? The most persuasive communicators in American history, including Abraham Lincoln, Martin Luther King Jr., Ronald Reagan, and Barack Obama, were exceptional in part because of their ability to make persuasive moral appeals.

Until now, MFT has remained primarily an academic endeavor. This chapter is the first ever extended effort to make MFT actionable for and central to persuasion in the wider world.

Before we begin, I recommend taking the test some researchers in this field have crafted at www.YourMorals.org to understand your moral tastes.

CARE/HARM

A mom runs into a burning building to save her kid. A brother beats up his sister's ex-boyfriend who abused her. You'll do just about anything for people you care about. You'll readily harm someone who hurts them. Because you care.

The care/harm foundation focuses our attention on suffering. People sensitive to care "show higher levels of empathic concern" and "take benevolence to be a guiding principle in their lives."[6] The care taste activates when you experience someone positively tending to you and your needs (or people you like), or posing a potential threat.

Activate the care taste bud on your audience's terms, not yours. Figure out what someone needs to *feel* cared for and to stop feeling harmed, including by recognizing and acknowledging their suffering.

Frustratingly, a message or gesture you intend to be caring can be experienced by your counterpart as uncaring or harmful. Consider romantic relationships. In *The Five Love Languages*, marriage counselor Gary Chapman discusses ways of expressing love: words of affirmation, acts of service, receiving gifts, quality time, and physical touch.[7] Different ones resonate more with different people.

Suppose a woman is having a bad day. Maybe something happened with a friend or at work. She needs some TLC. Her love languages are physical touch and time. She just wants a hug and time to talk. Her husband's language is gifts. So he gives her chocolate and flowers before heading to the gym. That doesn't go well! He needed to show her care by listening and giving her a hug. That's caring, and even saves him a few bucks.

A simple technique for showing the right kind of care is to ask, "How can I help you feel better?" Or, if they have a long history to look back on, think about a gift or gesture that meant a lot to them in the past, and use that as a guiding example. Too often, we show care on our terms, not theirs.

To maximize the persuasive potential of each moral foundation, it's important to communicate its opposite. With care, it's harm.[8] As a policy advocate, when I am for something, I also have to explain how a policy could work against my goal. As a poverty advocate, I explain how bad policies hurt the poor. An environmental advocate can explain how a regulation harms the environment. Harms can impede shared action, so you need to address them.

Lincoln's second inaugural address is a master class in communicating care. Delivered as America's awful Civil War neared the end, Lincoln made care appeals to help heal the nation's deep wounds:

> With *malice* toward none; with *charity* for all . . . let us strive on to finish the work we are in; to *bind* up the *Nation's wounds*; to *care* for him who shall have borne the battle, and for his widow, and his orphan—to do all which may achieve and cherish a just and lasting *peace*, among ourselves, and with all nations.[9]

Consider an alternative, hate-filled speech:

> With charity toward none; with malice for all . . . let us strive on to finish the work we are in; to wound our opponents fatally; to destroy those responsible for these battles, and those who supported their treason—to do all which may achieve and secure a just and lasting victory over all enemies, domestic and foreign.

How harmful.

Consider some uncaring comments from recent presidential elections. In the 2012 election, Mitt Romney was secretly recorded saying, "There are 47 percent of the people who will vote for the president [Barack Obama] no matter what. All right, there are 47 percent who are with him, who are dependent upon government, who believe that they are victims."[10] Not to be outdone, in 2016 Hillary Clinton said, "You know, to just be grossly generalistic, you could put half of Trump's supporters into what I call the basket of deplorables. Right? The racist, sexist, homophobic, xenophobic, Islamaphobic—you name it. And unfortunately there are people like that."[11] Gross indeed, both comments. And such uncaring rhetoric didn't work out well for either one.

To communicate care, explain how you or your plan are trying to support, empathize, or secure your audience and their needs. To communicate harm, show how an undesirable path will damage them and the things they care about.

FAIRNESS DIVIDED: EQUALITY AND PROPORTIONALITY

"That's not fair!" Something prompts you to feel this regularly. Your hard work wasn't rewarded. You feel like some people or groups aren't treated equally. Kids seem particularly adept at weaponizing those words: "But Mooooommmm! That's not fair!" You constantly assess situations with "fairness" as judge (and maybe jury and executioner).

Fairness motivates everyone. We equate "unfair" with "wrong." And yet two different notions of what's "fair" exist: equality (or equity) and proportionality.

Equality or equity is about the desire for equal treatment and equal outcomes, meaning receiving the same as someone else.[12] People driven by equality are motivated to distribute costs and benefits equally.[13] According to two researchers, equity prizes "equal say, equal opportunity, equal chance, even shares, even contributions, turn taking," and "balanced reciprocity."[14] Your starting place, your effort, or your inputs shouldn't determine your success.[15]

The equality taste makes people see wealth disparities between the rich and the poor as wrong. People sensitive to equality often assume massive wealth was accumulated by unfair means, like cheating. Their (often visceral) response is to be upset, criticize the situation, and seek to rectify it. For example, progressive taxation is meant to ensure the wealthy pay their "fair"—read: much higher—share, and then redistribute resources from those who have "too much" or "enough" to those who don't have "enough." The best predictor of equality on the MFT survey is someone's response to "The world would be a better place if everyone made the same amount of money."[16]

The proportionality taste, by contrast, focuses someone's attention on merit. An outcome is "fair" as long as it corresponds with someone's contribution or effort.[17] It would be unfair if differences in industriousness, productivity, and quality *didn't* result in different outcomes. Everyone needs to pull their weight. People generally get what they deserve.[18] How is it fair, someone may ask, for a lazy, unproductive worker to receive the same pay as (or more than) a hardworking, productive one? The best predictor of proportionality on the survey was the response to "In a fair society, those who work hard should live with higher standards of living."[19]

What's the difference between equality and proportionality? Proportionality is focused on what individuals deserve based on the merit of their contributions. Equality is concerned with the distribution of resources across a group.[20] Equality is also a "social" justice. Those highly sensitive to it are willing to address unfair outcomes at the expense of other groups (sometimes even their own).[21]

Someone can actually be sensitive to both tastes. Consider a rich person who feels they deserve all their wealth and also supports high taxes to pay for social programs for the poor.

Fairness is a potent persuasive cocktail. Mix up one *they* like. If you're low in equity while your counterpart is high, you need to explain how the action you want to share promotes equity. For example, if you work to alleviate poverty, you can explain how the free enterprise system has empowered billions of people to rise out of poverty, reducing inequality.

To figure out which appeals to make, probe what your counterpart means by "fair." You might say, "It seems like you have a particular idea of what's fair?" Then listen, because they'll tell you. Or ask, "What about that seems unfair to you?" Learning someone's views on income inequality and merit gives you a good idea of how they think about fairness.

How can you engage someone with radically different views about fairness? Ask them what makes them feel like a situation is unfair and immoral.

Truly listen. Make them feel understood. If someone is high in proportionality, you could say, "You probably think this policy is completely unfair because it rewards people who aren't pulling their weight, and punishes those who are." Talk to them about merit's importance, both in general and in the specific context.

Consider two persuasive appeals to fairness. In 2008, during a presidential primary debate, then-Senator Barack Obama was asked if he'd favor increasing the capital gains tax despite data showing government revenues decrease when this tax rate increases. He said:

> I would look at raising the capital gains tax for purposes of *fairness*. We saw an article today which showed that the top 50 hedge fund managers made $29 billion last year—$29 billion for 50 individuals. And part of what has happened is that those who are able to work the stock market and amass huge fortunes on capital gains are paying a lower tax rate than their secretaries. That's not *fair*.[22]

That's equity in action. While president, he insisted corporations needed to pay their fair share, and advocated for closing "tax loopholes" that corporations exploit.

Ronald Reagan communicated fairness as proportionality. In a 1985 "Radio Address to the Nation on Free and Fair Trade," Reagan advocated for trade that's free and fair. He promised to "move vigorously against *unfair* trading practices, using every legal recourse available to give American manufacturers a *fair* shake at home and open markets abroad." His fire was mainly aimed at protectionist tariffs.

> Protectionism is almost always *self-destructive*, doing more *harm* than good even to those it's supposed to be helping. Advocates of protectionism often ignore its huge hidden *costs* that far outweigh any temporary

> benefits . . . Protectionism almost always ends up making the protected industry *weaker* and less able to compete against foreign imports . . . Instead of protectionism, we should call it *destructionism.* It *destroys* jobs, *weakens* our industries, *harms* exports, *costs* billions of dollars to consumers, and *damages* our overall economy.[23]

It's unfair to punish hard work and destroy jobs, and hurt industries and the economy. Proportionality in action.

To communicate equity, show how a path supports or harms a group. To communicate proportionality, focus on merit and hard work.

LOYALTY/BETRAYAL

In his *Inferno,* Dante reserves the ninth and lowest circle of hell for the worst sinners: betrayers. Betrayal is worse than lust, gluttony, greed, wrath, heresy, violence, and fraud. Archetypal betrayers in this circle include Cain (who murdered his brother Abel) and Judas Iscariot (who handed over Jesus Christ). Take a moment to visualize, remember, and reexperience a time someone betrayed *you*—badly. You can readily agree with Dante: There's a special place in hell for betrayers.

At the same time, feelings of loyalty to a group or a person inspire us to do remarkable things, including sacrificing our life in extreme circumstances.

The loyalty taste is about how we relate to individuals and groups. We like cooperating with ingroups because of shared bonds (like sports, ideology, or geography), and competing against outgroups.[24] We assess whether we can work with someone. Are they a team player? We reward those we trust, and, as Haidt explains, "want to hurt, ostracize, or even kill those who betray us or our group."[25] People sensitive to loyalty tend to value group cohesion, and work to meet the duties and responsibilities of their social role in that group.[26]

The best predictor of whether someone is sensitive to loyalty appeals, according to the MFT survey, is whether they're upset "when people have no loyalty to their country."[27] A nation is an adhesive that can bind people together, like when men and women in uniform serve their nation. Loyalty also can pull us down to terrifying lows, like when we coalesce *against* alleged betrayers. Recall Senator Joseph McCarthy's witch hunts in the 1950s searching for alleged communist influence inside the U.S. government.

Some people aren't sensitive to loyalty appeals. They're drawn instead to universal values like human rights, and away from nationalism.[28] They don't identify with someone simply because they're from the same group (such as others from the same country, fellow school alums, and so on).

Loyalty appeals require tremendous caution because charges of disloyalty or betrayal whip your audience into a potentially uncontrollable emotional frenzy. Which means loyalty appeals require even more emotional intelligence. Here's how to do that.

The most persuasive way to make loyalty appeals is to be for positive values others can affirm. Celebrate what binds you together or attracts people to the group. Talk about what your group wants and needs, and how to address those wants and needs together.

Consider American patriotism as an example. Be for things like the beautiful ideas and principles found in the Declaration of Independence. The unifying narrative of "life, liberty, and the pursuit of happiness" has inspired billions of people around the world since it was written. Don't decry people you don't like as "un-American."

When you experience betrayal, tell the offender how their words and deeds hurt you or your group. Whenever possible, make the betrayal about the offense, not the offender.

A classic example is the case of Edward Snowden. While a government contractor in 2013, he betrayed America by stealing and disseminating a tremendous amount of national security information, then leaving the country, eventually settling in Russia. To discourage others from doing this, leaders in the national security space needed to explain how harmful Snowden's betrayal was. They could discuss how sharing that information puts Americans and our allies at risk, both on the battlefield and here at home. That's what the House Intelligence Committee did in a classified report, of which a summary was released. It explained how Snowden's disclosure "did tremendous damage to U.S. national security."[29]

You can also persuade someone to act differently by suggesting he's betraying his own professed beliefs. For example, suppose an employee comes into your office with a job offer and threatens to leave. You've invested tremendous time and company resources in him. Without calling him disloyal, remind him of your shared past, and ask him if he thinks the other company will really invest as much in him as you and your company have.

Or, without necessarily accusing someone of hypocrisy, you might point out instances of cognitive dissonance. For example, if a teammate prides themselves on putting the team first, then does some things that seem selfish, you might say, "It feels like we could focus more on putting the team first by [insert action]." Avoid making personal attacks, because they're never received kindly. For example, even if you think someone's actions aren't team oriented, it's not really helpful to call them out as selfish.

At the 2004 Democratic National Convention, Obama made persuasive patriotic appeals. He stood on the stage "knowing that my story is part of the larger American story, that I owe a debt to all of those that came before me. And that in no other country on earth is my story even possible." He then unleashed these lines:

> E pluribus unum: *out of many, one* . . . There is not a liberal America and a conservative America; there is the *United* States of *America*. There is not a Black America, and a white America, and Latino America, and Asian America. There's the *United* States of *America*. The pundits like to slice and

> dice our country into red states and blue states. Red states for Republicans, blue states for Democrats. But I've got news for them too: We worship an awesome God in the blue states, and we don't like federal agents poking around in our libraries in the red states. We coach little league in the blue states, and yes, we've got some gay friends in the red states. There are *patriots* who opposed the War in Iraq, and there are *patriots* who supported the War in Iraq. We are one people, all of us *pledging allegiance* to the *stars and stripes*, all of us *defending* the United States of America.[30]

Even his opponents are "patriots."

To communicate loyalty, focus on someone's allegiance or devotion to a person, family, community, nation, or some other unit. And explain how an undesirable action would harm that person or group.

AUTHORITY/SUBVERSION

"But Mom, I don't wanna. Do I *have* to?"

"Yes."

"Why?"

"Because I'm your mother and I said so. End of story!"

Parents are the first authority we all encounter. They want their authority respected, and it's generally legitimate. And all kids question their parents' authority at some point. Family conflict can result both from kids subversively not respecting legitimate parental authority, and from illegitimate parental tyranny.

The authority taste is about how much deference legitimate authorities and traditions deserve.[31] People sensitive to it see disrespecting legitimate authority or subverting tradition as destructive and wrong. Authority drives leadership and followership.[32] Hierarchies structure authority. We look for indicators of rank or status and where we fit vis-à-vis others. For example, you interact differently with your boss and subordinates.

Authority impacts persuasion in at least two important ways. First, when someone is sensitive to this taste, you need to know who or what they see as an authority, then appeal to it. For example, if the CEO makes a request, that's going to carry weight (unless the person dislikes the CEO and tries to subvert their wishes). Second, there's the authority status you have as a manager. As someone's boss, you have direct authority over them, and they're supposed to listen to you.

Only legitimate authorities are persuasive. What's the difference between legitimate authority and tyrannical, antisocial authority? According to evolutionary biologist and Harvard professor Joseph Henrich, it hinges on whether the authority is predicated on prestige or dominance. While coercion and command rule the roost in dominance hierarchies, people earn authority in hierarchies of prestige or competence on the basis of skill, knowledge, success, and effective leadership traits (like generosity, even-temperedness, and fairness).[33] We're biologically hardwired to seek out, defer to, and learn from prestigious (read: competent) members of the community.[34] For example, a young boy might look up to, defer to, and seek to emulate his older brother. The older brother maintains his place in this hierarchy only if he treats his brother properly—that is, teaching and mentoring, and not dominating, him. Subordinates within prestige hierarchies don't merely defer to the wishes of competent authorities to gain their patronage; they actually mimic the thinking, actions, and behavior of their superiors.[35]

Prestigious people *persuade and inspire* others to share action, which is prosocial.[36] Dominant people use force—not persuasion—to get others to do their bidding.

One great way to establish yourself as a legitimate authority is to demonstrate competence. Inspire someone to say, "Wow, she's good. I respect her.

Let's follow her." Be generous, too, because when competent people display generosity toward others, their prestige soars.[37]

When you see an authority as illegitimate, you consider subverting it. And that's not always a bad thing. Consider the American Revolution, or the rejection of Soviet rule among Central and Eastern European countries in the 1980s.

At its best, the authority foundation helps people form mutually beneficial relationships within hierarchies that yield shared action. At its worst, authority becomes coercive and turns into tyranny over an individual or a group.

Appeal to an authority they find persuasive. If someone identifies as an American patriot, cite the Declaration of Independence or Constitution, or the Founding Fathers. If someone loves Lionel Messi, telling them he endorses your product will be a selling point.

Next—and this one requires caution—consider how someone might be harmfully subverting the established order and the authorities that maintain it. For example, if your son won't obey your spouse, you can talk to him about the important role your spouse plays in the family and why it's important to respect their authority. Be cautious, because it's easy to turn people with different views into enemies, even traitors. For example, you probably wouldn't want to make your kid feel like a terrible, disrespectful child because they don't obey your spouse.

To communicate authority, focus on someone's respect for a person, group, or tradition, and the need to avoid subverting it.

PURITY/DEGRADATION

Over 2 billion Christians view Jesus Christ as their savior, the son of God, a sacred being who died on the cross for their sins. Imagine how a fervent

Christian would respond to a picture of a crucifix submerged in urine. Before you recoil from this book in disgust, know that such a piece of "artwork" exists and is called *Piss Christ*, by Andres Serrano. Many Christians (though not Serrano, who's Catholic) saw it as blasphemous. Responses ranged from death threats to an award sponsored in part by the National Endowment for the Arts.

The purity[38] taste points us up, toward things like a higher power (religion) or values (like virtue). It also alerts us to, and drives us to avoid, contamination and degradation of the body and spirit. Research shows people high in purity are more sensitive to "disgusting things (e.g., animal remains, corpses, rotten food)" and "value self-discipline and cleanliness." People sensitive to it "report higher frequency of attending religious rituals, both organizationally (e.g., in a church), and non-organizationally (e.g., saying prayers at home)."[39] The survey question most strongly correlated with purity was "I believe chastity is an important virtue."[40]

Purity is powerful because it binds people together into moral communities around higher ideals. Haidt explains that it inspires us to "invest objects with irrational and extreme values—both positive and negative—which are important for binding groups together."[41] Environmentalists, for example, tend to view nature as pure and sacred, and they want to keep it pristine.

At its best, purity motivates us to embrace higher, noble values, like when someone builds a basilica in service to God, while also eschewing lower thoughts and deeds like debauchery.

At its worst, purity can be a vehicle for harming those deemed "impure." For example, in the Indian subcontinent, there's a long history of deeming classes of people "untouchable." India, Pakistan, and Nepal formally outlawed the practice. And yet a survey in India from 2011 to 2012 revealed that 30 percent of Indian households, including 52 percent of Brahmins, the priestly class, admitted to practicing untouchability (the actual number was likely higher, since some won't admit to it).[42] The practice is dangerous, too.

From 2018 to 2020, India's National Crime Records Bureau registered over 180,000 anti-Dalit (the untouchable class) crimes.[43]

The purity taste might be the most promising *and* perilous to communicate. When you view something as pure or sacred, you can look up, reach high, and do inspirational things. The dangerous flipside is that when you see something or someone as disgusting, you might seek to rid yourself of them, figuratively or literally, gently or not.

How to persuade with purity? First, figure out how sensitive your audience is to purity by probing what they find pure and sacred, or disgusting. Ask them what, if anything, they hold sacred. Or ask if they're religious. If they don't offer much, they probably aren't sensitive to it, so avoid those appeals. If they do, home in on and appeal to those values. Second, set sights high—yours and theirs. For example, you can persuade a religious person to help the poor by presenting it as service to God.

Disgust can persuade, too, since it can serve as a reason to avoid undesirable paths. For example, one reason to maintain basic hygiene—doing things like showering regularly, wearing clean clothes, and combing your hair—is so you don't look and smell offensive to others.

Appeals to purity are a staple of American political discourse. It's almost mandatory (though decreasingly so) for presidents and many other elected officials to conclude their big speeches by saying, "May God bless America." In 1960, John F. Kennedy was trying to become the first Catholic elected president in a primarily Protestant nation. In an address to the Greater Houston Ministerial Association, he tried to remove purity from political conversation by insisting religious views are one's "private affair, neither imposed by him upon the nation or imposed by the nation upon him as a condition to holding that office."[44] Nothing to discuss!

Disgust appeals must be made with an abundance of caution because they can be highly destructive. Consider the most extreme example: Adolf Hitler. His violent ideology was driven in part by disgust of Jews, whom he saw as a "virus," a "parasite," and a "toxin" requiring elimination through the "Final Solution."[45] Even in everyday life, seeing and criticizing someone as disgusting can easily and quickly go off the rails.

To communicate purity, focus on higher bodily and spiritual values like faith, devotion, and virtue. To communicate disgust, identify wicked, sinful behaviors to avoid, such as profanity, greed, and boastfulness.

It's worth pausing to note that loyalty, authority, and purity appeals are more complicated, because they often take on an oppositional or adversarial tone. If someone isn't loyal, they're a *traitor*. If they question authority, they're *subversive*. If they eschew purity, they're *disgusting*. Be careful before you sharpen your negative knife to slice someone up. The aim is to inspire, not give way to negativity.

LIBERTY/OPPRESSION

"Life, liberty, and the pursuit of happiness." This epic language, from the Declaration of Independence, has inspired billions of people in their personal and political lives. We all want and need to be able to live and pursue happiness how *we* see fit.

The liberty taste[46] is about our desire to be free to think, say, and do what we want. We yearn for autonomy. We resent it when people attempt to dominate, bully, or constrain us. And when the oppression is substantial enough, we experience reactance, which Haidt describes as a "form of righteous anger" you experience "when an authority tells you you can't do something and you feel yourself wanting to do it even more strongly."[47] History is rife with examples of one group seeking to oppress, dominate, and conquer another.

There isn't one universal understanding of freedom, though. For conservatives and libertarians, liberty is being left alone to live as you choose. This "negative" conception of liberty prizes the absence or removal of constraints on our behavior.

People on the left, by contrast, adhere to a "positive" notion of liberty concerned with creating the conditions that allow people to be "free." The Left focuses especially on vulnerable groups and what they need to overcome obstacles to freedom. The weak must be defended against the strong (read: oppressors) and enabled to be free.

Consider government welfare programs. Leftists seek to address oppression by making the needy freer to act through financial support. Conservatives and libertarians oppose these programs, especially in their expansive forms. They see the steps the government takes (such as higher taxes and more regulations) as oppressive restrictions on freedom, and oppressive to the very groups they're meant to help.

In short, this moral taste is sensitive to whether you feel and think you're free to act. No one likes being dominated or bullied. We like expanding our space to live and flourish, and reject restraints on our lives. This taste is sensitive to the reality that the human condition leaves all of us with the potential to dominate others.

How do you weave liberty into persuasive endeavors? First, be sensitive to how you can make people feel free or oppressed. For example, boxing someone into a position (intentionally or not) and forcing them to act a certain way breeds resentment. Conversely, recognize how empowering it is to give someone the freedom to act (and the support needed to succeed). Second, explicitly express your ideas in terms of making people freer or less oppressed. If you're fighting for more choice, or against domination, say so. Third, figure out where your audience falls on the ideological spectrum, and couch your message in their terms. If you're talking to conservatives and propose a welfare program on the grounds that it'll make people freer, your proposal will irritate and potentially mobilize opponents. Instead, focus on how the group in question has been dominated and bullied. For example, you could advocate for mandatory financial literacy training in high schools to give people the knowledge they need to truly succeed. This can start a fruitful conversation.

There's a tension between the authority and liberty taste buds. Our longing for liberty impels us to remove restrictions, avoid domination, and open up space to live as we please. The authority taste bud, by contrast, inclines us to guide or be guided by others, which can infringe on freedom, especially when the authority is experienced as illegitimate.

Liberty looms large in persuasive rhetoric. Greeting immigrants when they arrived by ship to Ellis Island was the Statue of Liberty. Indeed, when I lived in Germany and France and asked people from those countries what they thought of when they thought of America, "freedom" was the most common response.

Throughout his "I Have a Dream" speech, Martin Luther King Jr. repeatedly rings the bell of freedom to advocate for civil rights for African Americans. He speaks of the "riches of freedom," "an invigorating autumn of freedom," a "thirst for freedom," and a "quest for freedom."[48]

To communicate freedom, focus on ideals like choice and autonomy. To convey oppression, consider themes like coercion and force.

HOW MFT FACILITATES POLITICAL PERSUASION

Leftists, conservatives, and libertarians are, on average, sensitive to different moral tastes. Those differing sensitivities *drive* commitment to a particular political ideology. You need to understand and adapt your persuasive strategies based on these psychological realities.

The phrase "on average" is crucial because the data represent averages across groups. There's variation (sometimes significantly so) within groups. While conservatives on average aren't sensitive to care, that doesn't mean *no* conservatives are.

For left-of-center folks, we adopt the term "leftist," which is more inclusive because it captures a greater share of people on the left, such as social democrats and Greens.[49] For right-of-center folks, we adopt the term "conservative" to capture folks who generally seek to conserve something (like institutions and traditions).

For people who don't comfortably fit into one of these categories, such as moderates and centrists, you need to work harder to understand their moral palates before you can make persuasive appeals. A moderate might be high, low, or right in the middle in their sensitivity to any of the moral tastes.

To follow the discussion, this table shows the moral tastes to which each group tends to be sensitive.

	Leftist	Conservative	Libertarian
Care	✓		
Equality	✓		
Authority	(left-wing authoritarians)	✓	
Purity		✓	
Loyalty		✓	
Proportionality	✓	✓	✓
Liberty	✓ (positive)	✓ (negative)	✓ (negative)

Before we proceed, it's crucial to note that since the moral tastes of these groups don't really overlap, it's challenging to persuade people with ideologies different from ours because there's no shared moral language. We're wired to appeal to our own values, even if our audience doesn't find them persuasive or, worse, finds them repulsive. This is ineffective or counterproductive.

Shared action requires you to observe and appeal to your audience's moral tastes.

Leftist morality rests primarily on care and equality, and, to a lesser extent, liberty. Care is the most important.[50] Left-of-center political programs generally focus on acknowledging and alleviating suffering, especially of the least well-off. Concerning equality, leftists see significant wealth disparities as unfair and oppressive to the disadvantaged. Social welfare programs are a prime example.

Leftists hold ambivalent views on proportionality.[51] They also embrace the positive conception of liberty discussed above, and they usually contend that the least well-off need active support (generally from the government) to be free.

Loyalty and purity are viewed with suspicion by leftists. Regarding loyalty, the object of our political loyalty is usually a nation. People on the left generally favor universalism over nationalism, meaning they're less "loyal" to a nation. Leftists favor universal values (especially care for the dispossessed) over what they see as the arbitrary group that is their nation. Purity, at least when it's related to religion or disgust, tends not to resonate with the Left.

The Left's relationship with authority is more complicated. Leftists often see authority as imposing harmful, unfair, oppressive policies on people who aren't in a position to speak up and fight for themselves. They look askance at hierarchies, upon which authority usually rests.[52]

There is, though, a distinctly leftist form of authoritarianism. It has three dimensions: antihierarchical aggression, anticonventionalism, and top-down censorship. Left-wing authoritarianism is associated with autocratic orientation, dogmatism, partisan violence, and anticapitalism. Left-wing authoritarians have traits like a preference for social uniformity, a willingness to wield group authority to coerce individual and group behavior, and moral absolutism.[53] The traits commonly associated with authoritarian personality—conventionalism, submission, and aggression—appear on the left, too.[54]

Leftists nonetheless remain sensitive to the loyalty, purity, and authority tastes in basic ways. Do leftists find loyalty among their spouse, friends, and colleagues unimportant? When leftists are in charge, do they accept or even welcome people disrespecting their authority? No and no. Purity appears in various places on the left. For example, environmental activists hold the environment up as pure and rail against things that degrade it, like pollution and development.

How can you persuade the Left? Appeal to leftists' concern for care, equality, and positive liberty. If a libertarian tries to insist to a leftist that proportionality is the only legitimate way to think about fairness, and concern for equality is *illegitimate*, persuasion is impossible; the libertarian is more likely to antagonize the leftist. As we consider conservative and libertarian morality, we'll see how the Left can persuade them.

Conservative morality is the broadest, resting on five of the seven moral tastes: proportionality, loyalty, authority, purity, and freedom.

Proportionality might be the *most* important foundation for conservatives.[55] Conservatives prioritize merit and the quality and quantity of inputs, outputs, and outcomes. The more you produce, the more you deserve. Conservatives see equal outcomes arising from unequal contributions as *un*fair, so they generally aren't sensitive to equality.

Conservatives are highly sensitive to matters of political loyalty and betrayal. Calls to serve one's nation and uphold its values are powerful motivators. For example, conservatives are more likely to display their nation's flag.

Let's contrast remarks from two presidents. Reagan spoke of America as a "shining city upon a hill," "a tall, proud city built on rocks stronger than oceans, wind-swept, God-blessed, and teeming with people of all kinds living in harmony and peace; a city with free ports that hummed with commerce and creativity."[56]

By contrast, Obama was asked whether he subscribed "to the school of

American exceptionalism that sees America as uniquely qualified to lead the world." Obama responded, "I believe in American exceptionalism, just as I suspect that the Brits believe in British exceptionalism and the Greeks believe in Greek exceptionalism." He said America was exceptional because it has the biggest economy in the world, "unmatched military capability," and democratic values that protect rights enshrined in the U.S. Constitution.[57] Reagan wore his patriotism on his sleeve; Obama brandished his universalism.

Conservatives' sensitivity to authority inclines them to be more respectful of hierarchies. Conservatives tend to trust and follow proper authority figures, usually out of respect, sometimes out of fear. Conservatives see the assumption of authority based on competence in social, economic, and political groups as fair because that authority and responsibility is commensurate with talents and abilities.

Purity is prominent on the conservative palate. In American politics, the Bible Belt refers to the large group of Southern states that tend to be socially conservative due to their predominantly Christian faith. They see the Bible and its teachings as sacred, and support politicians and policies that share those beliefs. For example, those in the pro-life movement oppose abortion because they believe life begins at conception, and all life is sacred.

Liberty is the final flavor on the conservative moral palate. Conservatives conceive of freedom as the ability to do what you want. Conservatives are wary of ideas, policies, and practices that either impede or restrict someone's ability to act as they see fit, or infringe on one person's freedom to attempt to enhance someone else's.

Care appears negatively correlated to conservatism.[58] So when leftists accuse conservatives of not caring, they're actually onto something. Talking to a conservative in terms of care usually won't be persuasive, and might be counterproductive. It also means conservatives lack the key moral language of leftists, creating a potential communications chasm.

With sensitivity to up to five moral tastes, conservatives have a broader moral palate than leftists. They're especially fierce when seeking to protect institutions (such as the family) and traditions.[59]

What's the best approach to persuading conservatives? Discuss issues in terms of proportionality, freedom, authority, loyalty, and purity. Avoid care and equity. This presents a big challenge for leftists, who usually aren't sensitive to the former five tastes, and are sensitive to the latter two.

Libertarians are generally sensitive to two of seven moral tastes: liberty and proportionality.[60] Libertarians strongly support maximum political, economic, and social liberty, with as few restrictions on behaviors that don't directly infringe on the rights of others as possible. Libertarians are even more supportive of economic liberty than conservatives.[61] Regarding proportionality, libertarians want people to pull their weight. They think supporting people who could produce, and choose not to, is unfair. Libertarians see punishing the wealthy as unfair because their wealth is the product of creating value for others. These shared conceptions of, and commitment to, liberty and proportionality have historically inclined conservatives and libertarians to make common political cause.

Libertarians aren't sensitive to the other five foundations. They score low on loyalty, authority, and purity.[62] On loyalty, libertarians value the universality of individual freedom over the particularity of a nation's or group's interests. They are skeptical of authority because it often infringes on freedom. Libertarians score extremely low on care, tending to be less compassionate and sensitive to suffering.[63] They're low in equity, too.

How to approach persuasive endeavors with libertarians? Appeal to their conception of liberty by showing how you seek to expand choice, remove restraints, or combat oppression. Tap into their sensitivity to fairness as proportionality by focusing on merit, hard work, and productivity. Appeals to the other five foundations will usually fall on deaf ears, or antagonize them.

While libertarians have a clear path to persuading conservatives—appeal to liberty and proportionality—their path to persuading leftists is narrow because their moralities don't obviously overlap. Libertarians' best strategy for persuading leftists is to couch their ideas in leftists' terms.

For example, libertarians are fervent supporters of capitalism and free markets. One result of the spread of both worldwide has been literally billions of people rising out of poverty.[64] If libertarians want to persuade leftists of the power of these ideas, they must communicate how they help the poor and dispossessed rather than focusing on the need to remove restrictions from people's economic behavior to protect their freedom.

So, too, with equity: Libertarians need to consider how their ideas and policies might promote more equitable outcomes that benefit the disadvantaged. The best way to help the poor, they can say, is to improve their living standards and expand their access to opportunity. Capitalism and free markets do that.

Another strategy for libertarians and leftists to share action is to focus on their distaste of loyalty, authority, and purity. They could rally around opposition to an oppressive authority or discuss their shared concern about the supposed necessity of being loyal to some group.

The bottom line is that we're wired to communicate effectively only with people who share our views. If you want to truly make a difference with people with diverse beliefs, you need to appeal to people of different political proclivities based on how *they* see things.

QUICK MORAL TASTE TESTS

Here are some simple techniques for quickly assessing someone's moral tastes so you know how to persuade them. Three simple queries can quickly tell you what someone's ideology is with a high degree of accuracy. Your situation will determine which one you use.

First, discern your counterpart's conception of fairness, with a focus on whether they're sensitive to equity. Reason being, someone high in equity almost always is a leftist, not a conservative or libertarian. By contrast, leftists can be sensitive to proportionality, so that's not a determinate.

Here are some ways to understand their conception of fairness. You can say, "It seems like you have an idea of what's fair." Or ask, "What does a fair outcome look like?" Or "How can we make sure people are treated fairly?" Basically, use a statement or question that reveals if they're driven by equity concerns. If they say something akin to "Fair means people having similar (or the same) amounts," they're high in equity and almost certainly on the left. If they say, "It depends on how hard people work," they're probably a conservative or libertarian.

Second, zero in on their sensitivity to care, since leftists are high in care, and conservatives and libertarians usually aren't. You might say, "How would this approach impact the poor?" Or "It feels like this idea would hurt the poor." If they dismiss the concern by saying something like "What really matters is whether it promotes economic growth" or "It protects property rights," they're probably conservative or libertarian. (Indeed, my libertarian friends do this all the time!)

Third, assessing sensitivity to authority can help you distinguish between conservatives and libertarians, or someone's kind of leftism. You might observe, "It looks like this policy might undermine [insert kind of authority, like tradition]." Or "How would this policy change impact [insert impacted party]'s authority?" If they dismiss the concern, they're probably not conservative. If they affirm antihierarchical aggression, anticonventionalism, or top-down censorship, chances are they're a leftist sensitive to authority.

CAN YOU CHANGE SOMEONE'S MORALS?

You might be tempted to think that by using the techniques in this chapter, you can change someone's moral tastes. By coloring your points with their moral language, maybe they'll actually start to think like you. What's more, even if only 30 percent of someone's morals are genetic, that still leaves up to 70 percent that isn't wired into them and is a product of their experiences.

However, attempting to change someone's morals is mostly a fool's errand. First, it's unlikely it'll actually happen, and it's even more unlikely that you'll be the one to cause this evolution. After all, they've grown up with lots of experiences that have led them to embrace their current moral framework. It would take a lot of counterexperiences to tip their morals in a different direction. That would require a lot of work—in most cases, far more than you can possibly put in.

Second, changing them is unnecessary. If you follow the techniques in this chapter, you can simply appeal to them to get what you want. This requires intentionality, which is much easier than radically shifting someone's perspective.

WHAT IF MORAL FOUNDATIONS THEORISTS ARE WRONG?

You might be wondering: Since this chapter is grounded in moral foundations theory, what if it's partly or entirely wrong?

MFT finds its footing in hundreds of thousands of survey responses. If better data support an alternative, I'd make a beeline for them. To date, no such data have emerged.

Does MFT oversell differences within groups? Data show averages, tendencies, and trends, which allow us to make predictions. Plenty of people in a group don't conform to the group's average. We need to account for individuals who diverge from group averages. For example, while leftists on average aren't sensitive to loyalty, many individual leftists are. Whenever possible, individualize your persuasion tactics by learning someone's particular moral tastes.

Is MFT right about leftist, conservative, and libertarian moralities being sensitive primarily to certain moral tastes? While that seems to be true on average, there's substantial variation.

Many leftists are sensitive to more than just care, fairness (equity and sometimes proportionality), and positive liberty. Consider a leftist politician who served in his nation's armed forces for twenty-five years, flies an American flag at his home, and has a flag tattoo on his arm. He's obviously loyal and patriotic.

Plenty of libertarians are passionate about capitalism because this economic system cares best for the poor. Some call themselves "bleeding-heart libertarians" and point to the "hockey stick" of economic history, where long periods of stagnation are followed by a surge of growth sparked by competition-motivated innovation.[65] They're almost certainly higher in care.

And some conservatives care. Reagan used care language frequently. Arthur Brooks, former president of the American Enterprise Institute, a conservative think tank, and now a professor at Harvard, penned a book called *The Conservative Heart*, in which he outlines a "vision for conservatism as a movement for social and economic justice."[66]

LET'S GET SPECIFIC

You're thinking: This stuff about moral tastes sounds good. Does it work? Here's how I use it in my public policy advocacy.

One of my primary advocacy areas is housing. We all deserve a good roof over our heads. And the best way to make housing affordable is to increase supply. We need diverse types of housing to meet people's diverse needs. Pretty much everyone agrees on this.

One great way to increase housing supply is to allow add-ons to properties called "accessory dwelling units" (ADUs): things like coach houses, English basements, and granny flats. Unfortunately, in Chicago, where I work, it's nearly impossible to build them. I'm advocating to remove restrictions so it's easier to make ADUs.

You now know it's necessary to tailor your advocacy to different audiences. Here's how I wrote two op-eds in premium local outlets making the exact same case: Remove restrictions to build more ADUs.

To a business-oriented newspaper, I made a conservative/libertarian economic freedom case. We need to increase supply and give people the freedom to use their property as they see fit. It has worked in other big cities like Los Angeles. Let's do it in Chicago. The newspaper accepted it right away.[67]

Then I turned to the premium progressive newspaper in town. The editor often just ignores emails, or quasi-responds and then ghosts you. So I thought: How can I frame this to appeal to her and her audience? Simple. It turns out the current restrictions on building ADUs in Chicago are deeply inequitable. They are much more restrictive in poor and minority areas, and much more permissive in richer, whiter areas.

So I appealed to progressive morals: ADU restrictions are inequitable.[68] I hit "send." And just a few hours later she replied enthusiastically and published the piece with almost no edits. If I had sent her the economically oriented piece, she might not have even bothered to respond.

The best part? Instead, I continue to grow a relationship with her and her audience. She quickly accepted my next op-ed—on occupational licensing with similar framing. That's persuasive.

LET'S REFLECT

Moral persuasion is simple and quite difficult. It's simple, because we know generally what sorts of appeals are persuasive to people of various political ideologies. It's difficult, though, because we're wired to find lots of moral appeals repulsive. Don't forget the wiring part. Recall that 30–60 percent of our morality is genetic.

Yet again, the persuader's mindset points the way: It's about them, not you. Serve leftists equity. Serve conservatives proportionality. Serve libertarians liberty.

Rather than force-feeding them dishes they don't like, cook them up a tasty moral dish they'll enjoy. Since persuasion geniuses want to make a difference, their cookbook has recipes for everyone.

Key Takeaways for Making Persuasive Moral Appeals

1. Morality doesn't just persuade people. It fires them up! Which means you need to make effective moral appeals to significantly increase your chances of sharing action with someone.
2. Psychologists have discovered how our moral minds actually work: just like our tongues! Humans have seven distinct moral taste receptors wired into our hearts and minds: care, equity, proportionality, authority, loyalty, purity, and liberty.
3. We don't really choose our morality. An estimated 30–60 percent of our morality is genetically wired into us. Instead of fighting this reality or trying to change someone's morality, figure how you can appeal to their morals to get what you want. The genetic reality is liberating, too, because it means you don't have to dislike someone for not sharing your morals.
4. People of different political ideologies are, on average, sensitive to different moral tastes. Leftists are sensitive to care and equity as well as to "positive" liberty (doing things to enable people to be free). Conservatives are sensitive to proportionality, authority, loyalty, purity, and "negative" liberty (removing restrictions on people's behavior). Libertarians are sensitive to proportionality and "negative" liberty.
5. Since everyone is sensitive to a kind of fairness (either equity or proportionality), always make some sort of fairness appeal. If they don't share your conception, speak broadly about "fairness" rather than focusing on equity or merit.
6. To persuade someone, cook up tasty moral dishes they like, rather than force-feeding them dishes they find distasteful. This requires you to figure out how to couch what you want in terms of their morals.

Moral Taste Focusing Question: What is the ONE Thing you can do to tap into your audience's moral taste buds?

Chapter 6

TELL MORALLY MOTIVATING, EMOTIONALLY INTELLIGENT STORIES

You're never going to kill storytelling, because it's built in the human plan. We come with it.

Margaret Atwood

We spend more time on stories than on anything else in our lives except sleep, where stories also appear in the form of dreams. In 2022 the media data company Nielsen showed Americans spend nearly one-third of our waking time (four hours and forty-nine minutes per day, to be precise) on TV and streaming services, where we mostly consume stories.[1] In February 2022 Americans streamed 169.4 *billion* minutes of content, up from 143.2 billion in February 2021. Those numbers continued to rise in 2023.[2]

And when we're not online? We tell stories all day long. "Honey, how was your day?" Story ensues. "Billy, how was school?" Story follows.

Our appetite for them is insatiable. One principal for whom I was a speechwriter got this intuitively, so much that they sometimes wanted speeches that were *only* stories (which went a bit too far when there wasn't enough analysis).

Storytelling is *the single most powerful persuasion tool.* Period. As Jonathan Haidt explains, "The human mind is a story processor, not a logic processor."[3] Stories persuade better than anything else. That's why persuasion geniuses work hard at becoming master storytellers.

The foundational question for persuasion is: What kinds of stories motivate people to share action with you? Here we reveal the secret formula for crafting persuasive stories: **Tell morally motivating, emotionally intelligent stories.** You'll learn exactly how to do that in any situation. I'll use a speech I wrote as an example.

Unfortunately, lots of smart people ignore the cognitive reality that we're story processors—to their detriment. Rather than using specific stories about an issue, and crafting meta-narratives, they write long reports and give long presentations chock-full of data and not much else. Snooze. Or worse.

Literally as I was revising this chapter, a buddy in the policy space texted me (modified only to remove the specific industry to protect his privacy): "I have no words. We have a decade of research and these 9 special interest groups have wild stories and no evidence. And they're winning. Vibes-based policy making right here." Emotive stories can work better than decades of research.

This chapter offers a way to turn just about any challenge into a persuasive story.

HOMO SAPIENS ARE STORYTELLING CREATURES

About a hundred thousand years ago, there were six species of man around the globe. Today, there's only one—us, *Homo sapiens.* We won. How?

Neanderthals (one of the six) were physically stronger than *Homo sapiens* and were almost certainly smarter—they had bigger brains. In a one-on-one brawl, a Neanderthal would easily dispense with an inferior *Homo sapiens*.[4] Nature *could* have selected them. And yet here *we* are. What happened?

Stories. *Homo sapiens* build everything—our lives, relationships, and experiences—around stories. Our sense of identity is one powerful kind of story; so is our sense of community. We tell stories about things like religion and nations that socialize us and bind us to others. Neanderthals, by contrast, weren't storytelling creatures, and weren't especially social, hanging out mostly in small groups. The result? Large groups of *Homo sapiens* bound together around stories, then ganged up and easily dispensed with smaller groups of Neanderthals.

This brief account, adapted from Yuval Noah Harari's 2011 book *Sapiens*, shows that our storytelling abilities lie at the heart of our species' success. In fact, Oxford evolutionary psychologist Robin Dunbar argues that human language first *evolved* to tell stories, especially gossip about who was and wasn't following social rules.[5] (Did you hear what he *did*?) Dunbar has, with others, argued that despite its bad reputation, gossip actually helps communities function better by policing moral infractions.[6]

Stories—fictional or not—facilitate cooperation. In *The Story Paradox*, Jonathan Gottschall suggests story "originated as a means for preserving and passing information about everything from religious and moral imperatives to specific advice about hunting or marriage."[7]

According to neuroscientist Antonio Damasio, stories are the solution to how to make wisdom understandable, transmissible, persuasive, enforceable—in a word, how to make it stick.[8]

We evolved to be storytelling creatures. And this starts at a remarkably young age. My two-year-old son, Thomas, doesn't just love Dr. Seuss stories. He *remembers* them, walking around reciting lines from the books.

The bottom line is that stories need to be at the heart of our persuasive strategies.

STORYTELLING 101

Let's start with the basics of storytelling. Stories have heroes (and villains), a plot, and some core characteristics. You need to incorporate these elements into your stories. If they're missing, your story will fall flat and won't inspire shared action.

Superman. Luke Skywalker. Katniss Everdeen. Standing front and center in every persuasive story is a compelling hero. They're the person saying and doing things, good and bad. Something about the hero has to draw you in and motivate you to keep watching or reading (and tell others to do the same), and ultimately to root for them. Maybe it's a great strength, like Superman. Or their determination, like Katniss. Heroes aren't perfect, though: They have flaws (say, anger) that get them into trouble, and from which they have to recover.

A hero partakes in a journey. Folklorist Joseph Campbell described this journey as "the call to adventure."[9] That journey unfolds through the plot. We even *know* the structure of a good plot. After examining over 100,000 fictional stories through statistical analysis, David Robinson, a data engineer with a Princeton PhD, concludes that the arc of the average story goes something like this: "Things get worse and worse until at the last minute they get better."[10] Typically, the hero explores the known or the unknown, confronts difficulty, and eventually overcomes it, usually by taking some sort of risk and transforming themselves into something better.

Central to most hero's journey is a foil: the villain. Lex Luthor—Superman. Darth Vader—Luke Skywalker. President Coriolanus Snow—Katniss

Everdeen. The villain usually creates challenges for the hero that capture your attention.

Don't forget that you're *always* the hero of your own story. This means your counterpart is always the hero of theirs. When their understanding of themselves as a hero aligns with what you're trying to persuade them to do, align your persuasion efforts behind this self-understanding. When the action you want to share runs counter to their self-narrative, you need to find another element of themselves to celebrate so they move in your direction. Otherwise, you're asking them to stop doing things they think are heroic, which is unlikely to pan out.

For example, suppose you run a daycare center. One kid, Bobby, refuses to help clean up. Turns out, his mom's story is that she shows heroic care for her kids by doing as much as possible for them. This often leads to her letting Bobby make a big mess, then cleaning up after him. Rather than chastising the parent, ask her about how she'd like to see Bobby develop as a playmate and teammate. When she discusses something that ties to getting Bobby to help, press on it and try to make that a part of her narrative about good parenting. Reinforce the heroic nature of the behavior (cleaning up) with her and with Bobby so they feel good about it.

Identifying your hero can come at the beginning, middle, or end of your story-crafting process. It's simplest when it comes at the beginning: You encounter someone (literally or figuratively), and their story (real or imagined) *is* the narrative. You just fill in the details.

Sometimes, though, you know what you want to say, and then you need to identify a hero to help persuade. In these cases, you need to either find or create a hero that fits the arc of your narrative.

For example, in my poverty advocacy, I work to eliminate unfair barriers to work like occupational licenses, which are government permission slips to work. I published an op-ed in a local newspaper explaining why they're unfair. Within thirty minutes of it posting online, I received an email from

"Ethan." He said he was a barber, loved my op-ed, and wanted to help any way he could. He's now the authentic face of our reform efforts in this policy space.

Stories generally follow one of three plots: challenge, connection, or creativity. Each plot is meant to teach, inspire, and motivate us to act. As Chip Heath and Dan Heath explain in *Made to Stick*, in the challenge plot, the protagonist faces a formidable obstacle and successfully overcomes it, which inspires us. A timeless example is the story of David and Goliath. Variations include "the underdog story, the rags-to-riches story, the triumph of sheer willpower over adversity."[11]

The connection plot centers on the formation of a relationship that bridges a gap in things like religion, class, and age, generally where we might not expect a relationship to form.[12] One example is the film *Up*, in which an old widower, Carl, forms a bond with a young boy, Russell, as they undertake their adventure in a house suspended by balloons.

The creativity plot revolves around someone making a "breakthrough, solving a long-standing puzzle, or attacking a problem in an innovative way."[13] A classic example is the story of the apple falling on Isaac Newton's head and inspiring his theory of gravity. Creativity plots usually include one or a few moments that serve as turning points. Something clicks, and off the protagonist goes to do great things.

Compelling plots tap into what people find meaningful. Harvard professor Arthur Brooks's research has shown the bulk of meaning comes from just a few things: "human relationships, productive work, and the transcendental elements of life."[14] That's why these things are at the center of just about any story, including popular songs, art, movies, and literature.

Love is the most prominent. One study found that 67.3 percent of Top 40 songs in the U.S. from 1960 to 2010 were about love.[15] A great example is Whitney Houston's song "I Will Always Love You." For friendship, check out "That's What Friends Are For" by Dionne Warwick. For faith, consider

Leonard Cohen's "Hallelujah." For work, give "A Hard Day's Night" by the Beatles a listen.

The best stories are "sticky." You remember them, they endure, and they persuade. According to Heath and Heath, sticky communications have six technical components: simplicity, unexpectedness, concreteness, credibility, emotions, and stories.

Simple stories have plots about just a few core things. They strip things down to their "critical essence" by weeding out information that's superficial, tangential, or just not directly relevant to the core, because it's distracting.[16] The Golden Rule "is the ultimate model of simplicity: a one-sentence statement so profound that an individual could spend a lifetime learning to follow it."[17] Simple isn't the same as short. Long stories can be simple. While the Harry Potter series and *The Lord of the Rings* each total thousands of pages, their basic plots are simple.

Here are two focusing questions to achieve simplicity:

1. What is the ONE Thing you need to convey in your story such that everything else will be easier or unnecessary? If you can't boil it down to one thing, then your story isn't sufficiently simple.
2. What would happen if I remove this idea, word, sentence, paragraph, section, or chapter? If the answer is "nothing," or "not much," probably remove it. Err on the side of short to maintain your audience's attention.

Simple phrases can be transformational. Standing in front of the Brandenburg Gate, which symbolized the separation of East and West Berlin, in 1987, Ronald Reagan said, "Mr. Gorbachev, tear down this wall!"[18] In his inaugural address, John F. Kennedy said, "Ask not what your country can do for you—ask what you can do for your country."[19] These powerful phrases persuaded because they simply encapsulated the right message at the right time by the right person.

Do you like encountering boring, mundane, thoughtless messaging? No one does. Unexpected elements can sear things into your audience's mind by breaking a pattern, violating expectations, or being counterintuitive.[20] They generate surprise, interest, and curiosity by grabbing our attention, and increasing alertness and causing focus through unforeseen twists and turns.[21] You generate interest by discussing things important to your audience in a thought-provoking manner. And you stimulate their curiosity by opening knowledge gaps and then filling them.

What does unexpectedness look like in practice? Consider *Star Wars: Episode V*'s ending: Darth Vader reveals he's Luke Skywalker's father—something no one expected. This undoubtedly sparked interest and curiosity in *Episode VI*. Would Luke succumb to the dark side, like his father? Or remain good and overcome evil? People flocked to theaters to see.

Concrete language is here, hard, and evocative. It points people in a clear direction. Abstract language, by contrast, is diffuse and distant, leaving too much open to interpretation. Human memory experiments reveal "people are better at remembering concrete, easily visualized nouns ('bicycle' or 'avocado') than abstract ones ('justice' or 'personality')."[22] If people have trouble even *remembering* abstract ideas, then they're not a good driver of shared action. Concrete language also ensures an idea "will mean the same thing to everyone in our audience," because they'll all visualize something similar.[23]

When discussing abstract ideas like "justice," be concrete. Don't follow the German philosopher Immanuel Kant. He proposed a categorical imperative: "Act only in accordance with that maxim through which you can at the same time will that it become a universal law."[24] Huh? Abstract garble. Martin Luther King Jr. is a model: "I have a dream that my four little children will one day live in a nation where they will not be judged by the color of their skin but by the content of their character."[25] King makes justice concrete, connecting his story and message: Don't judge by skin color. That's persuasive.

Credibility, the fourth component of stickiness, makes us *believe* what someone says. External credibility comes from things like status, degrees, rank, and previous experience. If a Nobel laureate in economics analyzes the economy on a news program, you're more likely to listen to them than if they endorse sneakers. Internal credibility is about the ideas in our stories. People need to be able to test the ideas themselves, to kick the tires and make sure they're consistent.[26]

Let's consider the emotional element of stories only briefly, since we discussed emotions in chapter 4. Decide what you want your audience to *feel* during and after your story. Tell stories about people, because, as Heath and Heath explain, we're "wired to feel things for people, not abstractions."[27] When telling a story about a thing, like the invention of the bicycle, make the story about the person who created it, or about how it has benefited people. Objects have no personality, and your audience can't relate to them.

You'll generate more positive feelings if you frame things around how your audience can benefit. For example, if you're selling grass seed, rather than advertising it as "the world's best seed," advertise is as the world's best surface for playing soccer with your kids, which shows how your customer benefits.[28] Make it about them.

Your experiences shape how *you* experience a story. Story formation is largely phenomenological. Taken to its Greek roots, *phainómenon* means "that which appears," and *lógos* means "study." Phenomenology is a philosophy of experience, literally the study of that which appears to you. It's about how we experience objects and events (phenomena). Since our experiences differ from everyone else's (a lot or a little), our stories differ, too.

What does phenomenology have to do with persuasion? Only stories sufficiently aligned with your audience's experiences will resonate with them.

You need to understand *their* realities, even if you don't like or agree with them, and operate within their context. Someone's story is real for them because they experience it, plain and simple. Persuasive stories resonate with your audience's experiences.

These questions will help you get the basics of storytelling right:

- Who's your audience? (Consult the stakeholder analysis from chapter 1.)
- What hero (and villain) would resonate with them?
- What journey would motivate your audience to share action? What obstacles would they find compelling for the hero to overcome?
- What plot type would appeal to them?
- Which of the technical elements (simplicity, unexpectedness, concreteness, credibility, and emotions) can you incorporate into your plot?

You need preliminary answers to all of these except the technical elements, because they're foundational to crafting a good story.

PERSONALIZE, HUMANIZE, DRAMATIZE

Great storytelling requires you to personalize, humanize, and dramatize.[29] This helps people understand, care about, and support the person, issue, problem, etc., at hand.

Craft personalized narratives that resonate with an audience. Focus on their specific issues, interests, or concerns. For example, I worked in fundraising for a nonprofit that partners with professors at a wide range of colleges and universities across America. Whenever possible, I personalized information for current or potential supporters by sharing information about our work at their alma mater. That meant far more to my audiences than general data points ever could.

Next, humanize. Always present your story—the twists, the turns, the victories, the defeats—in a human context. Don't just make abstract claims about something being good or bad, beneficial or not. Show how a policy, practice, idea, etc., will harm or help the hero of your story. Be specific. Humanizing stories makes them real, not abstract. For example, demonstrate unfairness through a story about how Susie was treated, not by philosophizing about "fairness."

Finally, dramatize. Dale Carnegie wrote nearly a century ago, "This is the day of dramatization . . . And you will have to do it if you want attention."[30] Stories need a plot centered around how something will make people better or worse off. The drama arrives as your hero either fights for a better, brighter future, or works to maintain the good status quo against some threat. The drama unfolds as the hero saves the day.

Personalizing, humanizing, and dramatizing require the right hero. Not just any ol' person will do. You need to put in the work to find or craft the right character to advance your goals. If you're using a real person, they need to be the right fit. Once you think you've found them, verify all the details of their story, because if a key detail cannot be proven—or worse, turns out to be false—then your credibility is shattered. For example, if a major newspaper runs your story, and inconsistencies or errors arise, your organization will look terrible.

The Institute for Justice, a nonprofit, public interest law firm, is a model for the personalize, humanize, and dramatize process. At the center of their stories is a dramatic moment, usually when the victim is sitting at their kitchen table and gets a letter from the government, out of the blue. The letter accuses them of having done something allegedly illegal, and their client's first reaction is, "Oh no! I'm in trouble." Off the hero goes on their journey, with IJ there to help them fight for their rights. They're especially good and intentional about putting a "human face" on the controversy.[31]

STORYTELLING'S SECRET FORMULA

You're finally ready for the secret formula for persuasive storytelling: Tell morally motivating, emotionally intelligent stories.

In chapter 5 you learned how to understand and appeal to *your audience's* morals, not yours. Ask yourself: How can my story activate their specific moral tastes? A tale on authority isn't going to resonate with a rebellious youth; but maybe they're high in the care taste, and you show them how their actions (like sneaking out at night) are hurting people they care about (their parents, for example). Then figure out how to have the hero activate their moral taste buds through words and deeds, like an act of care. The plot needs events, twists, and turns bringing moral matters to the fore and keeping your audience morally engaged.

Here's an example of what not to do from a conversation I had with my research assistant. I mentioned earlier that I'm passionate about capitalism because it cares best for the poor. When I told that story to him, he blankly stared at me, blinked, and said, "I'm an objectivist [a kind of libertarian]. That did nothing for me." My story missed the mark. To activate *his* moral taste buds, I needed to talk about how capitalism rewards people based on their merit (proportionality), and how it lets people be free to create and innovate (liberty).

Your stories need to be emotionally intelligent. Our Emotionally Intelligent Persuasion Model (EIPM) is central here. Recall the four steps: 1) Observe how you and your audience feel, 2) identify shared goals, 3) facilitate feelings necessary to share action, and 4) share action. Here's how to apply this to storytelling.

Begin by observing how you're feeling. If you're in a bad mood, now may not be the right time to engage. Next, gain clarity on how your audience is feeling. If they're happy, you probably don't want to tell a story that's going to make them sad. If they're anxious, you want a story that relieves some of their anxiety.

Your story needs to point toward shared goals. If there's agreement about what they are, then your story needs to illuminate and cement them. The hero's action might point toward them, or even take required actions. If no such agreement exists, then the goal of your story is to secure agreement on what those goals are. Your story could highlight problems your hero is facing that align with concerns for your audience in an effort to coalesce around a solution to address them.

You need to know what feelings will promote shared action. How do they feel about an issue? What feelings do you need to generate to motivate them to work with you? Excitement? Surprise? Anger? Your story needs to prompt the appropriate feelings. You achieve this through moments in your narrative that press your audience's emotional buttons. For example, if your goal is to inspire fellow members of your church community to volunteer to help with a charity drive, tell stories about how previous volunteers have helped the needy. Have videos from participants about how meaningful it was, or from recipients about how helpful it was.

If you can do all of this effectively, then step 4—sharing action—is more likely.

It's important to remind yourself that moral motivation and emotional intelligence require a high degree of intentionality because you're wired to launch *your* logic and lead with *your* morals. Persuasion geniuses never forget: It's about them, not you.

LET'S GET SPECIFIC: AN AIR FORCE MOMENT

To demonstrate how this storytelling formula works in practice, let's turn to a speech I wrote for the Air Force secretary as a model. I'll walk you through all parts of the speech so you see how to put this storytelling formula into practice.

The speech was delivered in the Pentagon's Hall of Heroes. Its purpose was to celebrate Air Force Master Sergeant John Chapman. Chapman was posthumously receiving the Medal of Honor, the highest military decoration an American can earn, in recognition of bravery while fighting and dying in battle in Afghanistan in 2002. Chapman was part of a unit searching for a lost soldier and walked into a hornet's nest of Taliban forces. He made the ultimate sacrifice to save others.

The event was particularly significant because fewer than 20 airmen have ever received the Medal of Honor, and none since Vietnam.

Chapman's Medal of Honor was truly seen as an Air Force "moment," which is exactly how we understood it in our planning meetings. That moment included multiple days of ceremonies at the White House, Pentagon, and Air Force Memorial. Everyone, including the president of the United States, knew we had to get this "right." For the secretary, getting it "right" meant memorably honoring Chapman as an individual, fallen soldiers generally, the Air Force, and America as a nation. No small task.

As I began conceptualizing the speech, I analyzed the audiences' moral tastes. The multiple audiences—Chapman's family, the Air Force, and America's armed forces—shared sensitivity to some tastes. The most obvious was loyalty, since it usually drives the choice to serve one's nation. We needed to appeal to their love of America.

They're probably also sensitive to freedom, since the desire to protect America's freedoms is one reason people wear a uniform. There are undercurrents of care in Chapman's story: care for his nation generally, and for the lost soldier he returned to find, Neil Roberts. Chapman was widely viewed as a standout soldier, so we could tap into proportionality. Authority, purity, and equality didn't really factor into the story, so I left them out.

Then I used the EIPM. Since the speaker (step 1: Observe how you want your audience to feel) was the secretary, I had to consider things from her perspective. She was a mixture of excited and anxious. Excited to honor Chapman and about the opportunity. Anxious because there was a lot of pressure to hit a home run. The audience (still step 1) mainly had feelings of excitement and sadness. Excited to celebrate Chapman and the Air Force, and sad because Chapman died in combat and is sorely missed. The secretary was (still step 1) well liked across the Air Force, so she was an excellent person to deliver the final speech at the event. The shared goals (step 2: Identify shared goals) were to celebrate Chapman's courage and sacrifice, and put the courage of airmen on par with that of services like the Army and Marines, which engage in more on-the-ground combat. The feelings necessary to achieve this (step 3: Facilitate feelings necessary to share action) were mainly a combination of enjoyment, love, and trust. The speech facilitated those feelings (step 3) remarkably well, and shared action followed (step 4: Share action).

I needed an unexpected framing to capture the audience's attention. Thinking primarily in terms of loyalty, my mind kept turning to a familiar song: "The Star-Spangled Banner." Specifically, the powerful words at the end of the first stanza: "O'er the land of the free, and the home of the brave."

At sporting events, Americans sing that line with an exclamation point. There's a problem with that: It's actually punctuated with a question mark. Reason being, when Francis Scott Key wrote it in 1814, it wasn't a foregone conclusion that America would remain free, given the ongoing War of 1812. There it was! By making the statement a question, we could wrap the whole speech in a song that resonates far and wide. This also provided a plot: Chapman's story is America's story. Our nation continues to exist only because brave people like Chapman fight to keep us free.

Now let's look at some of the details of the speech, which I recommend watching (link in endnotes), since the secretary nailed the delivery.[32]

The secretary began the speech by tapping into loyalty, with something unexpected: "You know, we don't focus on it very much, but the first verse of our *national anthem*, which we just heard so beautifully sung, is a series of questions." She immediately made it concrete: "Can you see our flag, as the dawn is breaking? It was 1814 and Francis Scott Key . . ." She then returned to loyalty, with an undercurrent of harm: "It was a tough time in our history. Washington, D.C., the capital of this young republic, had been sacked [harm] by the British a few weeks before. The Capitol [loyalty] had been set aflame [harm], and the White House [loyalty] was evacuated [harm]."

In her opening, the secretary tapped into loyalty with mention of our national anthem, the flag, our young republic, the Capitol, and the White House. And care-plus-harm arose when she talked about D.C. being sacked and evacuated.

The secretary then set the stage for tying Chapman's story to America's:

> That first verse ends with a question for us, a challenge: "O say does that star-spangled banner yet wave, O'er the land of the free [liberty] and the home of the brave?" Would our nation [loyalty] endure? Would we be protected [care] by the brave? Would we be able to produce the men and women [proportionality] it takes who swallow fear [emotions], who summon bravery [care], and act to protect freedom [liberty] and to protect [care] each other?

Enter Chapman, "who, by his actions [care], answered the question in our national anthem [loyalty] for his generation."

We crafted a refrain to bring Chapman's truly remarkable courage to the fore and make it stick with the audience. After describing each phase of his actions, the secretary said four times, "And he did it anyway." He went into the "hornet's nest" to try to rescue Roberts [care]. He charged the enemy, cleared a bunker, putting himself in harm's way, to protect [care] his fellow soldiers. Then, when a helicopter was sent to rescue him, "John knew he had to try to stop him [the gunman]. He was alone, outgunned. And he did it anyway." Because he cared.

We needed to show that our hero, John Chapman, was driven by the virtue he had spent his whole life cultivating, and that his behavior was emblematic, not an anomaly. I got on the phone and found a story to put Chapman's merit front and center.

> One of John's instructors recalled Sergeant Chapman's time at Combat Control School, one of the more grueling of Air Force training programs. In the Special Tactics Training pipeline, about 85 percent wash out. And his instructor recalls a smirk on Sergeant Chapman's face during training, as if the training was too easy for him. And, his instructor says, *it was* too easy [proportionality] for John. John Chapman never talked about how good he was [proportionality] at what he did. He didn't have to.

This story brings in an outside person to further establish Chapman's credibility as a deserving hero.

The secretary concluded by returning to "The Star-Spangled Banner," and making Chapman's story America's story:

> For his generation of Americans [loyalty], John Chapman was the answer [proportionality] to that lingering question. Our nation endures [loyalty] and continues to be the land of the free [liberty] because of brave [care] men. Because of John Chapman.

The audience was completely blown away. The secretary busily fulfilled requests for copies of the speech. People called me saying their offices were in tears. Mission accomplished—because we tapped into the audience's morals in an emotionally intelligent manner.

Most importantly, by successfully making this an Air Force "moment," people were even more eager to share action with the secretary. Which was crucial when she delivered another big speech a few weeks later, "The Air Force We Need," a significant and successful policy announcement. Ever since, *The Wall Street Journal* has repeatedly echoed her key recommendation for growing the Air Force.

BEWARE THE DARK SIDE OF STORYTELLING

Just like the rest of the persuasion techniques in this book, storytelling can be a force for evil, not just good. Doubtful? Stories about "equality" have resulted in death and misery for billions of people living under communist regimes. A pernicious story about purity and the need to exterminate parasites drove the Nazis to try to eliminate Jews.

The power of storytelling is much like "the Force" in Star Wars. The light side of the Force is beautiful and lifegiving. Think Yoda. And the dark side is menacing and destructive. Think the Death Star destroying entire planets. As Jonathan Gottschall, author of *The Story Paradox*, explains,

> Yes, narratives are the primary tools we use to make sense of the world. But they're also our main tools for fabricating dangerous nonsense.
>
> Yes, stories typically have moral dimensions that reinforce pro-social behavior. But in their monotonous obsession with plots of villainy and justice, they gratify and reinforce our instincts for savage retribution and moral sanctimony.[33]

Hence novelist John Gardner's characterization of storytellers as "secret propagandists,"[34] and of stories as the "greatest power" of anything in the world "to enslave."[35]

How do such evil stories come about? One of the most common ways is, we start blaming others, "them," for our problems and our group's problems. *They* harm us. "Them" easily becomes an "other," distant from, foreign to, and inferior to us. Their otherness makes "them" a villain, for whom we develop "a kind of moral blindness."[36] So we try to fight, defeat, and punish these enemies.

American politics largely has become a story about "them": crazy, stupid, evil "them." Because we need more enemies?

The scariest part about dark stories, especially conspiracies, is that they move fast. They can quickly spiral out of control, causing immense harm. Doubtful? In about one hundred days, the Rwanda genocide saw Hutus murder over half a million of their Tutsi neighbors through a dark story. Unfortunately, that's just one of many examples throughout history.

Avoid spinning dark tales. They're manipulative and harmful. They create a darker world. And they're usually counterproductive, as people come to view you in a darker light and become less inclined to work with you.

LET'S REFLECT

"Talk story" is a saying central to Hawaiian culture. It's also the key to persuasion. More than any other technique, stories persuade. When we hear them, something special happens that reason, data, analysis, or just plain talking simply can't replicate. Our hearts and minds open to people, situations, and issues when they'd otherwise remain closed. That's powerful. And crucially for persuasion, it helps us share understanding.

Every important situation needs a compelling story. Which means you always need to be equipped with a persuasive one. If you're a founder or executive, your organization needs a compelling origin story, and you need positive stories for your annual reports. In every job interview, you'll need a story of how you can add value in your next role—and specific stories to prove it! Every parent teaches their children values and ideals through stories about right and wrong. As psychologist Raymond Mar explains, "reader attitudes shift to become more congruent with the ideas expressed in a narrative."[37] This primes us to share action.

As tempting as it is to put the lion's share of your time into perfecting your analysis, it's more important to perfect the content and delivery of your stories.

All that said, stories cannot be a stand-in for analysis. Without a logical or rational foundation, your story will quickly crumble—and with it your chances of persuading. Without that firm foundation, people will hear you tell your story, feel good in the moment, then become skeptical once they have time to reflect.

Beware storytelling becoming a trope. Many people, when they learn how important stories are, tell them *too much*. When you overuse stories, they become less effective. And when you rely only on stories, you tell lots of stories lacking substance. The stories don't really have a point, so they don't stick. They just float away like a bubble, which usually bursts quickly.

Don't tell marshmallow stories, which are stories that provide a quick sugar rush, don't stick with you, and often make the recipient cringe because they're trite.

Transformative stories incorporate all the other principles in this book. They're crafted for the audience, since it's about them. They illuminate a vision that animates action. They're emotionally intelligent and morally motivating. They're upbeat. They help you negotiate. They're more than mere words. They're clear.

Now go talk story.

Key Takeaways for Telling Persuasive Stories

1. Humans are story processors before we're logic processors. That's why we spend more time on stories than anything else in our waking hours. That makes storytelling the single most powerful persuasive tool that exists.
2. The secret formula for the most persuasive stories is to tell morally motivating, emotionally intelligent stories. You learned in chapter 5 how to activate your audience's moral tastes. And in chapter 4 you learned the Emotionally Intelligent Persuasion Model as a proven way to generate persuasive feelings. Your story's plot needs to tap into your audience's morals and prompt the feelings necessary to share action. Both of these happen through the words and deeds of the characters.
3. The basics of storytelling are simple: You need a hero who partakes in a journey, usually with a villain as a foil. This happens in the context of a plot that grabs and maintains your audience's attention. While there are a few kinds of plots (challenge, connection, or creativity), they all tap into what an audience finds meaningful.
4. Great stories are personal, humanized, and dramatic. Personalized narratives resonate with an audience and center on their interests or concerns. Humanized stories and their twists and turns occur in a human context. Dramatic stories center on how a person or action will make people better off. Combined, these features help your audience care about and support the person or issue at hand.
5. While stories can be a force for great good, they can also be used for evil. Beware the dark side of storytelling.

Story Focusing Question: What is the ONE story you can tell that will morally motivate your audience to share understanding and action?

Part 3

APPLY TESTED TECHNIQUES TO ANY SITUATION

Part 1 walked you through the persuader's mindset: what it is, how it works, and how to embrace it. Part 2 dived deeply into the contours of the human brain to analyze how to use your cognitive wiring to get what you want. Parts 1 and 2 focused more on the vision and strategy required to become a persuasion genius (while providing highly actionable techniques).

Part 3 is more tactical. Building on the insights from the first two parts, what specific techniques will further enhance your ability to get what you want? These will help you move into the elite category of persuasion genius.

Chapter 7 brings negotiation strategy into your persuasion process. The best negotiators have proven techniques to navigate high-stakes situations and get what they want. You'll learn to use them everywhere, whether you're talking to the CEO, a customer service agent, or your child.

Chapter 8 builds on our earlier insights that persuasion isn't just about saying the "right" thing. Often, words are the *least* important part of a situation. How people experience you is crucial. For example, the wrong tone can make the "right" words toxic. The good news is that doing the things outlined in the chapter gives you the leeway to fumble your words and still get what you want.

Chapter 9 presents you with the simplest and often toughest test of all: the granny test. You'll learn how to ace it and bring optimal clarity into any communication.

Chapter 7

NEGOTIATE WHAT YOU WANT

The most dangerous negotiation is the one you don't know you're in.

Chris Voss, former FBI lead
international kidnapping negotiator

I wanted the job badly. It was big step up professionally. And I needed to know if I was *their* guy, and *why*, because that'd give me leverage. So when I got to ask my questions during each interview round, I unleashed a tremendously powerful technique, the "proof of life" question. The question reveals if they're serious about partnering with you, and why. I asked, "You've probably received lots of strong applications and talked to lots of great candidates. Why me?"

One executive responded that I had extremely strong credentials, especially my research skills. That distinguished me; so I leaned into them. The board chairman responded, "You're the first person who's gotten to me" (it was five months since the job posted). No one else had made it this far. Then I hit the president with the question. He meandered for a few minutes, then said, "That's a great question, and you know why." I smiled and said, "You don't have to answer it." He continued, "We're looking for a unicorn."

Translation: They weren't looking for a cookie-cutter candidate, and they saw a big horn on my forehead. *I* was their unicorn. Persuasion! I got the job because I knew how to open up the line of communication. And I got everything I asked for while negotiating the offer, too, including some things they had never given to anyone before me.

Classic negotiation situations include buying a car or scoring a big deal. In fact, every—yes, every—situation is some kind of negotiation. Even something as seemingly simple as starting a conversation is often a negotiation. Are they too busy? Do they have time for *you*? If you start talking to them, will they continue the conversation? Will you get what you want out of your interactions with them? You're negotiating every step of the way. That's why you'll learn to **negotiate what you want**.

If you don't know how to negotiate, the chances of people taking advantage of you are much higher, and you won't get what you want. This almost repeatedly happened at work to someone close to me. Her boss would come to her and tell her she was taking on significant new responsibilities without any indication she'd get a raise, promotion, or both. When she told me, I was angry and immediately said that was unacceptable, and that she needed to negotiate for herself. She was scared, because negotiation can be scary. She didn't want to upset anyone.

So I coached her using the techniques in this chapter. Three promotions that all came with raises and bonuses later, she's now able to negotiate on her behalf at work without any coaching from me. If she hadn't learned, she'd be frustrated about having a lot more work without any recognition.

The common conception is that negotiation is a zero-sum game, with a winner and a loser. Buying a car is a classic negotiation situation. You just grind the other person down until you get what you want, right? Nope. Negotiation, like any other persuasion situation, isn't about winning. Negotiation is about forming and growing a relationship to repeatedly secure durable deals with people. That's how you get what you want—not just once, but regularly.

This chapter is full of techniques to help you do that. Among other benefits, they unlock otherwise inaccessible information crucial to achieving shared action.

In my humble opinion, the best negotiation coach in the world is Chris Voss, former lead international kidnapping negotiator at the FBI. His *Never Split the Difference* is well worth your time. We'll draw on some of his techniques throughout.

NEGOTIATION IS AN EMOTIONAL ENTERPRISE

Empathy is a much better means to get what you want than sympathy. Yet we generally confuse them and deploy sympathy instead.

According to the American Psychological Association (APA), sympathy is "a capacity to share in and respond to the concerns or feelings of others."[1] In other words: I feel your pain. At most, this can be a starting point for persuasion. Often, though, sympathy derails persuasion, because as we share in someone's feelings, we can often exacerbate them. Since it's generally negative feelings that require sympathy, growing those feelings often hinders shared action for reasons we discussed in part 2. In short, they spiral into negativity.

Empathy is a better path to persuasion. The APA defines empathy as "understanding a person from his or her frame of reference rather than one's own."[2] The persuader's mindset starts with the insight that it's about them, not you. Rather than understanding them from your perspective, you need to do your very best to understand them from *their* perspective.

For example, you know a friend is upset with their situation at work. You assume that's because they haven't gotten the promotion you think they deserve, so you focus on that. Your friend is actually frustrated about not getting to work on a big project they're passionate about. Focus on demonstrating understanding of their concerns, not what you want their concerns to be.

It's far easier to be empathetic in person. Research shows face-to-face communications are more honest, cooperative, trusting, and ultimately more mutually beneficial.[3] This is easy to forget in an age of technology (text, email, and video calls) and telework.

That's why it's so important to set your default mode of communication to in-person. Whether you're discussing a big issue or just trying to connect with someone, the connection you'll form greases the wheels of shared action. For example, if you're negotiating a big sales deal, take the time to fly and go see your potential client. It'll pay big dividends. If there are problems, you're also more likely to uncover them in person. And if you don't uncover them, they'll get in the way at an inopportune moment.

Whenever I have to have tough conversations with my direct reports, I always do it in person. For example, a young buck on my team once completely failed to show up for an important event we were hosting that he was supposed to help execute. No one knew where he was. He rolled in a few hours late that day. No biggie? Not quite. Once everyone else left, I sat down and asked him what happened. He admitted to making a mistake, and I used it as an opportunity to offer additional feedback based on some other recent suboptimal behavior.

As I spoke, his body language (more on that in chapter 8) was visibly stressed. He said, "It feels like you're piling on." I said, "My goal is to help you grow." And I then laid out a pathway to that growth. He relaxed and, over the next few months, became a standout junior teammate. So much that he earned a sizable raise and promotion within a year. If I had tried to have that tough conversation over the phone, I can't imagine it would have gone nearly as well.

THINK LONG-TERM

Many people think of negotiation as "winning" and getting the absolute most they can, usually at the expense of their counterpart. They focus on what they want to get in the current moment. And sometimes they do get a short-term reward by giving their counterpart just barely enough to agree to something.

Now, how do *you* feel when someone does this to you? Not good. When you know a powerful counterpart is doing it, you feel cornered, with nowhere to go. You know they're taking advantage of you, because they're negotiating from a position of strength. They hold all the cards, and you don't have much choice. If you have a choice, often you just walk away. When you learn only later you've been taken advantage of, you're angry because you thought they were being fair and they weren't. You won't trust them again.

The core problem here is that many people focus only on the short-term gains in a negotiation. They think about what they can get today, and they neglect tomorrow. But the goal isn't to just "win" once and move on. The goal is to truly win over and over again.

That's why it's necessary to think long-term in your interactions. You will almost always see your counterpart again, whether you know it or not. And there usually aren't *that many* people you can make good deals with in the first place. You don't want to exhaust those options through one-time interactions.

Your goal is for them to feel good about interacting with you again tomorrow. That maximizes what you get in the long term. That means you have to understand their wants and needs, then work to satisfy them in a way and through a process they feel good about. Even if you give them what they want, if the process itself was unpleasant, they won't feel good about it.

This long-term mindset is better in the short term, too. When someone has negative feelings about their negotiation with you, or is even just lukewarm, they're not going to be eager to share action and implement your agreement. They'll do so reluctantly, slowly, inefficiently.

Real estate agents are a great example of why thinking long-term is so important. If they treat their client like a one-time transaction where they get their fee and move on, their client won't refer them to friends and family looking to buy or sell a house. Referrals are what distinguish top agents from everyone else.

My wife and I think long-term with our au pairs to ensure the highest-quality childcare. Technically, we're only required to pay them a paltry sum (less than two hundred dollars) per week, without any additional financial benefits. They can work 45 hours per week, including all but one weekend per month. Many families see their au pairs as cheap childcare with extended hours. Sweet!

While it's true that au pairs technically signed up for this, it gets exhausting quickly. Our current au pair has recounted how her friends have to start as early as 6:45 AM on Saturdays. They can barely travel to see this wonderful country, because they only get one weekend off per month.

My wife and I take a different approach: We think about what would motivate a great au pair to choose our family over others and do a great job for the entire twelve months. We advertise the following benefits on our profile: higher pay, other financial perks like a cell phone plan and a transportation stipend, no more than two weekend shifts per month, and regular hours. It doesn't cost that much more money to do all this, and it gets us great au pairs.

Even better: Once our au pair compares her situation to her other au pair friends in the area, she sees that, relative to them, she has it really good! Which makes her more eager to do a great job. This has been true with all our au pairs.

Interactions that seem purely transactional and one-off often aren't. If you go to the same coffee shop every day and form a good relationship with the barista, maybe they'll make your beverage first. If you're always nice to the hostess of a restaurant you like, she'll be much more likely to get you a nice table.

Thinking long-term requires patience. You don't have to rush into deals. One of my interns has a side business of reselling LEGOs (and making LEGO videos, his biggest passion). He said he often has "seller's remorse" because he prices his items too low. I asked him why he does that. He said, "Well, I want someone to buy them." I asked, "What bad thing happens if you price them at a higher price you think someone will pay, then see if there's a buyer at that price, then lower it if no one bites?" He said, "Nothing." So he's learning to be more patient.

PERSUADE WITH NEGOTIATION TECHNIQUES

The following sections provide seven negotiation techniques to help you uncover critical information, build a strong relationship with your counterpart, and move toward shared action.

Identify and Remove Barriers

We think persuasion is about getting someone to *do* something. So we ask the obvious question: How can I get them to do it? That's especially true when we're in some sort of negotiation.

There's a much more effective technique to get what you want: Figure out what's stopping them from doing something, then remove those barriers. Our feelings and logic cause us to erect barriers in our mind to shared action. Nobel laureate Daniel Kahneman suggests asking questions like "Why isn't she doing it already?" As your counterpart identifies barriers, "Then you go one by one systematically, and you ask, 'What can I do to make it easier for that person to move?'"[4]

The best way to identify barriers to shared action is . . . ask them. Ask someone what would stop them, or is stopping them, from doing something. Here's what this deeply counterintuitive approach looks like in practice.

In my current role, I lead a team of public policy researchers. I was hired to increase our research quality and quantity. When I started, I could have tried to tell people to produce more. That would have had the unhappy result of annoying people, stressing them out, and losing their trust before I ever had a chance to earn it. I didn't even know *why* they weren't maximizing productivity. So I asked about barriers to them producing more research.

There was a massive one: a process called "fact-checking," whereby we make sure every piece of information in our research is accurate. It was extremely burdensome, because it was ad hoc and haphazard. After weeks of lobbying the rest of the leadership team by showing them it was a huge barrier to productivity, I persuaded them to let me hire someone whose first task is to fact-check. Everyone across the organization is happier and more productive because I removed the biggest barrier to my team's success.

I identify barriers when I interview prospective employees, too. I ask them what would stop them from accepting an offer. They give remarkably honest, unguarded, and illuminating answers. And it tells me whether and how to proceed.

I even use this when my wife and I are interviewing au pairs to see if they're a good fit to move across the world, join our family, and care for our kids. I literally ask: What would stop you from coming here? One of three answers follows.

The best case is a quick response of "Nothing!" They're serious. That's what our current au pair said, and Emma is a wonderful part of our family. Sometimes, they hesitate, then say something like, "I'm anxious about living in a big city like Chicago." So we discuss whether our location is a good fit for them.

And sometimes they throw up a red flag. One candidate answered, "Well, you have to promise to buy me whatever food I want, never touch it, and buy me my favorite energy drink." That interview ended quickly.

Persuasion is also about knowing when you can't share action with someone and moving on. You can't make every deal—and you shouldn't.

Address Concerns Directly

It didn't make sense. My organization and his were completely aligned on the policy issue. We had a great lunch together and got along well. I independently wrote a report that complemented one he was writing. And for eight months, he ghosted me, despite me contacting him a few times.

Then, an opening: a carefully crafted op-ed I penned that resonated with him on the issue. Finally, he was willing to talk to me. Just barely.

For the first ten minutes, we outlined our legislative agendas—again, totally aligned. Then, overt hesitancy. He clammed up. Finally, he said, "Look, I know we're aligned, but I don't know if I can work with you."

I knew why. My organization had a reputation for being tied too closely to a previous administration, and as being too political. I had two choices: Ignore it, or address it directly.

Often, we hope problems will just go away if we hide them somewhere. In fact, that's counterproductive. As negotiation expert Jim Camp explains, we "try *not* to recognize our problems, or if we do recognize them, we're then tempted to sweep them under the carpet and hope they go away. If the problems seem insurmountable, we give up."[5]

Unrelated question: When you have a concern, do you like it when someone ignores it? Not exactly.

It wasn't the first time I encountered this response, so I wasn't surprised. I was ready. I knew just what to do: Address his concerns directly.

We just discussed the importance of identifying barriers to shared action. Otherwise, you can't move forward. Another technique for doing this is what Voss calls an "accusations audit." You identify, directly call out, and address the negative feelings, fears, frustrations, concerns, thoughts, etc., your counterpart might be harboring. You literally do an audit of the various accusations they could make against a person, situation, or any potential barrier to sharing action. You need to list all—yes, *all*—the negative things your counterpart could say, including about you personally.[6]

Identify things your counterpart sees, or could see, as a problem, even if you don't think they're problems. They see them as a problem, so they're real, which makes them *your* problem. Your goal is to acknowledge their concerns, *not* agree with them.

The very prospect of doing this terrifies most people for two reasons. They think it'll be unpleasant and make things worse!

First, yes, it's unpleasant and scary, but much less so than the alternative. The reality is that people sometimes have negative feelings about us and what we do. Just like in Alcoholics Anonymous, the first step is admitting you have a problem. And that problem could be *you*. Face the negatives head-on. Often, the only thing worse than identifying these barriers directly is neglecting to do so. Reason being, they'll still have these unresolved frustrations or concerns and will hold them against you and probably decide against sharing action with you. That's much worse! Decide if you prefer short-term or long-term pain.

Second, as it turns out, the best way to reduce negatives, Voss explains, is to address them directly. When you deny a negative, you give it credence.[7] When you tell someone, "I don't want you to get angry" or "Don't think I'm a jerk," it's *more* likely they'll get angry or think you're a jerk. When you instead put a negative front and center, you often diminish it, like letting air out of a balloon. Often, your counterpart says the negative isn't *that* bad. At a minimum, they'll appreciate you acknowledging and legitimizing their feelings. Your goal is to reduce, defuse, and ideally inoculate yourself against the negative.

The dynamic you're going for is to show understanding or change their baseline (or both). Showing understanding is simple enough: Identify what they're experiencing. Changing their baseline is trickier—and fun. I use it all the time to grease the wheels of shared action. For example, whenever I call customer service to make a special request, if I've made some sort of mistake, I'll say something like "You're going to think I'm the dumbest person you talk to all week." They usually respond with "Oh no, don't worry about it, how can I help?" They're expecting something pretty ridiculous. Then I share my relatively modest request. And they almost always fulfill it.

Your goal is to anticipate and openly identify the negative feelings someone is going to experience from what you say and do. I do this all the time wherever I am. If I have to make an unpleasant request of my direct reports, like working over the weekend (which is a rarity, and unfortunately sometimes unavoidable), I say, "I have an annoying request you're not going to like."

I once had to ask a new intern to undertake a tedious task on day one: Format two hundred footnotes. I said, "You're going to quit on day one because of this assignment." He probably thought I had an absolutely awful request coming his way. So the footnotes didn't seem so bad. (It was also a good test, which he passed with flying colors, earning a full-time job for being a hard worker and good teammate, among other qualities.)

You're better off going too far in calling out potential accusations, rather than not far enough. If you forget to identify something, and they think you should know better, they might be frustrated that you don't really understand them. On the plus side, if you do go too far, they often correct you.

After delivering an accusations audit, go silent. See what they say. If you hit the nail on the head, they'll indicate that. If you missed it, they'll say "No, that's not it." Then they'll either identify the problem, or you'll have to continue digging with accusations. It's imperative to resist the impulse to fill the painful silence with words. Definitely don't try to justify yourself. Don't say, "You're going to think I'm a jerk. But I'm not. It's not even my fault." This will just make matters worse, especially if they do think it's your fault.

The effectiveness of addressing concerns directly isn't limited to one-on-one communications. It's effective with groups with similar feelings and perspectives. Suppose you're a manager addressing skeptical or frustrated teammates. You can address the shared concerns of many (hopefully most) of your teammates directly. With groups it's especially important to make the list longer, because not everyone will have all the same negatives in their mind.

Now, back to where we started this section to see how this works. Rather than running from it, I laid it all out there. I said, "You're concerned our brand is toxic. You think we're too tied to the previous administration. We seem too political, and that's going to make working with us counterproductive. You're also concerned that some of our communications, like the cartoons, do more harm than good."

He looked at me, sighed in relief, and said, "Yes, those are my concerns." Next step? Lean into them. Which is what I did. I addressed each one in turn. I explained how we now work across the aisle as a matter of practice, both because it's good strategy and because it's the right thing to do. I highlighted how my work in particular explicitly talks to people across the political spectrum, not just folks on one side, and I highlighted the aforementioned op-ed.

Then? He sighed again in relief. He said, "I'm so glad to hear that." Then? For forty-five minutes we aligned our organizations on strategy and tactics. He recommended we have weekly calls to discuss. And we now coordinate closely, and he has brought me into a close-knit coalition. All because

I disarmed him by acknowledging his concerns and showing there was still a path to shared action.

Present Prospective Losses, Not Gains

Intuitively, we think showing our counterpart how they'll "win" by working with us is the path to persuasion. Behavioral economics reveals people are more inclined to share action when they see what they stand to *lose* (such as by *not* working with you). It's more persuasive to present loss (real or prospective) rather than gain (real or prospective).

"Prospect theory," developed by psychologists Daniel Kahneman and Amos Tversky, holds that most human beings are loss averse. "When directly compared or weighted against each other, *losses loom larger than gains*."[8] How much larger? Other researchers have shown we weigh losses up to five times more than gains of the same value.[9] If someone were to take one thousand dollars from you, you'd need to make another five thousand dollars to counteract the sting of having lost one thousand dollars.

Since we weigh losses disproportionately, we're strongly inclined to avoid loss. This molds how we feel, think, and act. Most people make risk-averse choices.

What does our loss aversion mean for persuasion? Move closer to shared action by focusing on losses your counterpart will face if they don't work with you, rather than gains they'd accrue. Which means you need to know what they care (most) about losing.

The simple formula for presenting loss is to identify what they're concerned about losing, then ask a question like: "Do you want to lose X?"

What does this look like in practice? Suppose you're an executive seeking to buy another company and merge operations. Your data and research indicate the company will grow 10 percent faster per year as a result of the merger. Rather than presenting the proposed merger as a chance for them to gain 10 percent more per year, tell them that every day they forgo the merger, they're *losing* 10 percent. Although the statements are logically equivalent—the difference is 10 percent either way—your counterpart will experience them differently.

"No"-oriented questions and labels are especially effective for presenting prospective losses. You can ask, "Are you OK losing market share while you wait to make this deal?" Or "It seems like you don't mind losing market share?" This will heighten their fear of loss, and better position you to reach an agreement.

Ditch the "win-win" proposals, and craft your message around your counterpart's potential and likely losses.

The Power of No

"Why say 'no' when it feels so good to say 'yes'?" That's the question Big Tom Callahan asks potential investors whose support he needs for a new business initiative in the movie *Tommy Boy*. It elicits a chuckle from his three visitors. And it aligns with your intuitions. "Yes" signals agreement. You get what you want—hooray! Ultimately, "yes" is victory. Right?

There's just one problem with our quest for "yes": It's an antipersuasion endeavor. You seek "yes" as affirmation you're on the right track. You structure questions to elicit that magic word. "Do you agree?" "You're good with this, right?" When they say "yes," you feel good and think you've sealed the deal.

Car salesmen go for "yes" compulsively and impulsively: "Isn't this a great car?" "This is just what you're looking for, isn't it?" If you say "yes," he whacks you over the head with it. "OK, so let's get you back to finance." Fun.

There's even a sales approach called "yes momentum." You begin by getting your counterpart to say "yes" to small or obvious asks ("You're looking to save time, right?"), and build up to bigger, more specific queries, culminating in a "yes" on the big agreement ("I think that's a great benefit—how about you?" Or "Are you with me here?").[10] Each "yes" allegedly builds momentum, inducing your counterpart to offer that big final "yes." Proponents actually coach people to "tie down" their counterpart with "yes." That's force, not persuasion.

The bestselling book *Getting to Yes* captures this allure. The authors counsel you to present your proposal as a "yesable proposition," to which "responding with the single word 'yes' would be sufficient, realistic, and operational."[11] No ifs, ands, or buts allowed. Just "yes!"

One problem, Voss explains, is that "yes" *is not necessarily a sign of agreement.* Sure, sometimes "yes" signals commitment—they're in. Sometimes, "yes" is a confirmation. It verifies information, like when your boss asks, "Does that make sense?" The confirmation "yes" affirms it does. It doesn't prove you agree with it. And some "yeses" are counterfeit. A counterfeit "yes" occurs when you say "yes" without really meaning it. Questions like "You're good with this, *right*?" pressure you into saying "yes." To get him to stop pestering you, you offer a counterfeit "yes." The person going for "yes" misinterprets this as true agreement where none exists.[12]

A variety of problems can come from this. Your counterpart might have regrets later on about saying "yes." Or they might not feel an authentic connection or have loyalty to you, making the "yes" worth little or nothing.

A "yes" that isn't really agreement can suggest you're on the road to shared action when you really aren't. You end up wasting lots of time and energy pursuing something that isn't likely to happen, either at all or until you address key barriers. That's why you need to poke and probe to be sure you fully understand them, even if they give you the "yes" you want.

Cutthroat negotiators know how to weaponize "yes" to get what they want, usually at your expense. Camp explains that "shrewd corporate negotiators" use the "trick" of offering an early "yes" all the time. They do it to get your adrenaline pumping. You get excited. And it "traps" you "in a cage."[13] What's not to love?

You can actually secure durable deals without anyone ever explicitly saying "yes." If you make an offer then ask, "What do you think?," your counterpart might say, "That sounds good. Where do I sign?" You didn't need to corner them with a phrase like "You're good with this, aren't you?"

If "yes" doesn't unlock persuasion, what does? The answer is extremely counterintuitive. "No" facilitates persuasion far more effectively than "yes."

Pause and think about what prompts you to say "no." "No" means you're declining something that doesn't work for you. Which prompts you to think more deeply about your reason for saying "no." As Camp explains, this helps you "focus on the real issues of the negotiation."[14]

"No" is the start—not the end—of a conversation. "No" pushes someone to a limit and defines boundaries for the conversation. You're saying anything beyond that point (price, duration, terms, time, etc.) doesn't work. As Voss explains, when you eliminate what you *don't* want, you gain clarity on what you *do*.[15] That's another avenue to shared action.

Seek "no" from your counterpart. As Camp says, "Don't fear the word, invite it."[16] How? It's simpler than you think. Just flip how you ask questions.

Whenever you'd normally yearn for "yes," try to elicit a "no" instead. Voss provides illustrative examples. For example, instead of "Do you agree?," ask "Do you disagree?" Instead of "Is this a good idea?," ask "Is this a bad idea?" Instead of "Are you good with this?," ask "Are you opposed to this?" Other formulations include "Is it silly . . . ," "Is it crazy . . . ," "Is it unreasonable . . . ," and "Do you mind . . ."[17] The goal in securing a "no" is to promote cooperation by creating an opportunity for them to define the contours of working together.

"No"-oriented questions invite your counterpart to disclose information that moves you toward shared action. While people could respond with a simple "no," they usually qualify it by saying more because you're asking for their perspective, which they love to share. For example, you might ask, "Is it a bad idea for me to do X?" Assuming it's not a terrible idea (they'll tell you if it is), they'll say something like, "No, it isn't a bad idea, but here are some problems with it." They'll list them, identifying barriers to shared action.

I always lead with "no"-oriented questions to get what I want. For example, I was invited to attend a working group of top professionals in my field on an important policy issue hosted by an elite organization. The organizer announced she was going to select a few people to form a smaller working group that'd drive strategy and create key products. Obviously, I needed to be a part of that.

I didn't know her well, so I needed to catch her attention. After a strong performance in the seminar, I walked over to her and said, "Is it crazy to ask if I can be a part of the smaller group?" She said, "No, that's not crazy." I explained how I could add value, and I was in. Now I'm working on prominent initiatives that are great for me professionally, including some big upcoming publications and the opportunity to share a stage with the organizer at an important event.

"No" even works with toddlers. Whenever I want to get my two-year-old son, Thomas, to do something, I get him to say "no" to an obviously bad option, leaving only the option I prefer. For example, I get him dressed in the morning. Sometimes, he has other plans. And his drive for independence is fierce, which includes picking what he wears every day. So I use "no" to get him to cooperate. I ask, "Do you want Dada to pick out your clothes for you?" Knowing that I'll do it if he doesn't come (yes, we've had some meltdowns over that), he says "no" and comes over and selects his outfit.

You might still be skeptical. Try it. Over the next week, add some "no"-oriented questions to your conversation. Just this week as I'm writing this, I wanted to sign up for an improv course. I had missed the early registration discount by two weeks. And obviously I wanted the lower rate. So in my email I wrote, "Is it crazy to ask if I can still access the discount?" Then

I explained my interest in the course. They wrote back, "We will try to help out to the best of our ability." And within a few hours, I had secured the discount. Not so crazy after all! Practicing in these low-stakes situations is also important for being prepared to do this in high-stakes situations.

While Voss tends to discount "yes," it certainly has a place in persuasion. For example, if you say to your friend, "It seems like you're frustrated?," and they say "yes," that's good, because you've correctly identified their feelings. They'll almost certainly elaborate: "Yeah, I'm frustrated because I feel like I'm not getting the credit I deserve at work."

When is "yes" helpful? It depends on the context and tone. Imagine someone sighing and saying "yes" in a heartfelt manner when you ask, "Is something wrong?" The point isn't to delete "yes" from your vocabulary. Rather, it's to be aware that "yes" is often deceptive, and "no" is usually much more illustrative.

Search for Proof of Life

Are they serious? How serious? Or are they playing you for a fool? You need to know. That's why you pose what Voss calls the "proof of life" question. Basically, you ask: Why me? Or, why us?

The story at the start of this chapter centered on this kind of question. A proof of life question uses "why" to determine if your counterpart is serious about sharing action with you. Every time I asked the executives, "You've probably received lots of strong applications and talked to lots of great candidates. Why me?," I got absolutely vital information about my prospects. And I used it to advance my candidacy.

Proof-of-life questions invite your counterpart to make your case for you on their terms. If what they say is compelling, then you know they're serious, and you have clarity about what attracts them to you. If it isn't, that's also critical information. You either address their concerns, or move on.

Proof-of-life questions are so powerful that I use one every time I interview someone to see if they're serious. Near the end of every interview, I ask, "You probably have lots of opportunities you're considering. Why this one?" Any answer here is illustrative. Here are examples of ones I've received:

- "I'm from Chicago and really want to improve the city." Great, they have a local connection and care about using policy to make things better.
- "This is my only opportunity, actually." They don't have any offers, so they'll almost certainly accept if I make an offer.
- "My girlfriend lives in Chicago, and I'd like to be closer to her." Aha—the job itself is not their primary motivator!

And if they don't have an answer—which, remarkably, some candidates don't—well, that sinks their chances.

I use proof of life questions to get what I want, too. To become a phenomenal public speaker (one of my big goals), I knew I needed a speaking coach. How else would I improve? So I scoured the internet to find top options. I narrowed down the list to three, then interviewed them. They were all expensive, so I needed to make sure I was investing both my time and money well. Which meant I needed to know if they truly wanted to invest in *me*.

I asked each one, "You probably have lots of potential clients. Why are you interested in working with me?" One said, "Well, I also care about doing social good" (I had mentioned my poverty work). She sounded remarkably inauthentic. I got the sense that she wasn't that interested, wouldn't do a good job, and would still be happy to take my money.

My eventual coach—the one I really wanted—said, "I have enough clients from Goldman Sachs. They're boring. Your project is interesting, and it'd be fun." She'd actually *enjoy* working with me! Sold. I had persuaded her

I'm a good fit, and she persuaded me that she had the expertise and energy I was looking for. Which she does.

Leverage Silence

When I taught university courses, after asking a question or making a thought-provoking (or simply provocative) statement, I'd go silent and patiently wait for students to respond. Often, they initially said nothing. Fortunately, I had all day (well, up to two and a half hours), so I waited, and waited, and . . . waited, embracing the silence. Eventually, I just asked the question again and told them I had all day. Finally, someone would say something to start a conversation, which usually led to fruitful conversation.

The harshest sound to most people's ears is the sound of silence. Cold, dark, scary silence. Since we experience silence as "the void that our nature abhors," Camp explains that we "rush to fill in the blank."[18] We start talking, blabbering away, spewing out information, and saying things we wish we hadn't. That's why silence is such a powerful technique: Your counterpart usually becomes uncomfortable, eventually can't stand it, and starts (or restarts) the conversation.

Silence is actually a powerful persuasive tool for ourselves, too. It's an opportunity for calm and tranquility. No noise. No static. Just you in your own head, and your counterpart in theirs. Silence gives everyone involved a chance to pause, reflect, and share what's on their mind.

There's no set timeframe for how much silence you need. It could be seconds, minutes, hours, or days. However long it takes them to respond. Still, your wait will feel like an eternity. Every second will feel like a minute. Count slowly in your head. Since silence is unbearable for most people, your counterpart usually will fill the void relatively quickly. And they'll usually fill it with critical information about whether and how you can get what you want.

Build Trust

I was absolutely furious. After working extremely hard for nearly two years on a project and receiving extensive external praise for the work, the guy who oversaw it blindsided me by "pivoting" the work in a radically different direction without even consulting me. He couldn't even deliver the news himself. He thought he could instead force my team to do this new work. Since I don't report to him, he couldn't force us, which meant he just lost crucial support for his work. Worse still, he completely destroyed trust by doing all this behind my back, which meant he wouldn't be receiving all the support he had been. How counterproductive.

Once you feel like you can't trust someone, it's hard to shake it. You can't confide in them. You're reluctant to interact with them. The flipside is, when trust is present, the wheels of persuasion are greased. How do we build trust?

In *The Speed of Trust*, Stephen M. R. Covey explains that trust is a function of character and competence. Character is who you are, and is composed of your integrity, motives, and interest. Competence is what you know, and is determined by your skills, results, and track record.

Trust has individual, relational, and organizational elements. Trust starts within ourselves. "Self-trust" arises when we have integrity, honesty, humility, good intent, capabilities (skills, knowledge, and style), and effectiveness. Start here, since you control them. Relational trust concerns how we interact with others. We earn it by being truthful, respectful, loyal, accountable, other-oriented, and continuously confronting and improving reality. Organizational trust is about creating an environment filled with trust across teams. Trustful organizations share information openly and candidly, the culture is innovative, mistakes are tolerated as a path to learning, and colleagues are collaborative.[19] All three kinds of trust facilitate persuasion.

Building trust is a slow process. We need to see and hear certain things from someone over a period of time to determine whether they're trustworthy. Lots of things can erode trust, and it can even disintegrate in an instant.

Fundraising and sales require supreme trust among the investor, the salesperson, and the organization. Consider these three investors from my fundraising career.

"Bob," we'll call him, had been supporting my organization for a long time at a relatively small annual sum (one thousand to two thousand dollars) compared to his massive financial capacity. He gave other organizations six figures. Why not us? Because we never listened to Bob. So he just wasn't that into us. When I started meeting with him, I changed that by understanding his interests and building trust. I crafted a few small proposals (about three thousand dollars) to support initiatives he liked. I reported on each investment. With trust soaring, we met, and I made the ask: Would he consider significantly increasing his investment? A check soon came in for twenty thousand dollars.

"Jim" committed to a huge (five hundred thousand–plus dollars) legacy gift to my institution to support interns. The fundraiser previously assigned to him left, and I quickly realized I was stepping into a hot mess: The investor had not been receiving any updates and was frustrated, and we hadn't even established the intern program we took money for. I mobilized, heading up to New York to understand his goals for the program. We got the program going. Then I sent Jim a robust report on the work the summer interns did. Then I went back to New York. And he was thrilled. Trust, which was strained, was fully restored. And so was his financial support.

"Andy" was a longtime supporter with $1 million–plus capacity. I met with him for breakfast. Odd meeting. Having never met me, he proceeded to tell me about how the president used to come see him, and now he was delegated down to me. Why? I didn't have an answer. (Turns out, the president didn't want to invest time in many relationships.) Andy was obviously hurt from the neglect. He literally got up, his words fading as he walked away. He never gave us another penny because trust had been shattered.

LET'S GET SPECIFIC

Every time I call or email her, she knows I want something. So much so that when I make the ask, she laughs out loud and says, "I knew you were going to ask for more." And she always gives it to me. How do I always get what I want with "Ann," who runs two professional development programs (one for interns, one for early-career employees, all of whom Ann's organization supports financially) from which my organization benefits?

I started by building a great relationship with Ann. It began with our first participant. Until I arrived, we hadn't worked with them for a long time, so they had to test us out again. We did a good job in the things they care about, from interviewing in a timely manner to good onboarding, responding to surveys about how the participant was doing, and checking in with Ann after the session ended. More than anything else, I demonstrated my passion for mentoring, which is crucial for interns' success.

As I regularly prove we're high-quality partners, I always ask for more. First, it was more interns for my team. We went from one participant per season to two. Then I asked for interns for other departments, and we soon expanded across three other departments. Then I asked them to start supporting full-time, early-career people, not just temporary participants. This was a big boost to our team. Most recently, I asked her to support two full-time employees, including a mid-career employee who already works for us. They don't usually do that. And she didn't hesitate to accept him into the program after I talked to her.

Still, when I call her, I need to prepare her for the ask. So I use some of the tactics in this chapter. Rather than letting her think, "Oh, here he goes again, asking for more," I just lean into it. I say, "Ann, you know I always ask you for more, and I'm going to do it again." I get her ready by saying something like "This request is going to seem completely unreasonable," then pause. Once I make it, I say, "It probably seems like I'm being greedy." If there's any hesitation, I ask, "What would stop us from making this work?," and she tells me directly, and I address her concerns. That's why I can ask for more interns and full-time employees. Even better, I can bring my own candidates rather than only selecting from their portal. We end up getting double what most organizations get.

Ann and I are to the point now that she reaches out to me about potential opportunities. Despite that, every time I make an ask, I use the techniques in this book to prepare her for it, just to make sure. And then I overdeliver so I continue to maintain and grow her trust in me.

LET'S REFLECT

Often, no deal is better than a bad deal. If you've used all your powers of persuasion, and your counterpart still can't or won't share understanding or action in a way that works for you, walk away in an emotionally intelligent manner. Don't reach this conclusion hastily—there's usually more you can do to engage in more fruitful conversation and demonstrate more understanding. Once you've exhausted reasonable options, if there's no clear, mutually acceptable path forward, then move on and conserve your most important resource—time.

The negotiation techniques in this chapter will help you assess whether shared action is possible and, if it is, how to unlock it. They're battle-tested and proven to consistently facilitate durable deals. That's why you need them in your persuasive toolbelt.

Key Takeaways for Successful Negotiations

1. Every time you're trying to get what you want, you're in a negotiation, from trying to start a conversation to sealing and implementing an agreement. While most people treat negotiation as a zero-sum game where you squeeze out as much as you can from your counterpart, this short-sighted mindset reduces what you get in both the short and long term.
2. Focus on building a trusting relationship with your counterpart and understanding their wants and needs. As your relationship with them grows, you'll be in a much better position to share action repeatedly.
3. Instead of trying to get someone to *do* something, figure out what's stopping them from doing it. Once you identify barriers to shared action, figure out how to remove them. Otherwise, a negotiation usually won't have the outcome you desire.
4. Rather than focusing on what your counterpart will "win" or "gain," Nobel Prize–winning research shows we're much more sensitive to losses than gains. Frame situations around what your counterpart will lose if they don't share action with you. A simple formula for this is, "Do you want to lose X?"
5. Go for "no" rather than "yes." Intuitively, we think "yes" signals agreement. Often, it doesn't, because someone just feels pressured to say it. Instead, invite your counterpart to say "no." This makes them feel safe and empowers them to decline something that doesn't work for them. It points toward how to share action, because they'll usually explain why something doesn't work for them, thus identifying a key barrier. "No" can even signal agreement when you flip how you ask questions to invite it.

Negotiation Focusing Question: What is the ONE negotiation technique best suited to facilitate shared action in this situation?

Chapter 8

GO BEYOND WORDS

Image is everything.

Nineteen-year-old Andre Agassi, stepping out of a Lamborghini for a TV commercial

Just about everyone wanted to dislike him, but they couldn't. Most people wanted to ignore him, yet he remained at the center of important conversations. A lot of folks thought his ideas were wacky, wrong, or both, yet his influence just kept growing, including with the president of the university. He was persuasive, because he had an abundance of intangibles that helped him get what he wanted.

I'm referring here to John Tomasi, formerly the Romeo Elton 1843 professor of natural theology at Brown University and the director of the Political Theory Project (PTP), where I was a postdoctoral fellow. He's now president of the Heterodox Academy.

John is one of the most persuasive people I've ever met. He always did things the right way. One reason people at Brown wanted to dislike him was because he brought libertarian and conservative ideas and scholars into one of the most leftist universities in America. He housed many such researchers at the PTP, and this was accepted because he also brought in leftist scholars. Brown was avant-garde in intellectual intolerance, including shouting down Ray Kelly, then commissioner of the New York City Police Department, in 2013. But they never shouted down any of John's speakers, because his hallmark events were debates, where two sides were represented. What's more, he's a passionate advocate for intellectual diversity, and he practiced it. For these and other reasons, he had the president's ear.

John didn't just do the right things. He did them the right way. His tone is always calm, curious, and conversational. He's relaxed and inviting. He's disarming. He's balanced. All this greased the wheels of shared action for John.

We all regularly fall into the trap of thinking the "right" words are the primary or only key to unlocking persuasion. Not exactly.

People who thread difficult needles regularly, like John, know how to **go beyond words**. Your character, likability, tone, body language, presentation skills, and planning efforts (among other things) are paramount to success in every persuasive endeavor.

How minor a factor can words be? Seven percent. Research by psychologist Albert Mehrabian shows there are situations when the words we say, our verbal communication, constitute as little as 7 percent of how people receive our communications.

When assessing how much we like someone, vocal liking (tone) can account for up to 38 percent of how much we like them. And facial liking (body language) can account for up to 55 percent.[1] Mehrabian emphasizes that these numbers apply only when we're talking about our feelings and attitudes. This does *not* mean that our words only ever constitute 7 percent of a communication. It does mean, though, that nonverbals play a massive role, given how important feelings and liking are in persuasion.

And this all happens at lightning speed. Research shows that people form first impressions of someone within thirty-nine milliseconds based on whatever information is available.[2] If you don't think fast about how to present yourself, they'll think fast about how to judge you.

The idea that words aren't the primary driver of our success is a tough pill to swallow for people who pride themselves on their intellectual abilities. It doesn't seem right that we can spend so much time crafting the perfect words, only to have something else get in the way.

By the time you're finished with this chapter, you'll come to see this reality as an opportunity. You'll learn to navigate it successfully by mastering commonly overlooked elements of persuasion with tangible, research-based techniques to put yourself in the best position possible right from the start.

PERCEPTION IS PERSUASION

This will sound like sophistry: For the purposes of persuasion, how your audience *perceives* you matters more than who you actually *are*. Reason being, how they perceive you is *their* reality. It colors everything they feel and think about you.

What associations do you have with the names Michael Jordan, Simone Biles, Taylor Swift, Jay-Z, Donald Trump, and Hillary Clinton? And how about the companies Whole Foods, Aldi, Nike, Payless, Pottery Barn, and IKEA?

Likewise, associations arise immediately when someone thinks about *you*. That's your "brand." Your brand is based on facts, and on emotions you elicit.[3] Persuasion requires you to manage it. That starts with credibility.

ESTABLISH CREDIBILITY

Your character, or ethos, is the biggest factor determining how people perceive you. Ethos combines external credentials (like actions and accomplishments) and internal factors (such as motivations) to establish your credibility. External credentials act as stamps of approval from others. They signal whether to listen to or ignore someone. For example, external credentials like awards (such as the Nobel Prize), fellowships (like the the Rhodes Scholarship), and schools attended (for example, Harvard) can establish someone's intellectual quality.

Credibility can emerge from someone's profession: A doctor's opinion generally gets special weight when they discuss medicine, and not when they talk about basketball. Credibility can arise from expertise combined with skill, as when someone is articulate.

Motives matter too. Are they just volunteering at a soup kitchen because they want something to write about in their college application essay? Or do they truly care? A good ethos establishes us as believable and worthy of conversation.

Establish credibility by reverse engineering your goals. Figure out how you want people to perceive you (for example, as highly qualified). Then identify what you need to accomplish, and the authentic characteristics you need to develop, to earn that ethos. Focus on processes you control, rather than things dependent on others. For example, athletes cannot completely control whether they win—their opponents have a say. They control whether they enhance their skills (for example, a basketball player can improve his dribbling or free-throw shooting). As your skills strengthen, you'll gradually earn the ethos you want and need.

Consider an undergraduate student whose goal is to become a professor at a research university. To accomplish that, they need to earn admission to a good graduate school. I've successfully advised students on getting into top doctoral, law, or medical schools like Oxford, Harvard, and the University of Virginia. The standard advice to students is: Get good grades, test scores, and letters of recommendation, and have a good writing sample and research plan. The problem? You present as a student.

The real secret is to get admissions committees to *perceive* you as someone who's on your way to becoming a tenured professor. How? Attend and present your research at a conference, because that's where professors share their work with the scholarly community. Rather than just having a writing sample, submit a high-quality article to a peer-reviewed journal, because that's the gold standard in academic publishing. Rather than just sketching out research interests (things you think you'd like to study), detail a research program you'll undertake through your early years as a professor.

When you ask professors for letters of recommendation, specifically ask them if they're prepared to write a strong, detailed letter. That's important, because many letters just aren't that strong. Then supply them with everything they need to do so. Figure out what assets your field values—language proficiency, data skills, high-level math abilities, practical experience, etc.—and bring those into focus in your application materials.

And yet all this will be for naught if you come across as unlikable.

BE LIKABLE

Likability prepares people for persuasion. We open ourselves up to people we like, and close ourselves off to those we dislike. We interact with people we dislike only as long as necessary, then stop as soon as we can. If we dislike someone enough, we'll actively work *against* them.

There are simple steps you can take to be more likable. Adopt a friendly, open demeanor. Friendly is *not* the same as fake—people quicky sniff out someone who's fake, disingenuous, or superficial. Your friendliness must be authentic. Look at others the way you'd like to be looked at: with respect, positivity, and a genuine sense you can learn something from them.

Even the most likable people aren't liked by everyone, but you can minimize that risk. Avoid things that make you unlikable, like being or even seeming unkind, mean, uncaring, rude, abrupt, inattentive, unreliable, selfish, or unstable, among other charming characteristics. That's especially important when someone doesn't know you. They don't have a baseline by which to judge your behavior.

If you're brusque and seem self-absorbed, they won't think, "I know they're having a rough week, so I'm not surprised they're in a bad mood." They'll just think, "What a jerk." When you do have a relationship with someone, avoid specific behaviors you know make them dislike you (such as phrases they don't like), even if you find them perfectly acceptable.

We like people who seem similar to us. One study showed the association between "interpersonal attraction" and both actual and perceived similarity was "significant and large." Especially important is *perceived* similarity because it "predicted attraction in no-interaction, short-interaction, and existing relationship studies."[4]

As similar as you may feel you are to someone, they have to feel that way, too. Finding similarities starts with listening and asking questions. How *else* would you get to know someone? When shared interest and beliefs arise in conversation, find ways to highlight similarities without interrupting your counterpart.

We don't like ungracious people. When someone says something nice, or pays you a compliment, receive it graciously. If someone says, "Wow, that was a truly amazing presentation," you could say something like, "Thank you. Hearing that feels good." Don't respond arrogantly, uttering something like "Yeah, I know" or "Well, the others were pretty weak."

Even more important, compliment others. People love knowing they did something well. Tell them! And always be genuine. People sniff out fake compliments a mile away. They'll rightfully resent you and won't trust you.

In grad school, being likable got me a grant I didn't even apply for. I had applied for a dissertation fellowship to go to Bordeaux from an institute on campus with which I had done a lot of work previously and had grown a warm relationship. While I wasn't the right fit for the specific fellowship, the associate director emailed me and asked, totally unsolicited, if I'd be open to receiving a smaller grant for the research. This was actually ideal because, in the meantime, I had secured another full-year fellowship, which meant this grant would be on top of that. I happily accepted it.

One basic thing you can do to get someone to like you is to learn their name right away, remember it, and use it. As Dale Carnegie said, "Remember that a person's name is to that person the sweetest and most important sound in any language."[5] Think of how much you dislike it when someone whom you think you know doesn't even remember your name.

Apologies go a long way. Recognizing your faults works wonders. This is hard, because we're averse to admitting we could ever, once, maybe, sometime, in a distant galaxy, have done something wrong. Muster the courage to face and address this fact. When you do something someone doesn't like and they let you know, tell them they have a point and apologize.[6]

Finally, bring the right amount of energy. Insufficient energy can cost you dearly. It almost totally derailed a highly credentialed guy I interviewed. On paper, he looked great. During the interview, he was flat as a pancake. So instead of moving him on in our search for a full-time position, I offered him an internship. Fortunately for him, his work was excellent, and I offered him a full-time position, which helped him secure admission to Harvard Law School.

Two personality types might have higher hurdles to being likable. Disagreeable people can come across as unlikable. Reason being, they can seem or actually be unkind, abrupt, dismissive, and argumentative. Individuals high in assertiveness (a component of extroversion) can come across as less likable because they feel compelled to share their feelings and thoughts clearly and firmly. Even if they intend no disrespect, their audience often doesn't appreciate the different opinion, and might even chafe at hearing it, especially when shared assertively. If someone is assertive and disagreeable, that's a double whammy impacting their likability.

Invariably, we all (yes, you and me, too) do things to make ourselves less likable. If you want to share action with someone, identify what exactly you're saying or doing to make them like you less. Then correct it to their (not your) satisfaction. Otherwise, barriers will remain, and you'll continue to damage the relationship.

What happens if, despite your best efforts, someone doesn't like you? Assess your chances of shared action. If the odds are too low, move on.

In an attempt to get people to like you, you'll be tempted to do things you aren't comfortable doing—maybe even things antithetical to who you are and what you believe. Don't do this! It won't work, because it's inauthentic, and they'll know it.

CULTIVATE CURIOSITY

Curious people are more likable. Research shows that curiosity predicts greater feelings of attraction and closeness, as well as positive relationship outcomes, even among strangers.[7] Curious people generate more closeness during both intimate and small-talk conversations, including with "unacquainted strangers during mundane conversations," according to one study.[8] Research shows a curious personality also has been linked "to a wide range of adaptive behaviors, including tolerance of anxiety and uncertainty, positive emotional expressiveness, initiation of humor and playfulness, unconventional thinking, and a nondefensive, noncritical attitude."[9] Higher curiosity even predicts greater interpersonally generated positive affect (the experience of positive emotions).[10]

Curious people ask open-ended questions ("how" and "what"), as well as thoughtful follow-up questions that probe more deeply. When someone pokes and probes in a thought-provoking manner, we enjoy the conversation more and feel more connected to them. Especially when they're curious about *us*.

People like—no, *love*—talking about themselves. Recall how we're wired to focus on ourselves. This psychological reality presents you with an opportunity to be more likable by being curious about them. Ask about and listen to them—a lot.

Be sure your curiosity doesn't lead you to interrupt people, because we dislike being interrupted, or feeling like someone has no interest in what we're saying.

If you dominate dialogue, that can make people dislike speaking with you. We don't like being on the receiving end of monologues. When it happens, we look to escape the interaction.

When you're curious about someone, they'll often talk about what's wrong in *their* world. When people complain, don't shut them down or tell them how misplaced their concerns are. They won't like this. Instead, show empathy. And if you really want to connect with them, you might even invite them to share their complaints, then listen attentively. Just make sure it doesn't turn into unproductive venting and points instead to shared action.

At the same time, and seemingly paradoxically, we don't like other people complaining, so avoid it when possible. People don't always like hearing what's wrong (especially what's wrong in *your* world). Try to share complaints only if someone asks, and if you know they're actually inclined to listen and converse.

People who bury themselves in their phones are less likable (unless you think the glow brightens you up, or that it's cool to fake looking busy).

There's nothing likable about being distracted by a screen or being constantly interrupted by pings and buzzes. Silence your phone and put it away so you can be present with someone.

SETTING THE TONE

Suppose your boss says, "*That's* a great idea." Wonderful praise, right? Could be, if it's enthusiastic, warm, and supportive. Maybe you'll get a promotion. What if it's said sarcastically? Or full of mockery? What if, instead of smiling, your boss rolls their eyes? You might need to start revising your resume. Exact same words, dramatically different meanings.

Tone and body language have an enormous impact on how people experience us. Recall the research from the start of this chapter: Together, they can account for 93 percent of how much people like us. Let's consider tone first.

Tone is *how* someone says something. It's composed especially of volume, pitch, and mood. Is your volume high or low? Do you sound happy or sad? Amused or annoyed? Confident or uneasy? The wrong tone quickly makes the "right" words offensive.[11] People experience tone similarly, too, regardless of whether we know the other person or not. One study showed that participants made consistent judgments about a stranger's voice based solely on hearing them say "hello."[12]

Tone is different from our technical, actual, unique voice. You sound like you, Morgan Freeman sounds like Morgan Freeman, and Taylor Swift sounds like, well, Taylor Swift. You can't change your voice. Your tone, though, is largely under your control.

The tone you adopt depends on who you want to be and how you want people to experience you. Fortunately, you (mostly) get to decide your tone (calm or frantic?). When emotions run high, it's hard to control your tone.

And it's in these situations that doing so is even more important, because it'll help determine whether situations stabilize or spiral out of control.

Tone is central to persuasion. Research shows tone (voice modulation for example) can facilitate persuasion when words are ineffective, even if your counterpart doesn't detect changes in your tone.[13] Another study found tone could be the most accurate means of communicating and assessing someone's feelings and internal state, better than just looking at them, or both seeing and hearing them.[14] There's an intimacy to hearing someone's voice: It's why podcasts can feel so direct and captivating.

Tone even predicts marital outcomes. One set of experiments found "acoustic features can predict marital outcome more accurately than those based on behavioral descriptors provided by human experts."[15] You're wondering: Well, what kind of tone will help me persuade?

In a word: calm. One study showed persuasion requires vocal tones denoting focus, low stress, and stable emotions. How come? "These three vocal tone dimensions . . . allow receivers to make inferences about a persuader's competence."[16] That's unsurprising. In difficult situations, we certainly don't turn to unhinged people for guidance. We turn to calm leaders. Calm conveys command of a situation. A calm, emotionally stable tone is a great default.

A particularly effective tone for promoting calm is what Chris Voss calls the late-night FM DJ voice. It's deep, soft, slow, and reassuring. It's downward inflecting. It says, "*I'm in control.*"[17] It exudes infectious calm. The neuroscience shows this sort of low voice works.[18] Just make sure your calm tone doesn't come off as emotionless. Be cool, like a DJ. Don't be detached or nonreactive.

Some research indicates men and women achieve vocal attractiveness through different tones. One study found that while both men and women increase their vocal attractiveness by increasing their valence (trust and likability), only men increase their vocal attractiveness by demonstrating dominance.[19]

Louder and varied volume signals confidence and can facilitate persuasion. This finding comes from a set of four experiments looking at the role of paralanguage, meaning acoustic properties of speech like pitch and volume. Speaking louder and varying volume serve "as a signal" the speaker more strongly endorses "the stance they take in their message."[20] If you want to exude and earn your audience's confidence, ditch the soft monotone delivery. Instead, bring enough energy to modulate your voice.

The audio experience is crucial, too. When you talk, how do you sound? On the phone or radio, it's all your audience encounters. We already discussed tone. How's your verbal pacing? Too fast, too slow, or just right?

From my time as a speechwriter, I recommend a range of 120–140 words per minute for most people. You need to know your baseline, your average words per minute. You learn this by recording yourself and counting your words per minute. Do you sound rushed? Calm and methodical? Slow and uncertain? Some people sound better with a quicker pace, others with a slower one.

Record yourself during a real presentation, because practice sessions don't have the same dynamics. Most people get nervous in front of an audience, causing them to speak more quickly. Your goal is to sound measured and speak slowly enough to give your words appropriate weight.

When someone doesn't like your tone, it's your problem and your fault. You must get it right. One technique for doing this is to assume people will interpret your tone as ungenerously as possible, especially in writing like email or text. Knowing that, get a clear picture of the tone you want or need to adopt—perhaps concerned, excited, or calmly positive. Then take an extra step or two to achieve the tone you want. This gives you more margin for error and reduces the chances you come across the wrong way.

You need lots of practice and effort to get your tone right, with heavy doses of trial and error. You'll mess up. Acknowledge, apologize, and adjust. Say, "I'm sorry. I didn't mean to sound annoyed," in a nice, calm tone. Then fix it. Or try "You're totally misunderstanding me!," and see how that goes.

At times, it can be (nearly) impossible to control your tone. When emotions are overflowing—maybe you're furious—your tone reflects this. How could it *not*? And yet it's precisely in difficult situations when tone disproportionately influences the outcome.

If you're angry and fighting with your spouse, do you think a venomous tone is going to make things better? Nope. It'd only throw kerosene on the fire. Think what might happen if you adopt a tone that isn't intended to actively antagonize the person you love.

That's true at work, too. If you're in a tense meeting and you're feeling stressed, expressing yourself in an anxious or annoyed tone is only going to make matters worse. Gather as much energy as you can, aided by the physiological sigh technique discussed earlier, and adopt the calmest tone possible.

Tone has a disproportionate effect on (de)escalating situations. Tone can turn molehills into Mount Everest. Or tone can reduce mountains in size, making them smaller even than molehills. Persuasion is infinitely easier when you have to walk over a few tiny hills instead of climbing thirty thousand feet.

ADOPT PERSUASIVE BODY LANGUAGE

I could see it in his throat. I suspected a cocky intern from an elite university hadn't been working hard, or doing much of anything for five weeks, while he insisted he was finding promising data. He was even writing code to use with AI! So we, along with the person on my team overseeing his work, sat down, and I asked the intern, calmly and firmly, what he had found so far.

His face dropped, and his throat got extremely tight, with lots of gulps, indicating a high level of stress. He fumbled around a bit, looking lost. But I already knew: He had nothing. Which meant he left the internship without a single thing to show for his time: not a good look for future opportunities.

Your body often reveals how you truly feel, even—sometimes especially—when your words tell a different story. You do this through nonverbal communication, which body language expert Joe Navarro defines as "a means of transmitting information—just like the spoken word—except it is achieved through facial expressions, gestures, touching (haptics), physical movements (kinesics), posture, body adornment (clothes, jewelry, hairstyle, tattoos, etc.), and even the tone, timbre, and volume of an individual's voice (rather than spoken content)."[21] Persuasion requires you to pay attention to the enormous amounts of information body language conveys—yours and theirs.

Since the literature on body language is vast, we'll focus on three key behaviors you can adopt, and three to avoid, to get what you want. We'll identify behaviors that are easy to adopt or avoid and are effective or undesirable.

First, you can take up space. After all, as nonverbal behavior expert Edward Hall observed, territory is in essence power. He found that people who take up more space tend to be more confident and of higher status (socioeconomically, hierarchically, or both).[22] Taking up space tells your counterpart that you feel comfortable, in your element.

Start with your hands, because, as an aptly titled piece in *Forbes* explains, "Great Leaders Talk With Their Hands."[23] A particularly persuasive hand gesture is called hand steepling. It involves "touching the spread fingertips of both hands, in a gesture similar to 'praying hands,' but the fingers are *not* interlocked and the palms may not be touching."[24] Your hands can point up (the most powerful position), out, or down when you're seated.

If you search the internet for pictures of former German Chancellor Angela Merkel standing, she's almost always steepling out, undoubtedly having trained it. Steepling signifies confidence in and dedication to your position. Other research shows steepling creates emotional connection, attraction, and immediacy between leaders and followers.[25]

Here are some ways to take up space with your legs. When standing, space your feet at least shoulder width apart, rather than having your feet too close to each other. When sitting, situate your feet as far apart as appropriate. It's generally deemed acceptable (fairly or not) for men to spread their legs farther apart than women. Splaying can be a sign of comfort or can be a dominance display.[26]

Confidence, not dominance, is our goal here. You don't want to dominate your counterpart, and don't want them to feel dominated. That inhibits persuasion. We're seeking connection instead. Be mindful of how your counterpart will experience your body language.

By contrast, search the internet for pictures of Russian President Vladimir Putin sitting, and he'll pretty much always have his legs dominantly splayed, never crossed, ankles never interlocked, both of which make people look smaller. He certainly trained to dominate.

Second, defying gravity also projects confidence. When you elevate something that otherwise is in a neutral or down position—your arms, hands, eyes, chin, etc.—you're defying gravity. As Navarro says, "Gravity-defying behaviors are associated with positive feelings." You exhibit them when you feel good, confident, or excited.[27] Observe them in others, too. When someone signals a lack of confidence, engage them in an emotionally intelligent manner that allows you to understand what's causing it.

Use your face to defy gravity. Start with your eyes, specifically the brows. "Arched eyebrows signify high confidence and positive feelings (a gravity-defying behavior), whereas lowered eyebrows are usually a sign of low confidence and negative feelings, a behavior that indicates weakness and insecurity in a person."[28] Lowered eyebrows can also signal someone has seen something unsettling and might be ill at ease. You lower your eyebrows when you sense a threat or are annoyed, displeased, or angry.[29] Recent research shows furrowed eyebrows can also signal, "I've not received enough information for current purposes," which can prompt the speaker to speak for longer.[30] You do it when you're focused or concerned.

Third, smile. You know this intuitively. Research shows "seeing someone else smile activates some of the same neurons as when *you* smile."[31] A confident-appearing smile (plus a confident chin) exudes competence.[32] Happy, smiling faces invite interaction and have strong motivational power.[33] Smiling brings positive psychological and physiological benefits, including better recovery from stress and a lower heart rate.[34] We even judge people who smile less harshly than those who don't.[35] It turns out truly smiling is a little more complicated.

Anyone can generate a fake smile on demand. Just engage the zygomatic major muscles in your cheeks and raise the corners of your mouth toward your ears. Voilà: a smile! You generate these sorts of smiles all the time, as a sort of social obligation. You learn from a young age to slap on a fake happy face even when you're sad.

A real smile works differently. The scientist Guillaume Duchenne de Boulogne "determined that a smile of real joy required the combined involuntary contraction of two muscles, the zygomatic major and the orbicularis oculi."[36] The latter muscle is actually in your eyes and can only be activated involuntarily, in contrast to the zygomatic major, which you can move at will. "A Duchenne smile is the one that reaches your eyes, making the corners wrinkle up with crow's feet."[37] To see what this smile looks like, search the internet for "Duchenne smile." You'll see people's eyes lighting up.

Since you can't generate a real smile at will, how is this useful for persuasion? First, when someone smiles at you, look quickly at their eyes. If they don't move, one study shows your counterpart is signaling distance.[38] It's then incumbent on you to figure out the cause and how to address it. Second, put yourself in situations and form relationships where everyone involved can generate real smiles on a regular basis.

When you choose to smile, it can look more authentic if you also raise your eyebrows. While this doesn't activate the orbicularis oculi, it does at least bring your eyes and face up a bit.

The first set of behaviors to be on the lookout for are pacifying behaviors, in yourself and others. They include touching your face, neck, or shoulder in response to a negative experience. We use these behaviors to calm ourselves. When you observe pacifying behaviors in yourself and your counterpart, figure out what's causing stress and how to alleviate it. For yourself, try to avoid pacifying behaviors, such as not touching your face or playing with your hair. When your counterpart does them, soothe them with EI by doing and saying things to calm them down and move closer to shared action.

The second behavior to note is when someone opens up or closes off their body to you. Navarro calls this "ventral fronting," which happens when you expose your front—your "eyes, mouth, chest, breasts, genitals, etc.," all sensitive areas—to someone you favor. When you dislike or are unsure of someone, a situation, or a subject, you engage in "ventral denial" and hide those sensitive areas.[39] Hence the phrase "turning our back," which you do physically or metaphorically to express negativity toward a person or situation. When you interact with someone, look for signs they're welcoming you—or not. And when you want or need to welcome someone else, make sure your body language aligns.

Remarkably, research actually shows that when judges adopt an open posture, they're better at detecting deception than if they have a closed posture.[40] So while you're on the lookout for someone turning away from you, stay open to them physically.

Finally, be mindful of expressions of contempt, because they make persuasion impossible. Eye-rolling is a classic sign of contempt. Another is the sneer. It demonstrates disrespect and lack of care or empathy.[41] Deep sighs and mimicking someone's body language in an unflattering manner can also be signs of contempt. Contempt corrodes relationships, comprehensively and quickly.

Contempt is so corrosive that it's the biggest predictor of divorce. John Gottman, a professor emeritus of psychology and one of the world's foremost experts on marital stability and divorce prediction, can observe married couples and literally, without hearing what the couples are saying, predict through body language and nonverbal behavior alone with 93.6 percent accuracy whether they'll divorce in the coming years.[42] What's he looking for? Eye-rolling, sneering, and negative facial expressions like frowns and winces.[43]

Great body language can't outweigh terrible tone. And insecure body language from your counterpart might just be signaling a barrier to shared action you need to investigate. Remember, body language is just one indicator of how someone is feeling and how they present themselves.

YOUR IMAGE IMPACTS PERSUASION

"Image is everything." That's what Canon had 19-year-old tennis phenom Andre Agassi say in 1990 as he stepped out of a Lamborghini during a commercial for their Rebel camera. When it comes to persuasion, sometimes image really *is* everything.

When someone looks at you, what do they see, feel, and think? How do they experience you? What's *your* image?

Image usually starts with how you look visually. This is partially a product of your immutable characteristics like height, age, gender, and skin color. Since you can't control these things, that might seem unfair.

Suppose a five-foot-three guy wants to train professional basketball players who are usually at least six-foot-four. His image seems incongruent with his role, unless his name is Muggsy Bogues. Or suppose a woman wants to coach American football at the professional level. It's pretty much exclusively a male sport. Her image is not that of someone who fits in that space. In both cases, the best way to address potential barriers to conversation and shared action is head-on. "Since I'm a woman, you're probably wondering if I have what it takes to coach men at this level. Here are my qualifications . . ."

More of your image is under your control than you might think. Focus on the elements that matter to your audience, because they will judge you based on what they see.

Look the part. If your counterpart can't visualize you doing the job, that's a big barrier to shared action. Project the image appropriate for the situation. For example, if you're interviewing for a job at an investment bank, wear a suit and tie, not shorts and a T-shirt. If you're interviewing for a job as a car mechanic, ditch the suit. When in doubt, err slightly in the direction of being overdressed to ensure you don't disrespect your audience, because being underdressed is usually taken as a slight. If you're unsure how to dress, do research. It'll pay dividends. Since we live in increasingly casual times, know today's standards in your field.

Similarly, don't overlook personal hygiene. Imagine if you walked into a store and the salesperson who comes over clearly hasn't showered in days. That doesn't make you more eager to make a purchase. Even in a world where so many people telework some or all the time, looking disheveled, neglecting to comb your hair, smelling musty, and the like won't help you get what you want.

How are your pronunciation and enunciation? People need to understand your words. Otherwise, conversation is challenging. Speak as clearly as possible. Especially problematic is someone misunderstanding your words. (Did they say "possibly" or "probably"?)

Account for accents. Someone from Arkansas speaking with a slow drawl might be hard for a group of New Yorkers to understand. A New Yorker sure will sound funny when they visit Arkansas. If you know you have an accent your audience will find difficult, do two things: Acknowledge it, and be as clear as possible in your pronunciation. A technique for doing this is to warm up speaking with a pen in your mouth, holding it in your teeth, for a few minutes.

Speeches deserve special mention. As a speechwriter for numerous senior government officials, I learned by doing and watching that no speech should ever be longer than twenty minutes. Ever. No, really. Abraham Lincoln's Gettysburg Address was less than three minutes. Martin Luther King Jr.'s "I Have a Dream" speech was about sixteen minutes. TED insists eighteen minutes is the magic number. What makes you think you need longer, even in this day and age?

Unfortunately, speeches have ballooned in length. When the president of the United States gives the State of the Union speech, it consumes more than an hour. Excruciating. If you think you have many equally important points to make (are you *sure* you do?), then you might just have to make multiple speeches. Squishing everything into one speech reduces your impact.

In a digital age, this will sound outdated: Beware using PowerPoint and other audio-visual tools. We know they're in no way necessary for delivering persuasive presentations. After all, what did people do forty years ago when they didn't exist? Speeches happened, and people still listened.

When I worked at the Pentagon, I saw generals and other high-ranking officials use PowerPoint as a crutch. Many of them hobbled along from slide to slide. The slides *became* the presentation, with the audience (you) becoming a mere afterthought. Presenters let videos, graphics, and other ornaments replace engaging their audience meaningfully. They crammed as much information as possible onto each poor little slide, helped by tiny fonts and lots of sub-bullets. You needed binoculars to read them. Audiences' eyes glazed over—if they even remained open. I'd be lying if I said I didn't almost doze off at least once!

If you must use PowerPoint or other audio-visuals, make them simple and supplemental. A slide with one word is far more compelling than one with fifty or one hundred words. Selecting one word forces you to boil things down all the way to their essence, to the ONE Thing. Your audience's attention needs to be on you, not on trying to read your seven bullet points, all with two sub-bullets. If you can do this, you'll even be more persuasive than many generals who love jam-packed PowerPoint slides.

Ask if you even need a PowerPoint in the first place. The most popular TED Talk of all time, by Sir Ken Robinson, has been watched nearly 79 million times, as of this writing. Without a PowerPoint. Five of the top ten most viewed don't have one. That's why I didn't use one in either of my two TEDx Talks on persuasion, despite the organizer of one of the events insisting I do so.

USE PERSUASIVE VISUALS

Someone once said, "A picture's worth a thousand words." All things being equal, we know that's true. It's called the "picture-superiority effect." It was first established in research from psychologists Allan Paivio and Kalman Csapo. They found free verbal recall, or our ability to remember or retrieve information, "is generally higher for items presented as pictures than for items presented as words."[44]

This of course begs the question: What *kinds* of visuals? Recent psychology research offers some guidance: photographs, positive images, and images about health issues.[45] Among other things, this offers further evidence that positivity is persuasive.

What do these insights on visuals mean for your persuasive endeavors? Whenever appropriate, include these kinds of visuals with your PowerPoints, articles, etc., because they'll make what you say stay with your audience for longer than words alone will.

LET'S GET SPECIFIC

Some examples from my perch as a hiring manager illustrate why it's critical to tend to much more than mere words.

During a video interview, a job candidate saw I wasn't in a shirt and tie (I think I was wearing a sweater), and literally took his tie off and threw it across the room, then unbuttoned his top button. That unprofessional behavior terminated his candidacy for the position immediately, even though his résumé suggested he was a good fit for the position.

Another candidate came into the office for a final-round interview. In our postinterview download, my colleague said she found it disrespectful that he wasn't wearing a suit. Some candidates even interviewed online in T-shirts. That doesn't signal you're taking the position seriously.

Lack of curiosity is killer. I always ask the candidates if they have questions. More than one has responded, "No, not really." Wrong answer! How can you really have no questions about a job you want? You need to have them prepared ahead of time.

Be assured without being cocky. One highly qualified candidate made himself extremely unlikable by literally saying that there are low-IQ people out there who weren't smart enough to see things the right way—that is, his way. That cost him the job.

And these are just some of the lowlights. I've experienced so many subpar performances from candidates who, on paper, seemed like great fits.

LET'S REFLECT

The reality that words are but a part of persuasion is liberating. It's an opportunity, because it means that you have a wide range of other techniques available to persuade. When you say the "right" thing and enhance it with persuasive tone and body language, make an effort to be likable, and project confidence, your chances of getting what you want skyrocket. And all this is directly under your control.

If you don't get your words quite right, yet you use other skills discussed in this chapter, that can more than make up for suboptimal messaging. That takes the pressure off.

In chapter 4 we discussed the "halo effect." Recall that it describes our "tendency to like (or dislike) everything about a person—including things you have not observed," based on how we perceive them. The flipside is the "horn effect." While we place halos over the heads of people we like, we put horns on the heads of people we dislike.

When you practice the skills in this chapter, you'll be much more likely to earn a halo with your counterpart, which makes it much easier to get what you want. You'll also avoid having your audience see horns on your head. Give your audience reasons to see you as an angel, not a demon.

Key Takeaways for Going Beyond Words to Persuade

1. Embrace the reality that persuasion requires you to go beyond words. See this reality as an opportunity to become even more persuasive. With the exact same words and better attention to the things discussed in this chapter, you'll significantly increase your chances of shared action. Even when your words aren't quite "right," you can use these other techniques to still succeed.
2. Be as likable as possible. Being likable doesn't necessarily mean someone will like you. It just maximizes your chances of this happening. Things you can do to be more likable include adopting a friendly, open demeanor; showing how you're similar to someone; being gracious in receiving praise, and being authentically generous in offering it; admitting mistakes when you make them. Avoid things you aren't comfortable doing to try to get someone to like you.
3. Get your tone right. It's so important that it can facilitate persuasion even if you can't find the right words. The best tone is a calm one.
4. Adopt persuasive body language because it gives off lots of crucial signals. Three things to do are to take up space (like through hand steepling), defy gravity (through arched eyebrows, for example), and authentically smile. Three behaviors to avoid are pacifying behaviors (such as touching your neck), closing off your body, and contemptuous expressions like eye-rolling.
5. At some level, image really is everything. How people perceive you is their reality. And if that perception isn't good, it has a negative impact on your reality. Make sure you cultivate the appropriate image with your audience to share action. Otherwise, their chances of disliking you increase.

Beyond-Words Focusing Question: What is the ONE Thing beyond mere words that you can do to increase your chances of persuasion?

Chapter 9

ACE THE GRANNY TEST

Those who know they are profound, strive for clarity; those who would like to seem profound to the crowd, strive for obscurity.

Friedrich Nietzsche, *The Gay Science*

When I was studying philosophy in Germany, I took a class on Martin Heidegger's *Being and Time.* Despite being fluent in German, I regularly left class wondering whether I spoke a word of it. (*Nein?*) Reading or listening to lectures on Heidegger left me absolutely confused. Even reading him in English didn't help.

Heidegger has a warranted reputation for being challenging to understand. It turns out that he intentionally strove for lack of clarity. He wrote, "Making itself intelligible is suicide for philosophy." That's dead wrong, for philosophy and any other form of communication. It's a fundamentally anti-persuasive mindset regardless of the situation.

Imagine someone, after reading something you wrote, or hearing you speak, praising how wonderfully unclear or unintelligible you were. That'd be absurd, and anything but a compliment. And yet many people think sounding smart and appearing sophisticated require using words and ideas that are complicated and hard to understand. Not at all.

Without clarity, which is the quality of being easy to understand and free from ambiguity, persuasion is impossible, because your audience can't understand you. If your audience doesn't understand you, it's your fault, because you didn't say things in a way that landed with them. And it's your problem, because if they don't understand you, you can't really get what you want.

With clarity, you're able to say what you want in a way your audience easily grasps. That's a crucial step on the path to persuasion.

To ensure you're clear, you need to talk to the right person. And the best person to gauge your clarity is pretty obvious: Granny. Persuasion geniuses know how to **ace the granny test**. In my experience teaching at elite universities, including Brown University and the University of Notre Dame, many students there can't pass this test. You'll learn how to be more persuasive than them.

We often don't have clarity at the start. We need time to think and talk things through, especially big ideas, important projects, and difficult situations. Persuasion geniuses know how to achieve clarity when it matters.

Clarity seems boring, like stating the obvious. And yet the success that comes from clarity is exhilarating.

THE GRANNY TEST

The simplest way to achieve clarity is to pretend like you're speaking to your granny. Granny usually isn't an expert in your particular field, which means you need to explain things to her in plain terms rather than technical jargon. For one, technical jargon won't resonate with her, because she doesn't know the terminology. More importantly, even if she knows it, it's often still confusing. "Experts" often use technical language as a crutch so they don't have to distill what they say enough to make it clear.

The best experts are able to make extremely complicated things simple and clear. The Nobel laureate economist Milton Friedman was a master of this. Take two minutes to watch his video "I, Pencil," in which he explains how no one person knows how to make a pencil, and yet they get made.[1] It's taken from his ten-episode series, *Free to Choose*, which is exemplary in its ability to discuss a wide range of economic issues in a highly accessible manner.

"Nontechnical" is not the same as "unintelligent." Normal counterparts aren't incapable of understanding concepts. They're just usually busy or uninterested in monkish details. Focus on the key things you need to convey, and provide details only when they ask for them. Indeed, Granny's lack of expertise on a particular subject actually makes her an ideal judge of clarity, because she will only accept easy-to-understand explanations. That's one of Granny's many virtues.

When you aren't clear to Granny, the consequences are minimal. Granny just smiles, nods, says "That's nice, dear," and proceeds with her day. Your audience usually isn't so kind. If you aren't clear, they'll either ignore or dismiss you, or get frustrated and like you less. It's up to no one but you to fill in the gaps of what you're trying to say. Lack of clarity makes it hard for you to engage Granny (or anyone else) in fruitful conversation.

Here's the granny test: Would your granny understand what you're saying? Use it with every important communication (and preferably all communications).

Here's the same message delivered two different ways—one passes the granny test, the other doesn't.

1. The ultrasound showed a pregnancy in the uterus about nine weeks along, and the baby's heartbeat was seen.
2. The ultrasound revealed an intrauterine gestation consistent with an estimated gestational age of nine weeks, with fetal cardiac activity present.

Granny needs accessible language free of unnecessary or overly abstract words. How else would she understand you? Unfortunately, many people think they need to use the most complex language possible. They mistake it as a sign of their erudition. How else would they prove they're smart? Or they think big ideas can only be explained in erudite-sounding ways with hifalutin language. There's an impulse that using simple language is tantamount to dumbing down their ideas.

In turns out, though, that unnecessarily complex language makes it harder to get what you want. Research shows that needless complexity makes you less, not more, persuasive by having your audience assess what you write and say more negatively and assess you as less intelligent. The author concludes, "Write clearly and simply if you can, and you'll be more likely to be thought of as intelligent."[2]

I once attended a political economy lecture with a famous professor. He was a prominent faculty member at the top-ranked program in his field. He said, "My superpower is that I make complex things seem simple." At first I thought, "Hmm, that sounds arrogant." Then, for the next hour, he systematically explained a wide range of complicated economic concepts in remarkably simple language. It was Friedman-esque. I thought, "Wow, that *is* his superpower." This is the type of skillset that produces bestselling books and a wide sphere of influence. Granny would have followed every word.

Later, I was in a workshop for graduate students (which I was at the time) with this professor. A graduate student from another highly ranked program presented his research. I couldn't follow a word of his extremely complex technical language. I felt dumb. Once the presentation was over, this professor said, "I didn't understand anything you just said." Not even an internationally famous professor could follow him!

Passing the granny test is harder than it seems because of the curse of knowledge. As Chip Heath and Dan Heath explain in *Made to Stick*, "Once we know something, we find it hard to imagine what it was like not to know it. Our knowledge has 'cursed' us. And it becomes difficult for us to share our knowledge with others, because we can't readily re-create our listeners' state of mind."[3] You'd never deliberately be thoughtless with Granny, so don't start now.

Granny needs you to be easy to follow. Communications shouldn't be a labyrinth—windy and confusing. Your points need to follow sequentially: A to B to C to D, not A to Q to J to F. Make sure what you say flows logically.

Granny needs you to clearly state your purpose up front—don't bury or hide it. One great way to do this in your writing is with clear topic sentences. One of my direct reports—a supersmart woman with an Ivy League degree—likes to bury her main point in the middle of a paragraph. Hard to follow. When she puts it at the top (which she's slowly learning to do), it makes a world of difference.

"Clear" isn't the same as "short." Many podcasts are two, three, four hours long and get hundreds of thousands of downloads per episode. Think Joe Rogan. People binge-watch shows on streaming services, one after another, for hours, enraptured by stories. Our appetite for great content is insatiable, as long as it captures our attention.

Here's a practical technique for acing the granny test. Condense what you want to say to one page. Then, whittle it down to a three-by-five-inch index card containing a story and your two or three most compelling facts. This is how you boil your issue down to its essence. Granny will be pleased.

If you work in a highly technical field, you might be thinking that this doesn't apply to you. Au contraire: In technical fields, clarity might be *more* important. If engineers misunderstand how to build something like a bridge because the instructor didn't convey it clearly in class, the consequences can literally be lethal.

Granny needs to know your thesis. A thesis is the argument, hypothesis, or idea that you want to put forward, test, or advocate for. It's the heart of what you want to say or investigate, and it usually comes near the top of what you're writing or saying. Without a thesis, it's hard to persuade.

An example of a thesis is "Lincoln was America's greatest president" or "Lincoln was America's worst president." These are claims you'd then try to support with compelling evidence. Your thesis could be descriptive—football is the most popular sport in America. You could support this with viewership data. Whatever the case, you need something substantive to convey.

Here are some tips for crafting a thesis. Be able to boil what you want to say down to one sentence. It should fit into the formulation "In this communication I will argue that . . ." For example, "In this paper, I will argue that Lincoln was the greatest American president." Even better if you can add a "because": ". . . because he saved the Union and ended slavery." Once you know how to put it into that simple formulation, you can spruce it up stylistically and leave behind the "In this paper I will argue that . . ."

Clearly presenting your thesis is important in everyday conversations, too. Suppose you're concerned your family isn't managing its finances properly. You're paying a lot of money in credit card interest every month. Your thesis might be "We should budget better to pay off our balance in full every month." You'd support your thesis with evidence, such as how much you've spent just on interest over the last year, then ask your spouse how they feel about that.

One "thesis" I had for my family was "We should get a dog. They're great companions and are a lot of fun." My wife was skeptical for a few years. Initially, I wanted a basset hound because I find them adorable. She found their slobber unbecoming. In order for her to find my thesis persuasive, I had to understand her barriers. She didn't want a large dog. That was reinforced when we went to a dog show, talked to a breeder of old English sheepdogs, and my wife felt like she was walking a bear. (It did look like a crossbreed.) She also didn't want a dog that sheds. Then one day, I read an article in *The Wall Street Journal* about a rare wooly pooch: the barbet. It checked off all her boxes, and she was persuaded by my thesis, so we added Pascal to our family.

To truly ace the granny test, you also need simplicity and precision.

Simplicity is found in uncomplicated words free of pretense and unnecessary elements. Consider iconic words from Martin Luther King Jr.'s "I Have a Dream" speech: "I have a dream that my four little children will one day live in a nation where they will not be judged by the color of their skin but by the content of their character." Nice and simple, no unnecessary or pretentious words.

King could have said something like "I have a dream, a vision, a hope that my four children—wonderful, inspiring as they are, the apples of my eye—will one day, hopefully in my lifetime, but perhaps not, have the opportunity to live in a society—America, the land of the free, the home of the brave—where our fellow brothers and sisters will not look at them and judge them based purely or primarily by the color of their skin but, rather, will have the opportunity to inhabit a nation where they are judged by the content of who they are and of who they want to become." That bloated sentence weighs in at 103 words, nearly three times longer than the original 35 words. It's full of pomp and sentiment, leaving the reader lost. It was actually easier to write, because short sentences require more thought and intentionality. As the French philosopher Blaise Pascal wrote in a letter, "I have made this [letter] longer only because I have not had the time to make it shorter."

Simple communications aren't easy. Consider how simple most sports are. Basketball: Throw the ball through the hoop. Soccer: Kick the ball into the net. Tennis: Hit the ball in the court one more time than your opponent. Running is the simplest sport of all: left foot, right foot, as fast as you can. None of these sports is easy. They require a tremendous amount of skill and practice. Just ask Michael Jordan, Pelé, Roger Federer, and Usain Bolt. The same is true with communications. Simplicity requires much thought and revision to achieve. You need to be able to slow down your thinking and sort through the clutter. Simplicity is almost always the last stop, rarely the first.

Simple communications pack more punch because they're not watered down. Imagine your favorite alcoholic beverage: wine, for example. While you can have more liquid by adding water to your glass, it'd taste worse. Don't water down what you say, either.

Groom your thoughts and words to achieve simplicity with Occam's razor: "Entities should not be multiplied beyond necessity." Applied to persuasion, this means when deciding which explanation to offer, choose the simpler one.

At the same time, don't *over*simplify things. In a famous misquotation of Albert Einstein (he didn't say it), "Everything should be made as simple as possible, but not simpler."[4] By oversimplifying, you risk suggesting difficult problems have easy or simple solutions. We almost invariably miss key aspects of what we most want to communicate, which often leads to incomplete and unsound recommendations. This sets you up for trouble later. For example, in my poverty advocacy, if I oversimplified work as a solution to poverty without recognizing the regulatory, social, and cultural barriers (among others) poor people face in finding and holding a job, my oversimplification would harm my credibility and maybe even offend some people.

Granny craves simplicity not because she's stupid but because she's smart. She appreciates the effort the writer or speaker puts into crafting careful messages. Rather than getting distracted by prolixity, she insists on clarity so she can absorb more of what the speaker says.

Precision ensures we're aiming at and hitting the right target by being exact and accurate. In medicine, for example, precision surgery uses images, robotics, and minimally invasive techniques to address a medical issue. If a surgery is imprecise and cuts too much, or overlooks part of the problem, the patient will suffer harm.

Precision is the ability to specify what you're saying as exactly as possible. It's not, like, umm, you know. Precision isn't saying something in the vicinity of what you mean. It's expressing just what you mean—no more, no less. This requires removing uncertainty, ambiguity, and vagueness. When they exist, figure out why and address them.

To achieve precision, omit as much unnecessary information from your thoughts and words as you can. This clutter gets in the way of hitting your target. Declutter, one unnecessary word at a time.

At times, a desire to be as precise as possible can make you less persuasive, because you dive into too much detail and make too many points. Be sure your precision is also concise in what you convey. More is often less.

To achieve clarity, simplicity, and precision, you often need to slow things down to speed them up. If you proceed too hastily, your thinking and communicating will usually be muddled. Don't rush. By investing time at the beginning of your process, you can usually save yourself much more time later because you're focused on the right things.

CLARIFY YOUR ONE THING

A core speechwriters' mantra is that a speech about everything is a speech about nothing. Every time I wrote a speech, I worked with the principal to home in on what the speech was really about. It couldn't be everything, or even a few things. The best speeches were always about one thing.

For example, I wrote a speech to be delivered at Harvard. The temptation when speaking at such an elite institution is to try to showcase your intelligence by discussing too many things. Fortunately, my principal (the deputy director of a national agency) knew better. So we crafted a speech about one thing—innovation. She talked about how innovation was central to our enterprise, what drives it, and how we could work with academics at Harvard and elsewhere to accelerate it. Because the remarks were focused, the audience easily followed and was engaged, as evidenced by their good questions. That greased the wheels for further engagement, including a visit by the director to campus.

You need to be able to identify and focus on important things, and ultimately the *most* important thing. We'll adapt the ONE Thing, an idea from Gary Keller and Jay Papasan, here to help you pass the granny test.

To figure out what matters and what to do, Keller and Papasan offer what they call the "focusing question": "What is the ONE Thing I can do such that by doing it everything else will be easier or unnecessary?"[5] When you try to do too many things, you lack focus and don't see clearly. You waste resources and spin your wheels. Identify your goal, engage in activities that maximize your chances of getting there, and stop doing things that don't.

To make this more concrete, let's consider some examples. A focusing question for our health could be "What's the ONE Thing I can do to achieve my diet goals?" The answer might be "Eat significantly less sugar." For business, the question could be "What's the ONE Thing I can do to make us more competitive?" You might respond, "Retain talent more effectively."[6] Pause and take a moment to identify an important issue you want to address, and craft your focusing question for it. Here's how all this applies to persuasion.

Persuasion geniuses ask this focusing question: What's the ONE Thing you can communicate such that everything else in your persuasive endeavor will be easier or unnecessary? Ask this question every time. It focuses you on the most important thing required to share action. For example, if your ONE Thing is to boost customer retention, figure out what to say and do to get more customers to come back. You might revise your marketing strategy, or interview people who buy from you once and never return.

The focusing question is so powerful that we included one at the end of each chapter. Recall for example the one from chapter 6: What is the ONE story you can tell that will morally motivate your audience to share understanding and action?

Persuasion geniuses have ONE Thing at the heart of their initiatives. In politics, Nelson Mandela's ONE Thing was to defeat South Africa's apartheid regime. Winston Churchill's foreign policy ONE Thing upon becoming prime minister of the United Kingdom was to defeat the Nazis. During his famous speech "We Shall Fight on the Beaches," he declared, "We shall not flag or fail. We shall go on to the end" to defeat the Nazis.[7]

Over twenty-five hundred years ago, the Greek poet Archilochus wrote, "The fox knows many things, but the hedgehog knows one big thing." In order to be a hedgehog, you need to be able to step back and identify your one big thing. While the fox's mind is full of many smaller things, the most impactful people have the ability to step back, zoom out, and think big. Widen your persuasive horizons by thinking like a hedgehog.

CLARITY REQUIRES REVISION

Einmal ist keinmal: "Once is never." This German saying encapsulates the reality that you rarely if ever get things right the first time. Only through trial and error, practice, reworking, and repeating this process do you master something. So, too, with clarity. For this you must commit the resources—above all, time and energy—to revise enough to achieve the clarity necessary to persuade.

One principal for whom I wrote speeches despised feedback. On my very first day, the other speechwriter warned me: If you disagree with them, they'll probably take the metaphorical sword out of their sheath and cut you down to size. He had seen this happen on multiple occasions. It wasn't pretty.

I almost got slashed on my first trip with this person. They asked how a speech went. I gently tried to suggest one or two simple ways to enhance an already good speech. I got a look that said, "Stop talking, now!" I learned quickly. This person refused to learn. So I didn't bother with feedback.

Feedback facilitates clarity. You need to bounce ideas off others to improve them. Others see things you can't, don't, or won't. Conversation helps highlight issues you hadn't thought of, and sparks questions about things that aren't clear. After all, everyone's vision is limited to their field of sight. You usually need multiple people to help you see clearly.

Before you can revise effectively, you need to know how you generate ideas and content. There are two kinds of writers and, by extension, thinkers: outline and process. An outline writer produces an outline in their head or on paper before writing. They figure out what they want to say, then write a draft that conforms to that outline.

A process writer, by contrast, gains clarity by actually going through the writing process. Since they don't know what they want to say at the start, they must get their ideas on the page to sort through them. Usually only after drafting something do they figure out where they're going. Once they know, they must revise in light of the clarity they achieved. For the outline writer, clarity needs to come before they start writing, whereas process writers find clarity at the end.

While it would be easy to think that one style (intuitively, probably the outline writer's) is better, this isn't a matter of better or worse; rather, it's a matter of understanding and working within the contours of how your mind works.

You need to know whether you're an outline or process persuader so you adopt the right methods to succeed. The outline thinker needs clarity before feeling comfortable enough to engage their counterpart. The process thinker might gain clarity only by going through the process of engaging their counterpart.

BARRIERS TO CLARITY

Everyone faces barriers to achieving clarity. Here we consider how to overcome two of the most common: uncertainty and insecurity.

Uncertainty can occur when you don't know what you want to say. It can also arise by not knowing how to convey what you want to say. How do you overcome uncertainty? Don't fear it. Everyone experiences it. Rarely (if ever) do you start with certainty. Don't judge uncertainty. Start by observing it. Consider its cause. Reflect and rethink. Write things down and converse with others. Figure out what's not clear. Is it an idea? A part in a process? The proposed solution? Or something else? Attack the uncertainty head-on, poking and probing until you understand what's unclear and how you can remove the uncertainty. As long and winding as the path may be, it only gets longer if you wait to walk it, which can actually increase uncertainty.

Insecurity is another barrier to clarity. It's common to lack confidence in your thoughts and words. Perhaps you're afraid of embarrassing or undermining yourself (which you might indeed do!). You might lack confidence in what you want to say and how to say it. You could be unsure of your ability to craft a persuasive message (perhaps you can't yet).

Whatever the cause of insecurity, when someone lets insecurity get the better of them, their performance suffers. Perhaps they audibly sound nervous or unsure. They might sway because they're nervous. They might forget to make some of their important points.

Overcoming insecurity has two steps. First, gently observe what's making you feel insecure. Maybe you are uncomfortable with an idea or some data. Or perhaps you're simply uncomfortable speaking in front of people. Without knowing the source of your insecurity, you can't address it. Avoid judging your insecurity, because you'll often end up judging yourself harshly, which is counterproductive.

Second, attack your uncertainty head-on, one tiny step at a time. Let's suppose you're uncomfortable with public speaking. Many people are! Practice in low-stakes situations. You can practice by yourself, first just speaking in a room, then speaking into a mirror. If you have pets, you can practice with them. My wife practiced with our dog Pascal when she was preparing for an important professional presentation. Pascal was a sympathetic listener.

Then, practice with sympathetic humans. When I was preparing for my two TEDx Talks, I practiced with my two-year-old son, Thomas. Ask your friends and family if you can practice in front of them. Moms and grannies are great sympathetic audiences.

As you slowly build your comfort, you can practice in front of professional colleagues. Find the nicest people and ask if they can spare a few minutes. You'll notice that each time you practice, your insecurity will decrease a tiny bit. Remarkably, with enough practice and intentional training (including with the techniques in this book), you'll end up with a high level of security and confidence.

When you overcome insecurity, instead of sounding nervous, you sound calm and confident. Instead of swaying and distracting your audience with your movement, you firmly plant yourself when talking and use persuasive body language. Instead of skipping over important points, you clearly share your thoughts, one at a time.

It's important to realize that your communications are almost never as bad as you think. We're usually our own toughest critics, which often is an impediment to feeling secure in who you are, and what you feel, think, and say. You'll notice things in your head and think they're a big problem, while your audience has no clue something like forgetting some lines in a presentation is happening.

We certainly have not exhausted barriers to clarity here. If you face other ones, observe them and figure out how to address them effectively.

LAND MINES LURK IN THE FOG

Lack of clarity can lead to a lack of trust. Sometimes, people are intentionally unclear. Deception often lies at the heart of this. The speaker is obtuse or unclear because they want to hide or obscure their real meaning. Politicians notoriously craft phrases to intentionally leave their meaning ambiguous. "Mistakes were made." By whom? Certainly not the politician!

A classic example from George Orwell illustrates how dangerous lack of clarity can be. In "Politics and the English Language," written as the Cold War was starting, Orwell shows how an English professor can defend Russian totalitarianism:

> He cannot say outright, "I believe in killing off your opponents when you can get good results by doing so." Probably, therefore, he will say something like this:
>
> "While freely conceding that the Soviet régime exhibits certain features which the humanitarian may be inclined to deplore, we must, I think, agree that a certain curtailment of the right to political opposition is an unavoidable concomitant of transitional periods, and that the rigors which the Russian people have been called upon to undergo have been amply justified in the sphere of concrete achievement."[8]

Bad actors often hide bad deeds behind unclear, complicated, imprecise prose. To persuade your counterpart to share action, you need to be able to break through their unclear words. That requires a heightened ability to think clearly.

Unintentional lack of clarity poses problems, too. Recall a text chain where you and the other person have different interpretations of what was said: "That's not how I meant it!" These things happen every day. When the resulting misunderstandings are large, trouble lies ahead. Lack of clarity breeds confusion. Confusion means there's no shared understanding of the issue or situation, and thus on how best to proceed.

Sometimes we choose to not be as clear as possible, or as clear as necessary, because we want to protect someone. We fear clearly saying something will hurt them. So we avoid it. For example, if a friend asks you about behavior you find inappropriate, like lewd comments, you might hesitate to say anything because you don't want to offend them. So you say something like "Well, we all have our way of expressing ourselves" or "We joke in different ways." Or we tell them it's not a problem, when we know it is.

The desire to avoid upsetting them is understandable. Unfortunately, it sets up everyone involved for trouble, because it makes space for ambiguities. They linger and grow, lurking in the shadows until they jump out. It's better for you to be open and honest with your friend than for them to embarrass themselves in front of others.

Ask yourself: How do I need to present my feelings and thoughts to make them clear to my audience?

LET'S GET SPECIFIC

If you apply the techniques in this chapter, you'll be far better equipped to pass the granny test than many graduates of elite universities.

In my last semester of graduate school at Notre Dame, as I was finishing my dissertation, I had the privilege of teaching an upper-level political science course. As their first paper approached, I said, "Make sure your paper has a thesis." There were audible snickers in the room, as if to say, "You silly grad student, we know how to write papers!" After all, they had gotten through most of their undergraduate careers with good grades. They obviously knew something so basic!

Well. They turned in their essays. And? Fully one-third had no thesis. No argument! Instead, their papers were full of summary, mostly just regurgitating the text, either by paraphrasing or directly quoting it. Every now and again, they'd offer some musings that pointed in the direction of analysis. But that was about it. All description, no real thinking.

In the margins I wrote comments like "thesis?," wondering where it was. Students questioned me, saying, "What do you *mean* my paper has no thesis?" They thought mere summary more than sufficed. I responded, "What do you *mean* what do I *mean*?! Your paper needs an argument." I explained that their papers weren't really saying anything.

Sadly, this wasn't an anomaly at Notre Dame. I saw it there as a teaching assistant in numerous courses where I graded papers. And I saw it with students at Brown University and the University of Wisconsin–Madison, where I taught for two years each. I've experienced it with recent graduates from Harvard and interns from the University of Chicago and Duke University, all top universities.

With my students, I offered to look at as many iterations of a thesis as necessary until it was clear and usable. I asked them to fill in the simple formulation, "In this paper I will argue that . . ." The first time a student did this with me, it took a few iterations, sometimes as many as ten, back and forth via email or in office hours, until Granny would understand. Usually, though, once they got it the first time, it clicked, and we'd only need two to three iterations for future papers.

Then, as they actually wrote their paper, I made sure their thesis drove their prose and analysis. I made sure they had sufficient evidence to support it. Otherwise, the paper was deficient. For that, I reviewed outlines or drafts of introductions to make sure they were on the right track. Then, I provided extensive feedback on every paper. Students often remarked that they never got feedback like that from other professors.

Here's the best part: For students who wanted to learn (which, alas, isn't every student), their writing always improved by leaps and bounds, and they eventually could pass the granny test with flying colors. This helps them throughout their professional lives. They produce better cover letters and writing samples. They impress their bosses with clearer ideas.

LET'S REFLECT

I returned to Germany the year after studying Heidegger for a seminar on Jean-Jacques Rousseau, another challenging philosopher. What a difference a professor can make! I have never experienced anyone bringing more clarity to a complicated text than this professor, all *auf Deutsch*. Everyone—even me!—could understand.

He walked through the sequence of ideas calmly, showing us the flow and why Rousseau laid things out the way he did. He paused on every important concept and explained it thoroughly. He never used pretentious language, despite being the smartest person I've ever met. His granny would have been proud.

Without clarity, it's much harder to get what you want. Your audience won't understand you. Worse, they might *mis*understand you. The reason behind the lack of clarity might be that you don't even understand yourself. These are all barriers to getting what you want. If you don't overcome them, your cause is lost.

Skeptical? Just think about all your good ideas sitting on the shelf because you haven't explained them clearly enough in conversation. I see this all the time in public policy. I encounter what looks like an excellent idea, with data to support it. But it's presented in a way that is so unclear and hard to understand that trying to grasp it literally makes my head hurt.

Without clarity, your vision is blurry, and you can't see where you're going, so you won't achieve the shared action necessary to get there.

With clarity, though, success follows. And that gets your juices flowing. Just ask Granny.

Key Takeaways for Acing the Granny Test

1. Clarity is the unsung hero of persuasion. Without it, people don't understand you. That's your fault, because you didn't express yourself in a way your audience could follow. And it's your problem, because without clarity, shared action is much less likely. With clarity, though, you're able to say what you want so your audience readily grasps it. Clarity at the highest level is a persuasion superpower.
2. The best way to achieve clarity is to ace the granny test: Would your granny understand what you're saying? Since Granny usually isn't an expert in your particular field, you need to explain things to her in plain terms and accessible language rather than technical jargon.
3. Clearly communicating to others starts by knowing your thesis, which is your argument, hypothesis, or idea you want to put forward. Without one, it's not clear what you're trying to say. The simplest way to craft a thesis is to fit it into this sentence: "In this communication, I will argue that . . ."
4. To master clarity, identify your ONE Thing, which is a way to identify and focus on the most important thing. In each persuasive endeavor, ask: What's the ONE Thing you can communicate such that everything else in your persuasive endeavor will be easier or unnecessary?
5. Observe and identify your barriers to clarity. The two most common are uncertainty and insecurity. Yours might be different. Whatever they are, address them head-on.

Clarity Focusing Question: What is the ONE Thing you can communicate such that everything else in your persuasive endeavor will be easier or unnecessary?

Conclusion

Your journey to becoming a persuasion genius will be uniquely yours. While this book provides a general road map, you need to individualize your training and practice. We all have our strengths and weaknesses. Mine are different from yours. You need to start by openly and honestly observing yours. One alternative is to ignore them. That's not exactly a recipe for success. Another is judging them, getting frustrated, and being harsh on yourself. If you've ever seen a professional athlete berating themself for making a mistake during a game, completely melting down as their performance spirals, you know this probably isn't effective either. So just observe. That can be challenging enough!

You need to enhance your strengths, because that's what will set you apart and help you achieve your goals. People generally are selected for opportunities because of strengths, not lack of weaknesses. Maybe you're a good storyteller. Become a great one. At the same time, you need to at least mitigate your weaknesses, because if you don't, they'll hold you back. If you can turn your weaknesses into strengths, that'll be especially powerful. Your goal is to simply be a little better than you were yesterday; after all, we can all be so much more than we are. Judging yourself for not being the absolute best version of yourself is unhelpful. So is judging yourself against others. Be the best version of you possible, not the best version of your friend or coworker.

Throughout your learning process, look for and celebrate moments when you feel, "I'm doing this!" That will bring you great satisfaction and give you confidence and motivation to keep growing. When you're frustrated, remember those moments to help you get back to work. As you progress, you'll start to create opportunities that otherwise wouldn't have existed. And you'll capitalize on ones that you would have been scared to pursue, like when you raise your hand at a big meeting and share great insights.

There will be peaks and valleys on your journey, too. Just because you did something right once doesn't mean you'll nail it every time; nor does it mean it'll always land the same way with different audiences. And sometimes, you'll mess up. Making mistakes makes you human. Mistakes help you improve, too.

Learn to fail better. In "Worstward Ho," Samuel Beckett writes, "Ever tried. Ever failed. No matter. Try again. Fail again. Fail better." Persuasion geniuses reach that level not by making no mistakes, but rather by failing better by learning from their mistakes and how to not make them repeatedly.

Writing this book has been a personal and professional journey for me, full of mistakes. I've encountered so many realities, especially about the remarkable object that is the human brain, that have been deeply uncomfortable for me. For example, as a former academic who was trained to rigorously analyze texts and ideas, my default at one point was to launch my logic at people. As a result, I also didn't default to telling stories, because they didn't seem analytical enough. My tone can still sound professorial at times, like I'm delivering a lecture, when it needs to be more conversational. And that whole judgment thing? I used to judge myself far too harshly when my performance fell even a tiny bit short of what I expected. Unhelpful!

What are some of the biggest changes I've made? Instead of leading with "logic," I now lead with morally motivating, emotionally intelligent stories whenever possible. For example, as an antipoverty advocate with a PhD who usually wears dressier clothes, I don't exactly look the part of someone in poverty. I know this. Recall that I start my talks by saying, "You're probably wondering why I care about poverty. Well, it's seared into my family's history. My mom grew up dirt poor. My granny raised five kids by herself. They were so poor, my granny literally had to count pennies. Every year, my mom wondered if there would be presents around the Christmas tree, because most years, there weren't. My mom and her siblings bear the psychological scars of this poverty to this day. I want to make sure as few people as possible experience this kind of depravity."

I've actually welled up a few times, fighting tears, because it's true, and their suffering still hurts me. That authentic story earns me instant credibility.

Instead of judging myself, I observe and work hard to grow. It's not wrong that I sometimes fall into a professorial tone, because that's how I was trained. Instead, I've honed a more conversational tone so I'm talking with, not at, my audience.

At the start of this book, I quoted the Greek poet Archilochus, who said, "We don't rise to the level of our expectations; we fall to the level of our training." Big personal and professional successes don't come out of nowhere. They're the product of intentionally working to grow. Practice in low-stakes situations gets you ready to perform when it matters. That's what happened to me for my TEDx Talk.

Once I got the official invitation to deliver my TEDx Talk from Mohammed, there was just one little problem: You normally get at least two or three months (sometimes more) to prepare one of these big talks. Due to the challenges he faced with his university, I got three weeks. Three weeks to craft, practice, memorize, and perfect a huge speaking engagement that would appear on one of the biggest platforms in the world. Which is, well, nowhere near enough time. Especially because I was preparing another big talk I was delivering the week before the TEDx talk.

Fortunately, I was ready. I knew what to do. TED Talks are about big ideas. I thought: What's my ONE Thing? Mine was that by rewiring yourself in three simple ways (put feelings first, be *for* something, and appeal to their morals), your chances of getting what you want would skyrocket. I outlined a vision for achieving shared action by doing this. I knew the audience would feel uncomfortable about this, so I addressed their misgivings and made them feel good about trying this out. I was upbeat and *for* something.

I knew I needed stories, so I added them throughout the talk. I made sure my tone was conversational and my body language was powerful (I used hand steepling and kept my eyebrows arched for almost the entire talk). And I continued to simplify the talk until the day before I delivered it, making sure Granny would easily follow it.

The best part is that with this book, you have the tools to deliver powerful talks, write great things, and engage people the right way.

But maybe you're thinking: Some of this seems pretty tough. Can I really rewire myself in the ways outlined in this book?

There's a foundational irony that's cause for tremendous optimism about your ability to make the adjustments necessary to get what you want when it matters. While our cognitive wiring makes persuasion challenging in the ways we've discussed, you just have to flip your frame of reference and ask yourself: How would I feel if someone did these things to me? *Not good* is usually the answer. So don't do it to others! Let's unpack this, starting with part 1.

You know that we're wired to think and talk primarily about ourselves. Do you like being on the receiving end when someone else does that? Nope. Which is why it's in your interest to rewire yourself and not do that to others. Apply the persuader's mindset to everything you do. That's also why you need a vision that appeals to your audience. What else would motivate them, at the highest level possible, to share action with you, especially in the medium and long term? Nothing.

Now, let's consider part 2. While it feels good to insist you're right, be negative, and showcase your values, we don't like being on the receiving end of a steamroller. So don't steamroll others! It's not easy to accept that persuasion starts with feelings, that negativity is usually counterproductive, and that our values aren't the only right ones. Alas, it's also illogical to disregard neuroscience and psychology. Which is why we need to operate within these realities, ideally with stories.

We bring a lot of other prior assumptions that make it harder to get what we want. We think negotiation and persuasion are zero-sum games where we win and they lose, yet we certainly don't like it when people treat us that way.

We like to think persuasion is about finding the right words. So we're always searching for them. And yet when people use the wrong tone, or have uncomfortable body language (especially toward us), or do a host of other things that make us not want to work with them, we pull back rather than lean in.

We take for granted that because something is clear to us, it's clear to others. So we present things in ways our audience doesn't really grasp. And what do you do when someone delivers an unclear presentation, or writes something unclear? You either ignore it, or you get annoyed that they didn't present it clearly.

Once you flip your frame of reference on all these items, you're ready to become a persuasion genius. Sooner than you think, it'll stop feeling like you're talking to a brick wall, and start to feel like you're winning hearts and minds. Because you will be.

Remember, you won't always be perfect. You'll need the presence of mind to execute when it matters. That comes through knowledge and training.

Persuasion isn't about being right. When we approach it like it is, our chances of getting what we want fade quickly. Persuasion is about making a difference. By rewiring yourself in ways we've discussed in this book to bring people in rather than push them away, your chances of persuading people will skyrocket, and you can finally make the difference you care about. And you'll even create a more functional society along the way.

You now know that true persuasion starts with empathy, positivity, and shared purpose. That's how you make a difference. And that's how you get what you want.

Acknowledgments

About a decade ago, I started to notice some things I felt were amiss in society. It felt like we were drifting apart from others, and seeing people who don't think like us in an increasingly negative light. We were losing the ability to even talk to others. I knew it wasn't good, and it didn't have to be this way. I wanted to know why this was happening, and how to make it better. This book is my attempt to do that.

This book exists because so many people have generously supported me in more ways than I could recount throughout the research, writing, and rewriting process. They have made my thinking, writing, speaking, and persuasive abilities much better.

The manuscript was completed and then revised many times while I was a research fellow at the Competitive Enterprise Institute. I'm grateful to Kent Lassman, Iain Murray, Travis Burk, Richard Morrison, and Ryan Young for being so supportive. I also profited immensely from one of my interns, Jack Nicastro, who was remarkably helpful. John Phillips, another intern for a shorter period, also made the book better.

At the Illinois Policy Institute, I also received good insights and assistance from LyLena Estabine, Larry Han, Jack Knorr, Lilly Rossi, and Rich Wetzel.

I have profited from conversations about persuasion with many people over the past decade. These include Matt Abrahams, Connor Boyack, Corey Burres, Dick Carpenter, Carrie Conko, Nick Eberstadt, Tammy Hensch, John Hood, John Kramer, Randy Lee, John Mozena, Larry Reed, Terry Saeger, Sean Stevens, Marian Tupy, Bridgett Wagner, Stone Washington, and Marty Zupan.

Special thanks for people who read parts of the manuscript, were especially generous with feedback, or helped in other key ways: Nic Dunn, Carmine Gallo, Jim Hickel, Aaron Pomerantz, Peter Salovey, Lynn Scarlett, and Aigul Yangalina.

The Leadership Institute has served as a venue for me to test out many of the ideas in this book in my workshops on persuasive communications. I'm grateful to Ryan Brann for the opportunity to continue partnering with them, as well as Matthew Patella.

My speaking coach, Caroline Goyder, helped me better understand how to make more of the advice in this book actionable and digestible. Joe Ross, another helpful speaking coach, helped me refine the book's tone.

My agent, Jennifer Lyons, has been supportive from our very first conversation. She has helped me navigate all aspects of the publishing process, especially pushing me to think about what sets this book apart.

BenBella Books has been a great publisher, providing great expertise at every stage of the process. Many thanks to the entire team there. Special thanks there go to Glenn Yeffeth, Claire Schulz, Alicia Kania, Jennifer Canzoneri, Heather Butterfield, Kim Broderick, and Sarah Avinger. My editor, Stephanie Gorton, has provided numerous rounds of excellent feedback, making this a better book in every way. Evan Herrington provided careful copyediting.

ACKNOWLEDGMENTS

My family has been an unending source of support from the very beginning. This book would not exist if my wife, Maria, hadn't fully supported me writing it on nights and weekends for almost two years before starting my research fellowship, then continuing with every single step that has followed. She's a thought partner in everything I do. Her love has been a source of energy and inspiration. I tested out many of the ideas in this book on my son, Thomas, on our morning walks with our dogs, Pascal and Pierre, every day. He's a great sounding board. My daughter, Elizabeth, came along at the end of the process and helped me fine-tune things. My mom, Cheryl, always supports me in everything I do, cheering me every step of the way.

More gratitude than I could ever express goes to Kent Lawrence. His unending generosity and support have done more for me and this project than I could ever recount. My best attempt at a thank-you is to pay it forward. That's why this book is dedicated to him.

Notes

INTRODUCTION

1. CBS Miami, "Elementary School Students Prep for Debate Championship," published April 19, 2024, accessed August 13, 2025, https://www.youtube.com/watch?v=Q88ZIhsSWm0.
2. Levi Boxell, Matthew Gentzkow, and Jesse M. Shapiro, "Cross-Country Trends in Affective Polarization," *Review of Economics and Statistics* 106, no. 2 (March 2024): 557–65.
3. "Americans' Feelings About Politics, Polarization and the Tone of Political Discourse," Pew Research Center, September 19, 2023, https://www.pewresearch.org/politics/2023/09/19/americans-feelings-about-politics-polarization-and-the-tone-of-political-discourse/.
4. Alexus Bazen, "Cell Phone Statistics 2025," Consumer Affairs, March 20, 2025, https://www.consumeraffairs.com/cell_phones/cell-phone-statistics.html.
5. N. F. Mendoza, "66% of Americans Admit to Sleeping with Their Phone at Night," TechRepublic, February 20, 2020, https://www.techrepublic.com/article/66-of-americans-admit-to-sleeping-with-their-phone-at-night/.
6. John D. Mayer and Peter Salovey, "The Intelligence of Emotional Intelligence," *Intelligence* 17, no. 4 (October 1993): 433; Peter Salovey and John D. Mayer, "Emotional Intelligence," *Imagination, Cognition and Personality* 9, no. 3 (March 1990): 185–211, https://doi.org/10.2190/dugg-p24e-52wk-6cdg.

NOTES

CHAPTER 1

1. Diana I. Tamir and Jason P. Mitchell, "Disclosing Information About the Self Is Intrinsically Rewarding," *Proceedings of the National Academy of Sciences* 109, no. 21 (May 7, 2012): 8038–43, https://doi.org/10.1073/pnas.1202129109.
2. Adrian F. Ward, "The Neuroscience of Everybody's Favorite Topic," *Scientific American*, July 16, 2023, https://www.scientificamerican.com/article/the-neuroscience-of-everybody-favorite-topic-themselves/.
3. Mark Goulston, *Just Listen: Discover the Secret to Getting Through to Absolutely Anyone* (Amacom, 2015), 103.
4. Elizabeth C. Pinel and Anson E. Long, "When I's Meet," *Personality and Social Psychology Bulletin* 38, no. 3 (February 22, 2012): 296–307, https://doi.org/10.1177/0146167211433878; Elizabeth C. Pinel, "Existential Isolation and I-Sharing: Interpersonal and Intergroup Implications," *Current Opinion in Psychology* 23 (October 2018): 84–87, https://doi.org/10.1016/j.copsyc.2018.01.002; Elizabeth C. Pinel, "I-Sharing, the Problem of Existential Isolation, and Their Implications for Interpersonal and Intergroup Phenomena," in *Handbook of Experimental Existential Psychology* (Guilford Press, 2004), 352–68.
5. Bob Burg and John David Mann, *The Go-Giver: A Little Story About a Powerful Business Idea* (Portfolio, 2010), 37, 139–40; Douglas Stone, Bruce Patton, and Sheila Heen, *Difficult Conversations: How to Discuss What Matters Most* (Penguin Books, 2023), 172.
6. "Bill Clinton Has a Superpower, and Mastering It Can Make You Successful Beyond Belief," *HuffPost*, August 8, 2013, https://www.huffpost.com/entry/bill-clinton_n_3718956.
7. Stone et al., *Difficult Conversations*, 168.
8. Goulston, *Just Listen*, 59.
9. Goulston, *Just Listen*, 156.
10. Stone et al., *Difficult Conversations*, 37.
11. Burg and Mann, *The Go-Giver*, 68.
12. Jim Camp, *Start with No: The Negotiating Tools that the Pros Don't Want You to Know* (Crown Publishing Group, 2011), 159–60.
13. Madeleine E. Gross and Jonathan W. Schooler, "Smartphone-Based Program for Enhancing Curiosity and Its Associated Virtues: A Randomized Waitlist-Controlled Pilot Study," *Journal of Positive Psychology* (May 2025): 1–14, https://doi.org/10.1080/17439760.2025.2500566.
14. Sandy Hein, "What Is the Black Swan Group's Negotiation 9™ (N9™)?," Negotiation Training and Live Events, February 8, 2021, https://www.blackswanltd.com/newsletter/what-is-the-black-swan-groups-negotiation-9-n9.
15. Daryl Davis, "Why I, as a Black Man, Attend KKK Rallies: Daryl Davis:

TEDxNaperville," TEDx, November 2017, https://www.ted.com/talks/daryl_davis_why_i_as_a_black_man_attend_kkk_rallies?language=en.

16. Nicholas Kristof, "'How Can You Hate Me When You Don't Even Know Me?,'" *The New York Times*, June 26, 2021, https://www.nytimes.com/2021/06/26/opinion/racism-politics-daryl-davis.html.
17. Thomas F. Pettigrew and Linda R. Tropp, "A Meta-Analytic Test of Intergroup Contact Theory," *Journal of Personality and Social Psychology* 90, no. 5 (2006): 751–83, https://doi.org/10.1037/0022-3514.90.5.751.
18. Pam A. Mueller and Daniel M. Oppenheimer, "The Pen Is Mightier Than the Keyboard: Advantages of Longhand Over Laptop Note Taking," *Psychological Science* 25, no. 6 (2014): 1159–68, https://doi.org/10.1177/0956797614524581.

CHAPTER 2

1. "Our Purpose," Ford, accessed June 22, 2023, https://corporate.ford.com/about/purpose.html.
2. "Delusional Disorder: Causes, Symptoms, Types & Treatment," Cleveland Clinic, May 22, 2022, https://my.clevelandclinic.org/health/diseases/9599-delusional-disorder.
3. Emma, "The Joe Rogan Experience: 4 Lessons from the #1 Podcast," Ausha, January 2, 2025, https://www.ausha.co/blog/joe-rogan-experience/.
4. Vatsal Sanghavi, "Everything You Need to Know About the Joe Rogan Experience Podcast," Podnotes, accessed June 4, 2025, https://www.podnotes.app/blog/everything-you-need-to-know-about-the-joe-rogan-experience-podcast.
5. "2022 National Defense Strategy," U.S. Department of Defense, 2022, https://media.defense.gov/2022/Oct/27/2003103845/-1/-1/1/2022-national-defense-strategy-npr-mdr.pdf.
6. Cynthia Ejike, "Strategic Plan vs. Operational Plan vs. Tactical Plan: What Is the Difference?," Profitable Venture, accessed April 17, 2025, https://www.profitableventure.com/strategic-plan-operational-tactical-difference/.

CHAPTER 3

1. Lokman I. Meho, "The Rise and Rise of Citation Analysis," *Physics World* 20, no. 1 2007: 32, https://doi.org/10.1088/2058-7058/20/1/33.
2. Antonio Damasio, interview by Kristin Gillespie, University of Southern California, posted May 10, 2021, by Deconstructing Sentience, https://www.youtube.com/watch?v=9LFUUdSeMPs.
3. Mayer and Salovey, "The Intelligence of Emotional Intelligence," 433.
4. Richard J. Haier, *The Neuroscience of Intelligence* (Cambridge University Press, 2017).
5. John Mayer, Peter Salovey, and David Caruso, *Mayer-Salovey-Caruso Emotional*

Intelligence Test (MSCEIT): User's Manual (Multi-Health Systems, Inc., 2002), 32. I'm grateful to Peter Salovey for sharing these data.

6. Aristotle, *On Rhetoric: A Theory of Civic Discourse*, trans. George A. Kennedy (Oxford University Press, 2007), 39.
7. Tenelle Porter, Abdo Elnakouri, Ethan A. Meyers, et al., "Predictors and Consequences of Intellectual Humility," *Nature Reviews Psychology* 1, no. 9 (June 27, 2022): 524–36, https://doi.org/10.1038/s44159-022-00081-9..
8. Daniel Kahneman, *Thinking, Fast and Slow* (Farrar, Straus and Giroux, 2011), 224–5.
9. Philip E. Tetlock, *Expert Political Judgment: How Good Is It? How Can We Know?* (Princeton University Press, 2006), 233.
10. Kahneman, *Thinking*, 174. He goes on to explain that "surprising individual cases have a powerful impact and are a more effective tool for teaching psychology because the incongruity must be resolved and embedded in a causal story."
11. Philip E. Converse, "The Nature of Belief Systems in Mass Publics (1964)." *Critical Review* 18, no. 1–3 (2006): 1–74, https://doi.org/10.1080/08913810608443650, 3.
12. Converse, "The Nature of Belief Systems," 14.
13. Converse, "The Nature of Belief Systems," 14, 16..
14. Converse, "The Nature of Belief Systems," 51–52.
15. Converse, "The Nature of Belief Systems," 45.
16. See, for example, Gregory B. Markus, "Stability and Change in Political Attitudes: Observed, Recalled, and 'Explained,'" *Political Behavior* 8, no. 1 (1986): 21–44, https://doi.org/10.1007/bf00987591. He finds that "policy attitudes generally do not have strong cognitive representations, are eminently changeable, and once they are changed, an individual's cognitive autobiography is revised so as to render the changes invisible."
17. Roy Pierce and Philip E. Converse, *Political Representation in France* (Harvard University Press, 1986).
18. Philip E. Converse, "Assessing the Capacity of Mass Electorates." *Annual Review of Political Science* 3, no. 1 (June 2000): 331–53, https://doi.org/10.1146/annurev.polisci.3.1.331.
19. Daniel Kahneman, Olivier Sibony, and Cass R. Sunstein, *Noise: A Flaw in Human Judgment* (Little, Brown Spark, 2021), 4, 66.
20. Kahneman et al., *Noise*, 4.
21. Jeff Desjardins, "Every Single Cognitive Bias in One Infographic," Visual Capitalist, August 26, 2021, https://www.visualcapitalist.com/every-single-cognitive-bias/.
22. Jonathan Haidt, *The Righteous Mind: Why Good People are Divided by Politics and Religion* (Pantheon, 2012), 55. See also 64, 83, 189.
23. Anne-Laure Sellier, Irene Scopelliti, and Carey K. Morewedge, "Debiasing Training

Improves Decision Making in the Field," *Psychological Science* 30, no. 9 (2019): 1371–79, https://doi.org/10.1177/0956797619861429.

24. Kahneman, *Thinking*, 82.
25. Kahneman, *Thinking*, 124.
26. Kahneman et al., *Noise*, 12. Emphasis in original.
27. Kahneman et al., *Noise*, 21, 78.
28. Kahneman et al., *Noise*, 73–5, 78.
29. Kahneman et al., *Noise*, 81, 86–93.
30. Richard E. Nisbett, *Mindware: Tools for Smart Thinking* (Farrar, Straus and Giroux, 2015). Nisbett offers an optimistic, change-oriented toolkit for reframing common problems to apply scientific and psychological concepts to them. Kahneman is skeptical of Nisbett's tools. On Nisbett's methods, Kahneman says, "Pencil-and-paper doesn't convince me . . . A test can be given even a couple of years later. But the test cues the test-taker. It reminds him what it's all about."; Ben Yagoda, "The Cognitive Biases Tricking Your Brain," *The Atlantic*, September 7, 2018, https://www.theatlantic.com/magazine/archive/2018/09/cognitive-bias/565775/.
31. Antonio R. Damasio, *Descartes' Error: Emotion, Reason, and the Human Brain* (G. P. Putnam's Sons, 1994), 143, 159. Feelings, Damasio explains, are "first and foremost about the body." He continues: "They offer us *the cognition of our visceral and musculoskeletal state* as it becomes affected by preorganized mechanisms and by the cognitive structures we have developed under their influence. Feelings let us *mind the body*, attentively, as during an emotional state, or faintly, as during a background state." Feelings include both emotional experiences and physical sensations. We can feel emotions, like anger or surprise. We also can feel hungry and tired, neither of which are emotions (and can combine to make you feel "hangry"). Damasio explains that "all emotions generate feelings if you are awake and alert, but not all feelings originate in emotions."
32. Carroll E. Izard, "Four Systems for Emotion Activation: Cognitive and Noncognitive Processes," *Psychological Review* 100, no. 1 (1993): 68–90, https://doi.org/10.1037/0033-295x.100.1.68, 72–3; Damasio, *Descartes' Error*, 139. Psychologist Carroll Izard describes an emotion as a physiological response to an event, issue, or idea that motivates action. Neuroscientist Antonio Damasio also explains that emotions entail a "collection of changes in body state that are induced in myriad organs by nerve cell terminals." Damasio elaborates: "In conclusion, emotion is the combination of a mental evaluative process, simple or complex, with *dispositional responses to that process*, mostly *toward the body proper*, resulting in an emotional body state, but also toward *the brain itself* (neurotransmitter nuclei in the brain stem), resulting in additional mental changes." These bodily changes can be physiological (like goosebumps), behavioral (like laughing or frowning), and experiential (like someone's face reddening from embarrassment).

33. Damasio, *Descartes' Error*, 146. Many researchers use the terms interchangeably. We'll ultimately do the same here. See, for example, Damasio: "Other authors often use these words interchangeably, or 'feeling' may not be used at all and 'emotion' divided into expressive and experienced components."; Izard, "Four Systems," 72: "Many writers use the terms emotion, feeling, and emotion experience interchangeably."
34. Damasio, *Descartes' Error*, 159.
35. Haidt, *The Righteous Mind*, 61. Emphasis in original.
36. Tchiki Davis, "List of Emotions: 271 Emotion Words." Berkeley Well-Being Institute, accessed March 28, 2022, https://www.berkeleywellbeing.com/list-of-emotions.html; Alan Cowen and Dacher Keltner's research reports also captured 27 distinct categories of emotion. The list includes: admiration, adoration, aesthetic appreciation, amusement, anger, anxiety, awe, awkwardness, boredom, calmness, confusion, contempt, craving, disappointment, disgust, empathic pain, entrancement, excitement, envy, fear, guilt, horror, interest, joy, nostalgia, pride, relief, romance, sadness, satisfaction, sexual desire, surprise, sympathy, and triumph; Alan S. Cowen and Dacher Keltner, "Self-Report Captures 27 Distinct Categories of Emotion Bridged by Continuous Gradients," *Proceedings of the National Academy of Sciences* 114, no. 38 (September 5, 2017), https://doi.org/10.1073/pnas.1702247114.
37. Izard, "Four Systems," 70, 73.
38. Robert Earl Patterson, "Intuitive Cognition and Models of Human–Automation Interaction," *Human Factors: The Journal of the Human Factors and Ergonomics Society* 59, no. 1 (February 2017): 101–15, https://doi.org/10.1177/0018720816659796.; see also Damasio, Descartes' Error, xiii.
39. Damasio, *Descartes' Error*, xii–xiii.
40. Kahneman, *Thinking*, 4, 20, 24, 105.
41. Kahneman, *Thinking*, 13, 21.
42. Kahneman, *Thinking*, 21.
43. Kahneman, *Thinking*, 21, 24–5.
44. Kahneman, *Thinking*, 86.
45. Kahneman, *Thinking*, 416
46. Damasio, *Descartes' Error*, x–xi, 53. Damasio offers the "somatic marker hypothesis," which posits that "emotion is in the loop of reason, and that emotion could assist the reasoning process rather than necessarily disturb it, as was commonly assumed." He explains: "Reduction in emotion may constitute an equally important source of irrational behavior." And the shocking conclusion: When "emotion is entirely left out of the reasoning picture, as happens in certain neurological conditions, reason turns out to be even more flawed than when emotion plays bad tricks on our decisions."
47. Daniel Goleman, *Emotional Intelligence: Why It Can Matter More Than IQ* (Bantam Books, 2005), 97.

48. Josh Bandoch and Joe Tabor, "Regulatory Reform Can Make Housing More Affordable for Illinois Families," Illinois Policy Institute, July 9, 2024, https://www.illinoispolicy.org/reports/regulatory-reform-can-make-housing-more-affordable-for-illinois-families/.
49. "Reduce Anxiety & Stress with the Physiological Sigh," Huberman Lab, posted April 7, 2021, https://www.youtube.com/watch?v=rBdhqBGqiMc; Melis Yilmaz Balban, Eric Neri, Manuela M. Kogon, Lara Weed, Bita Nouriani, Booil Jo, et al., "Brief Structured Respiration Practices Enhance Mood and Reduce Physiological Arousal," *Cell Reports Medicine* 4, no. 1 (January 10, 2023), https://doi.org/10.1016/j.xcrm.2022.100895.
50. Roger Fisher and Daniel Shapiro, *Beyond Reason: Using Emotions as You Negotiate* (Penguin Books, 2006), 157.
51. "GRIT Tension Reduction Strategy," Psychology.Iresearch.net.com, accessed August 13, 2025, https://psychology.iresearchnet.com/social-psychology/antisocial-behavior/grit-tension-reduction-strategy/.
52. I'm grateful to Carmine Gallo for emphasizing some of these points.
53. Chip Heath and Karla Starr, *Making Numbers Count: The Art and Science of Communicating Numbers* (Avid Reader Press/Simon & Schuster, 2022).
54. Carmine Gallo, *The Presentation Secrets of Steve Jobs: How to Be Insanely Great in Front of Any Audience* (McGraw Hill Publishing, 2009).
55. Interview with Carmine Gallo, September 17, 2025.
56. Sally Planalp, "Communication, Cognition, and Emotion," *Communication Monographs* 60, no. 1 (March 1993): 3–9, https://doi.org/10.1080/03637759309376288.

CHAPTER 4

1. Joyce E. Bono and Remus Ilies, "Charisma, Positive Emotions and Mood Contagion," *The Leadership Quarterly* 17, no. 4 (2006): 330, https://doi.org/10.1016/j.leaqua.2006.04.008.
2. Marianne Sonnby-Borgström and Peter Jönsson, "Dismissing-Avoidant Pattern of Attachment and Mimicry Reactions at Different Levels of Information Processing." *Scandinavian Journal of Psychology* 45, no. 2 (February 25, 2004): 103–13, https://doi.org/10.1111/j.1467-9450.2004.00385.x.
3. George Orwell, *The Orwell Reader* (Harcourt, Brace and Company, 1956), 405–6.
4. Amrisha Vais, Tobias Grossman, and Amanda Woodward, "Not All Motions Are Created Equal: The Negativity Bias in Social-Emotional Development," *Psychological Bulletin* 134, no. 3 (May 2008): 383–403, https://pubmed.ncbi.nlm.nih.gov/18444702/; Furthermore, Rozin and Royzman argue that there are four elements of negativity bias: negative potency, steeper negative gradients, negativity dominance, and negative differentiation; Paul Rozin and Edward B. Royzman, "Negativity Bias, Negativity Dominance, and Contagion," *Personality and Social Psychology Review* 5, no. 4 (November 2001): 296–320, https://doi.org/10.1207/s15327957pspr0504_2.

5. Kahneman, *Thinking*, 301.
6. Roy F. Baumeister, Ellen Bratslavsky, Catrin Finkenauer, and Kathleen D. Vohs, "Bad Is Stronger Than Good," *Review of General Psychology* 5, no. 4 (December 2001): 323–70, https://doi.org/10.1037/1089-2680.5.4.323.
7. Qais AbuHasan, Vamsi Reddy, and Waquar Siddiqui, "Neuroanatomy, Amygdala," *National Library of Medicine*, July 17, 2023, https://www.ncbi.nlm.nih.gov/books/NBK537102/.
8. Kahneman, *Thinking*, 301.
9. Paul E. Stillman, Jay J. Van Bavel, and William A. Cunningham, "Valence Asymmetries in the Human Amygdala: Task Relevance Modulates Amygdala Responses to Positive More Than Negative Affective Cues," *Journal of Cognitive Neuroscience* 27, no. 4 (April 2015): 842–51, https://doi.org/https://doi.org/10.1162/jocn_a_00756; Lisa Feldman Barrett, Eliza Bliss-Moreau, Seth L. Duncan, et al., "The Amygdala and the Experience of Affect," *Social Cognitive and Affective Neuroscience* 2, no. 2 (2007): 73–83, https://doi.org/10.1093/scan/nsl042.
10. Goleman, *Emotional Intelligence*, 14.
11. "Amygdala Hijack: Symptoms, Causes, and Prevention," Medical News Today, accessed November 6, 2021, https://www.medicalnewstoday.com/articles/amygdala-hijack#what-is-it.
12. John T. Cacioppo and Gary G. Berntson, "The Affect System," *Current Directions in Psychological Science* 8, no. 5 (October 1999): 133–37, https://doi.org/10.1111/1467-8721.00031; Greg J. Norman, Catherine J. Norris, Jackie Gollan, Tiffany A. Ito, Louise C. Hawkley, Jeff T. Larsen, et al., "Current Emotion Research in Psychophysiology: The Neurobiology of Evaluative Bivalence," *Emotion Review* 3, no. 3 (June 28, 2011): 349–59.
13. Planalp, "Communication, Cognition, and Emotion."
14. Louisa C. Michl, Katie A. McLaughlin, Kathrine Shepherd, and Susan Nolen-Hoeksema, "Rumination as a Mechanism Linking Stressful Life Events to Symptoms of Depression and Anxiety: Longitudinal Evidence in Early Adolescents and Adults," *Journal of Abnormal Psychology* 122, no. 2 (2013): 339–52, https://doi.org/10.1037/a0031994. PMID: 23713497.
15. Susan Nolen-Hoeksema, Blair E Wisco, and Sonja Lyubomirsky, "Rethinking Rumination," *Perspectives on Psychological Science* 3, no. 5 (2008): 400–24, https://doi.org/10.1111/j.1745-6924.2008.00088.x.
16. Christine D. Scher, Rick E. Ingram, and Zindel V. Segal, "Cognitive Reactivity and Vulnerability: Empirical Evaluation of Construct Activation and Cognitive Diatheses in Unipolar Depression," *Clinical Psychology Review* 25, no. 4 (2005): 487–510, https://doi.org/10.1016/j.cpr.2005.01.005; Zindel V. Segal and Rick E. Ingram, "Mood Priming and Construct Activation in Tests of Cognitive Vulnerability to

Unipolar Depression," *Clinical Psychology Review* 14, no. 7 (1994): 663–95, https://doi.org/10.1016/0272-7358(94)90003-5.

17. Shawn Achor, "The Happiness Advantage: Linking Positive Brains to Performance," TEDx Bloomington, YouTube, posted June 30, 2011, https://www.youtube.com/watch?v=GXy__kBVq1M.
18. David Rozado, Ruth Hughes, and Jamin Halberstadt, "Longitudinal Analysis of Sentiment and Emotion in News Media Headlines Using Automated Labelling with Transformer Language Models," *PLOS ONE* 17, no. 10 (October 18, 2022), https://doi.org/10.1371/journal.pone.0276367..
19. Achor, "Happiness Advantage."
20. Abraham Lincoln, "First Inaugural Address of Abraham Lincoln," Avalon Project: Documents in Law, History and Diplomacy, accessed November 22, 2022, https://avalon.law.yale.edu/19th_century/lincoln1.asp.
21. Franklin D. Roosevelt, "First Inaugural Address of Franklin D. Roosevelt," Avalon Project: Documents in Law, History and Diplomacy, accessed November 24, 2021, https://avalon.law.yale.edu/20th_century/froos1.asp.
22. Ronald Reagan, "Farewell Address to the Nation," Ronald Reagan Presidential Library and Museum, accessed November 30, 2021, https://www.reaganlibrary.gov/archives/speech/farewell-address-nation.

CHAPTER 5

1. Researchers have found evidence for oleogustus as a sixth taste receptor. See: Cordelia A. Running, Bruce A. Craig, and Richard D. Mattes, "Oleogustus: The Unique Taste of Fat," *Chemical Senses* 40, no. 7 (July 3, 2015): 507–16, https://doi.org/10.1093/chemse/bjv036; Philippe Besnard, Patricia Passilly-Degrace, and Naim A. Khan, "Taste of Fat: A Sixth Taste Modality?," *Physiological Reviews* 96, no. 1 (January 2016): 151–76, https://doi.org/10.1152/physrev.00002.2015; Russell S.J. Keast and Andrew Costanzo, "Is Fat the Sixth Taste Primary? Evidence and Implications," *Flavour* 4, no. 1 (February 3, 2015), https://doi.org/10.1186/2044-7248-4-5.
2. Researchers acknowledge there might be additional foundations not yet captured by their model, so the list might grow. See: Ronnie Janoff-Bulman and Nate C. Carnes, "Surveying the Moral Landscape," *Personality and Social Psychology Review* 17, no. 3 (March 16, 2013): 219–36, https://doi.org/10.1177/1088868313480274; Tage Shakti Rai and Alan Page Fiske, "Moral Psychology Is Relationship Regulation: Moral Motives for Unity, Hierarchy, Equality, and Proportionality," *Psychological Review* 118, no. 1 (January 2011): 57–75, https://doi.org/10.1037/a0021867; Jesse Graham, Jonathan Haidt, Sena Koleva, Matt Motyl, Ravi Iyer, Sean P. Wojcik, et al., "Moral Foundations Theory: The Pragmatic Validity of Moral Pluralism," *Advances in Experimental Social*

Psychology 47 (2013): 55–130, https://doi.org/10.1016/b978-0-12-407236-7.00002-4. Separately, there's also no consensus that liberty is definitively a moral taste bud.

3. Haidt, *Righteous Mind*, 144. Emphasis added.
4. Carolyn L. Funk, Kevin B. Smith, John R. Alford, Matthew V. Hibbing, Nicholas R. Eaton, Robert F. Krueger, et al., "Genetic and Environmental Transmission of Political Orientations," *Political Psychology* 34, no. 6 (October 17, 2012): 805–19, https://doi.org/10.1111/j.1467-9221.2012.00915.x; Peter K. Hatemi, John R. Hibbing, Sarah E. Medland, Matthew C. Keller, John R. Alford, Kevin B. Smith, et al., "Not by Twins Alone: Using the Extended Family Design to Investigate Genetic Influence on Political Belief," *American Journal of Political Science* 54, no. 3 (June 21, 2010): 798–814, https://doi.org/10.1111/j.1540-5907.2010.00461.x; Nancy L. Segal, "Twins Reared Apart Design," *Wiley StatsRef: Statistics Reference Online*, September 29, 2014, https://doi.org/10.1002/9781118445112.stat06696; Kevin Smith, John R. Alford, Peter K. Hatemi, Lindon J. Eaves, Carolyn Funk, and John R. Hibbing, "Biology, Ideology, and Epistemology: How Do We Know Political Attitudes Are Inherited and Why Should We Care?," *American Journal of Political Science* 56, no. 1 (November 28, 2011): 17–33, https://doi.org/10.1111/j.1540-5907.2011.00560.x; Haidt, *Righteous Mind*, 323. Pinker also argues the correlation coefficient might be as high as 0.62. See Pinker, *The Blank Slate: The Modern Denial of Human Nature* (Penguin Books, 2016), 283. For a discussion of family relationships beyond twins, see: K. R. Truett, L. J. Eaves, E. E. Walters, A. C. Heath, J. K. Hewitt, J. M. Meyer, et al., "A Model System for Analysis of Family Resemblance in Extended Kinships of Twins," *Behavior Genetics* 24, no. 1 (January 1994): 35–49, https://doi.org/10.1007/bf01067927.
5. Peter K. Hatemi, Sarah E. Medland, Robert Klemmensen, Sven Oskarsson, Levente Littvay, Christopher T. Dawes, et al., "Genetic Influences on Political Ideologies: Twin Analyses of 19 Measures of Political Ideologies from Five Democracies and Genome-Wide Findings from Three Populations," *Behavior Genetics* 44, no. 3 (February 26, 2014): 282–94, https://doi.org/10.1007/s10519-014-9648-8.
6. Mohammad Atari, Jonathan Haidt, Jesse Graham, Sena Koleva, Sean T. Stevens, and Morteza Dehghani, "Morality Beyond the WEIRD: How the Nomological Network of Morality Varies Across Cultures," *Journal of Personality and Social Psychology* 125, no. 5 (November 2023): 1157–88, https://doi.org/10.1037/pspp0000470.
7. Gary Chapman, *The 5 Love Languages: The Secret to Love that Lasts* (Northfield Publishing, 2015).
8. Some researchers argue "all morality is understood through the lens of harm." See: Kurt Gray, Liane Young, and Adam Waytz, "Mind Perception Is the Essence of Morality," *Psychological Inquiry* 23, no. 2 (May 2012): 101–24, https://doi.org/10.1080/1047840x.2012.651387, 108. Their alternative approach, called "dyadic morality," deemphasizes the other six moral foundations. It focuses on the

intention and pain caused in actions involving an "intentional moral agent and a suffering moral patient"; Gray et al., "Mind Perception,", 101; Haidt offers a persuasive response to "dyadic" morality, showing harm isn't the only moral taste; Jonathan Haidt, "A Straw Man Can Never Beat a Shapeshifter: Response to Schein and Gray (2015)," YourMorals Blog, October 27, 2015, https://ymblog.jonathanhaidt.org/2015/10/a-straw-man-can-never-beat-a-shapeshifter/.

9. Abraham Lincoln, "Second Inaugural Address of Abraham Lincoln," Avalon Project - Documents in Law, History and Diplomacy, accessed November 6, 2025, https://avalon.law.yale.edu/19th_century/lincoln2.asp. Emphasis added.
10. Emma Margolin, "Romney's 47% Comment Named Quote of the Year," MSNBC, December 10, 2012, https://www.msnbc.com/hardball/romneys-47-comment-named-quote-the-year-msna16754.
11. Katie Reilly, "Hillary Clinton Transcript: 'Basket of Deplorables' Comment," *Time*, September 10, 2016, https://time.com/4486502/hillary-clinton-basket-of-deplorables-transcript/.
12. Atari et al., "Morality Beyond," 1161, 1180; Chris Skurka, Liana B. Winett, Hannah Jarman-Miller, and Jeff Niederdeppe, "All Things Being Equal: Distinguishing Proportionality and Equity in Moral Reasoning," *Social Psychological and Personality Science* 11, no. 3 (August 7, 2019): 374–87, https://doi.org/10.1177/1948550619862261, 375.
13. Morton Deutsch, "Equity, Equality, and Need: What Determines Which Value Will Be Used as the Basis of Distributive Justice?," *Journal of Social Issues* 31, no. 3 (Summer 1975): 137–49, https://doi.org/10.1111/j.1540-4560.1975.tb01000.x.
14. Rai and Fiske, "Relationship Regulation."
15. Skurka et al., "Things Being Equal," 375.
16. Atari et al., "Morality Beyond," 1187.
17. Atari et al., "Morality Beyond," 1159, 1161, 1180; Haidt, *Righteous Mind*, 161; Skurka et al., "All Things Being Equal," 375; Rai and Fiske, "Moral Psychology is Relationship Regulation," 57, 64.
18. Atari et al., "Morality Beyond," 1176.
19. Atari et al., "Morality Beyond," 1188.
20. Ronnie Janoff-Bulman and Nate C. Carnes, "Social Justice and Social Order: Binding Moralities Across the Political Spectrum," *PLOS ONE* 11, no. 3 (March 31, 2016), https://doi.org/10.1371/journal.pone.0152479, 3; Ronnie Janoff-Bulman and Nate C. Carnes, "Moral Context Matters," *Personality and Social Psychology Review* 17, no. 3 (July 16, 2013): 242–47, https://doi.org/10.1177/1088868313492021; Ronnie Janoff-Bulman and Nate C. Carnes, "Surveying the Moral Landscape," *Personality and Social Psychology Review* 17, no. 3 (March 16, 2013): 219–36, https://doi.org/10.1177/1088868313480274.

21. Janoff-Bulman and Carnes, "Binding Moralities"; "Moral Context Matters"; and "Surveying the Moral Landscape."
22. "User Clip: Obama to Increase Capital Gains Tax Because of 'Fairness.'" C-SPAN, April 16, 2008, https://www.c-span.org/clip/public-affairs-event/user-clip-obama-to-increase-capital-gains-tax-because-of-fairness/4830724. Emphasis added.
23. Ronald Reagan, "Radio Address to the Nation on Free and Fair Trade," The American Presidency Project, August 31, 1985, https://www.presidency.ucsb.edu/documents/radio-address-the-nation-free-and-fair-trade-0. Emphasis added.
24. Atari et al., "Morality Beyond," 1161.
25. Haidt, *Righteous Mind*, 179.
26. Atari et al., "Morality Beyond," 1176.
27. Atari et al., "Morality Beyond," 1187.
28. Haidt, *Righteous Mind*, 164.
29. "Highlights House Intelligence Committee Review of Edward Snowden Disclosures." House Intelligence Committee, accessed June 4, 2025, https://intelligence.house.gov/uploadedfiles/snowden_report_highlights.pdf, 2.
30. Barack Obama, "C-SPAN: Barack Obama Speech at 2004 DNC Convention," YouTube, 2008, https://www.youtube.com/watch?v=eWynt87PaJ0.
31. Atari et al., "Morality Beyond," 1158, 1161, 1187; Haidt, *Righteous Mind*, 168.
32. "Moral Foundations Theory," Moral Foundations, accessed February 22, 2022, https://moralfoundations.org/.
33. Joseph Henrich, *The Secret of Our Success: How Culture Is Driving Human Evolution, Domesticating Our Species, and Making Us Smarter* (Princeton University Press, 2015), 347.
34. Henrich, *Secret of Our Success*, 43.
35. Henrich, *Secret of Our Success*, 347–48.
36. Haidt, *Righteous Mind*, 167.
37. Henrich, *Secret of Our Success*, 129.
38. Atari et al., "Morality Beyond," 1158-9. Earlier MFT research referred to this taste bud as "sanctity/degradation." We'll also employ the terms sacred/sanctity when it fits the discussion.
39. Atari et al., "Morality Beyond," 1177 .
40. Atari et al., "Morality Beyond," 1187. It correlated at 0.84.
41. Haidt, *Righteous Mind*, 179.
42. Amit Thorat and Omkar Joshi, "The Continuing Practice of Untouchability in India: Patterns and Mitigating Influences," *Economic & Political Weekly* 5, no. 2 (January 11, 2020): 36–45.
43. Kavita Chowdhury, "Seven Decades After It Was Abolished, 'Untouchability'

Continues to be Practiced in India," *The Diplomat*, August 23, 2022, https://thediplomat.com/2022/08/seven-decades-after-it-was-abolished-untouchability-continues-to-be-practiced-in-india/.

44. John F. Kennedy, "Address to the Greater Houston Ministerial Association," John F. Kennedy Presidential Library and Museum, September 12, 1960, https://www.jfklibrary.org/learn/about-jfk/historic-speeches/address-to-the-greater-houston-ministerial-association.
45. Paul Julian Weindling, "Eradicating Parasites," *Epidemics and Genocide in Eastern Europe, 1890–1945*, February 2000, 19–48, https://doi.org/10.1093/acprof:oso/9780198206910.003.0016.
46. While not all MFT researchers agree liberty is a foundation, at a minimum it's the next best candidate, so we include it here with the caveat that it remains an open question.
47. Haidt, *Righteous Mind*, 200–201.
48. Martin Luther King Jr., "Read Martin Luther King Jr.'s 'I Have a Dream' Speech in Its Entirety," NPR, January 16, 2023, https://www.npr.org/2010/01/18/122701268/i-have-a-dream-speech-in-its-entirety.
49. Joshua Bandoch, "The Right Way to Label the Left," *National Review*, July 2, 2023, https://www.nationalreview.com/2023/07/the-right-way-to-label-the-left/.
50. Haidt, *Righteous Mind*, 157, 345; for more on how care is central to leftist ideology, see: Atari et al., "Morality Beyond," 1158, 1171 ; J. Matias Kivikangas, Belén Fernández-Castilla, Simo Järvelä, Niklas Ravaja, and Jan-Erik Lönnqvist, "Moral Foundations and Political Orientation: Systematic Review and Meta-Analysis," *Psychological Bulletin* 147, no. 1 (January 2021): 55–94, https://doi.org/10.1037/bul0000308; Richard A. Klein, Michelangelo Vianello, Fred Hasselman, Byron G. Adams, Reginald B. Adams, Sinan Alper, et al., "Many Labs 2: Investigating Variation in Replicability Across Samples and Settings," *Advances in Methods and Practices in Psychological Science* 1, no. 4 (December 2018): 443–90, https://doi.org/10.1177/2515245918810225; Jesse Graham, Jonathan Haidt, and Brian A. Nosek, "Liberals and Conservatives Rely on Different Sets of Moral Foundations," *Journal of Personality and Social Psychology* 96, no. 5 (May 2009): 1029–46, https://doi.org/10.1037/a0015141; Jesse Graham, Brian A. Nosek, Jonathan Haidt, Ravi Iyer, Spassena Koleva, and Peter H. Ditto, "Mapping the Moral Domain," *Journal of Personality and Social Psychology* 101, no. 2 (2011): 366–85, https://doi.org/10.1037/a0021847.
51. Atari et al., "Morality Beyond," 1171, 1180; Haidt, *Righteous Mind*, 213; Skurka et al., "All Things Being Equal." Skurka et al. find that although leftists "did not endorse Equity and Proportionality as much as they endorsed Harm or Fairness, they did endorse Equity and Proportionality more than Loyalty, Authority, or Purity," 380.
52. Haidt, *Righteous Mind*, 168.

53. Thomas H. Costello, Shauna M. Bowes, Sean T. Stevens, Irwin D. Waldman, Arber Tasimi, and Scott O. Lilienfeld, "Clarifying the Structure and Nature of Left-Wing Authoritarianism," *Journal of Personality and Social Psychology* 122, no. 1 (January 2022): 135–70, https://doi.org/10.1037/pspp0000341, 145, 160, 162–3.
54. Matthew Kugler, John T. Jost, and Sharareh Noorbaloochi, "Another Look at Moral Foundations Theory: Do Authoritarianism and Social Dominance Orientation Explain Liberal-Conservative Differences in 'Moral' Intuitions?," *Social Justice Research* 27, no. 4 (November 16, 2014): 413–31, https://doi.org/10.1007/s11211-014-0223-5, 416.
55. Skurka et al., "Things Being Equal," 376, 381; Atari et al., "Morality Beyond," 1171, 1180; Wil Arts and John Gelissen, "Welfare States, Solidarity and Justice Principles: Does the Type Really Matter?," *Acta Sociologica* 44, no. 4 (December 2001): 283–99, https://doi.org/10.1177/000169930104400401.
56. Reagan, "Farewell Address."
57. "News Conference by President Obama, 4/04/2009," National Archives and Records Administration, April 4, 2009, https://obamawhitehouse.archives.gov/the-press-office/news-conference-president-obama-4042009.
58. Atari et al., "Morality Beyond," 1171.
59. Haidt, *Righteous Mind*, 356–7.
60. Ravi Iyer, Spassena Koleva, Jesse Graham, Peter Ditto, and Jonathan Haidt, "Understanding Libertarian Morality: The Psychological Dispositions of Self-Identified Libertarians," *PLOS ONE* 7, no. 8 (August 21, 2012), https://doi.org/10.1371/journal.pone.0042366.
61. Haidt, *Righteous Mind*, 352.
62. Iyer et al., "Libertarian Morality," 8.
63. Iyer et al., "Libertarian Morality," 8, 12, 15.
64. Ronald Bailey and Marian L. Tupy, *Ten Global Trends Every Smart Person Should Know: And Many Others You Will Find Interesting* (Cato Institute, 2020); Steven Pinker, *Enlightenment Now: The Case for Reason, Science, Humanism, and Progress* (Penguin Books, 2019).
65. "History's hockey stick: Real gross domestic product per capita using the ratio scale," Our World in Data, 2018, https://ourworldindata.org/grapher/historys-hockey-stick-gross-domestic-product-per-capita-using-the-ratio-scale-1990; Don Boudreaux, "The Hockey Stick of Human Prosperity," YouTube, posted June 24, 2014, https://www.youtube.com/watch?v=t9FSnvtcEbg; "History's Hockey Stick: Growth in Income," The Economy 1.0, 2017, https://core-econ.org/the-economy/v1/book/text/01.html.
66. Arthur C. Brooks, *The Conservative Heart: How to Build a Fairer, Happier, and More Prosperous America* (Broadside Books, 2015).
67. Joshua Bandoch, "Expanding Alternative Housing Will Make Chicago More

Affordable," *Crain's Chicago Business*, September 24, 2024, https://www.chicagobusiness.com/opinion/key-affordable-housing-could-be-adus-illinois-policy-op-ed.

68. Joshua Bandoch and LyLena Estabine, "Coach Houses, Other Accessory Dwelling Units Would Boost Housing Equity in Black Neighborhoods," *Chicago Sun-Times*, November 4, 2024, https://chicago.suntimes.com/other-views/2024/11/04/accessory-dwelling-units-black-neighborhoods-housing-equity-bandoch-illinois-policy-institute.

CHAPTER 6

1. For a summary of the report, see "Nielsen's State of Play Report Reveals That Streaming Is the Future, but Consumers Are Currently Overwhelmed by Choice," Nielsen, April 6, 2022, https://www.nielsen.com/news-center/2022/nielsens-state-of-play-report-reveals-that-streaming-is-the-future-but-consumers-are-currently-overwhelmed-by-choice/.
2. Nielsen, "Streaming Unwrapped: Streaming Viewership Goes to the Library in 2023," January 2024, https://www.nielsen.com/insights/2024/streaming-unwrapped-streaming-viewership-goes-to-the-library-in-2023/.
3. Haidt, *Righteous Mind*, 328.
4. Yuval Noah Harari, *Sapiens: A Brief History of Humankind* (HarperCollins, 2015), 34.
5. Robin Dunbar, *Grooming, Gossip, and the Evolution of Language* (Harvard University Press, 1998).
6. R. I. Dunbar, Ben Teasdale, Jackie Thompson, Felix Budelmann, Sophie Duncan, Evert van Emde Boas, et al., "Emotional Arousal When Watching Drama Increases Pain Threshold and Social Bonding," *Royal Society Open Science* 3, no. 9 (September 2016), https://doi.org/10.1098/rsos.160288.
7. Jonathan Gottschall, *The Story Paradox: How Our Love of Storytelling Builds Societies and Tears Them Down* (Basic Books, 2021), 26.
8. Antonio Damasio, *Self Comes to Mind: Constructing the Conscious Brain* (Pantheon, 2010), 293.
9. Joseph Campbell, *The Hero with a Thousand Faces* (New World Library, 1949), 41-48.
10. David Robinson, "Examining the Arc of 100,000 Stories: A Tidy Analysis," *Variance Explained*, April 26, 2017, http://varianceexplained.org/r/tidytext-plots/.
11. Chip Heath and Dan Heath, *Made to Stick: Why Some Ideas Survive and Others Die* (Random House, 2007), 226–7.
12. Heath and Heath, *Made to Stick*, 228.
13. Heath and Heath, *Made to Stick*, 229.
14. Arthur C. Brooks, "The 3 Equations for a Happy Life, Even During a Pandemic," *The Atlantic*, April 9, 2020, https://www.theatlantic.com/family/archive/2020/04/how-increase-happiness-according-research/609619/.
15. Peter G. Christenson, Silvia de Haan-Rietdijk, Donald F. Roberts, and Tom F. M. ter

Bogt, "What Has America Been Singing About? Trends in Themes in the U.S. Top-40 Songs: 1960–2010," *Psychology of Music* 47, no. 2 (January 23, 2018): 194–212, https://doi.org/10.1177/0305735617748205.

16. Heath and Heath, *Made to Stick*, 28.
17. Heath and Heath, *Made to Stick*, 16.
18. Ronald Reagan, "Tear Down This Wall," The History Place: Great Speeches collection, accessed June 4, 2025, https://www.historyplace.com/speeches/reagan-tear-down.htm.
19. "President John F. Kennedy's Inaugural Address," National Archives and Records Administration, accessed June 4, 2025, https://www.archives.gov/milestone-documents/president-john-f-kennedys-inaugural-address.
20. Heath and Heath, *Made to Stick*, 16, 64, 68.
21. Heath and Heath, *Made to Stick*, 16.
22. Heath and Heath, *Made to Stick*, 106.
23. Heath and Heath, *Made to Stick*, 17.
24. Immanuel Kant, *Groundwork of the Metaphysics of Morals*, ed. Mary Gregor (Cambridge University Press, 1997), 31.
25. Martin Luther King Jr., *A Testament of Hope: The Essential Writings and Speeches* (HarperCollins, 1991).
26. Kahneman, *Thinking*, 87.
27. Heath and Heath, *Made to Stick*, 17–18, 168.
28. Heath and Heath, *Made to Stick*, 179.
29. The Institute for Justice's John Kramer shared this formula with me, and he has truly mastered using it.
30. Dale Carnegie, *How to Win Friends and Influence People* (Simon & Schuster, 1936), 182.
31. "Working with the Media," Institute for Justice, accessed October 11, 2022, https://ij.org/report/entrepreneurs-survival-guide/working-with-the-media/.
32. "Medal of Honor Hall of Heroes Induction Ceremony: Tech Sgt John A. Chapman, USAF," DVIDS, August 23, 2018, https://www.dvidshub.net/video/620841medal-honor-hall-heroes-induction-ceremony-tech-sgt-john-chapman-usaf.
33. Gottschall, *Story Paradox*, 13.
34. John Gardner, *On Moral Fiction* (Basic Books, 1979), 39.
35. John Gardner, *The Art of Fiction: Notes on Craft for Young Writers* (Vintage, 1991), 87.
36. Gottschall, *Story Paradox*, 128.
37. Raymond A. Mar, "The Neuropsychology of Narrative: Story Comprehension, Story Production and Their Interrelation," *Neuropsychologia* 42, no. 10 (January 2004): 1414–34, https://doi.org/10.1016/j.neuropsychologia.2003.12.016, 1425.

NOTES

CHAPTER 7

1. "Sympathy," American Psychological Association, accessed November 10, 2022, https://dictionary.apa.org/sympathy.
2. "Empathy," American Psychological Association, accessed November 10, 2022, https://dictionary.apa.org/empathy.
3. Kathleen L. Valley, Joseph Moag, and Max H. Bazerman, "'A Matter of Trust': Effects of Communication on the Efficiency and Distribution of Outcomes," *Journal of Economic Behavior and Organization* 34, no. 2 (February 1998): 211–38, https://doi.org/10.1016/s0167-2681(97)00054-1.
4. Daniel Kahneman, Stephen J. Dubner, and Greg Rosalsky, "Episode 306: How to Launch a Behavior-Change Revolution," Freakonomics, October 25, 2017, https://frekonomics.com/podcast/how-to-launch-a-behavior-change-revolution/.
5. Camp, *Start with No*, 215.
6. Chris Voss with Tahl Raz, *Never Split the Difference: Negotiating as If Your Life Depended on It* (Harper Business, 2016), 65.
7. Voss, *Never Split*, 64, 72.
8. Kahneman, *Thinking*, 282. Emphasis added.
9. Baumeister et al., "Bad Is Stronger."
10. Mike Brooks, "How to Build Yes Momentum," Sales Gravy, Accessed November 24, 2025, https://salesgravy.com/how-to-build-yes-momentum/.
11. Roger Fisher, William L. Ury, and Bruce Patton, *Getting to Yes: Negotiating Agreement Without Giving In* (Penguin, 2011), 81.
12. Voss, *Never Split*, 80–81.
13. Camp, *Start with No*, 47.
14. Camp, *Start with No*, 45.
15. Voss, *Never Split*, 75.
16. Camp, *Start with No*, 48.
17. Voss, *Never Split*. Voss provides the Black Swan Group's top 10 no-oriented questions in "Three Types of Yeses."
18. Camp, *Start with No*, 124.
19. Stephen M. R. Covey, *The Speed of Trust: Why Trust Is the Ultimate Determinate of Success or Failure in Your Relationships, Career and Life* (Simon & Schuster, 2006).

CHAPTER 8

1. Mehrabian offers a summary of his research findings here: Albert Mehrabian, "'Silent Messages': A Wealth of Information About Nonverbal Communication (Body Language)," Personality & Communication: Psychological Books & Articles of Popular Interest, 2016, https://www.kaaj.com/psych/smorder.html; For an in-depth consideration

of his finding, see Albert Mehrabian, *Silent Messages: Implicit Communication of Emotions and Attitudes* (Wadsworth, 1981).

2. Moshe Bar, Maital Neta, and Heather Linz, "Very First Impressions," *Emotion* 6, no. 2, (2006): 269–78, https://doi.org/10.1037/1528-3542.6.2.269.
3. Jerry McLaughlin, "What Is a Brand, Anyway?," *Forbes*, January 9, 2012, https://www.forbes.com/sites/jerrymclaughlin/2011/12/21/what-is-a-brand-anyway/?sh=12b255cf2a1b.
4. R. Matthew Montoya, Robert S. Horton, and Jeffrey Kirchner, "Is Actual Similarity Necessary for Attraction? A Meta-Analysis of Actual and Perceived Similarity," *Journal of Social and Personal Relationships* 25, no. 6 (December 2008): 889–922, https://doi.org/10.1177/0265407508096700; See also Hampton et al. replicated the finding of a positive association between similarity and liking: Adam J. Hampton, Amanda Fisher Boyd, and Susan Sprecher, "You're Like Me and I Like You: Mediators of the Similarity-Liking Link Assessed Before and After a Getting-Acquainted Social Interaction," *Journal of Social and Personal Relationships* 36, no. 7 (July 2019): 2221–44, https://doi.org/10.1177/0265407518790411.
5. Carnegie, *How to Win Friends*, 105.
6. Guy Winch, "10 Ways to Become More Likable," *Psychology Today*, September 6, 2020, https://www.psychologytoday.com/us/blog/the-squeaky-wheel/202009/10-ways-become-more-likable; Rachel Gillett, "19 Simple Social Skills That Will Instantly Make You More Likable," *Business Insider*, February 7, 2018, https://www.businessinsider.com/how-to-be-more-likable-2017-12; Brianna Wiest, "How to Be the Most Likable Person in the Room," *Forbes*, December 11, 2018, https://www.forbes.com/sites/briannawiest/2018/12/11/how-to-be-the-most-likable-person-in-the-room/?sh=386761b26642; Deep Patel, "10 Ways to Become a Super-Likable Person," *Entrepreneur*, April 28, 2017, https://www.entrepreneur.com/leadership/10-ways-to-become-a-super-likable-person/293343; Travis Bradberry, "13 Habits of Exceptionally Likeable People," TalentSmartEQ, February 14, 2023, https://www.talentsmarteq.com/13-habits-of-exceptionally-likeable-people/.
7. Todd B. Kashdan and John E. Roberts, "Trait and State Curiosity in the Genesis of Intimacy: Differentiation from Related Constructs," *Journal of Social and Clinical Psychology* 23, no. 6 (December 2004): 792–816, https://doi.org/10.1521/jscp.23.6.792.54800.
8. Todd B. Kashdan, Patrick E. McKnight, Frank D. Fincham, and Paul Rose, "When Curiosity Breeds Intimacy: Taking Advantage of Intimacy Opportunities and Transforming Boring Conversations," *Journal of Personality* 79, no. 6 (October 19, 2011): 1369–1402, https://doi.org/10.1111/j.1467-6494.2010.00697.x.
9. Todd B. Kashdan, Ryne A. Sherman, Jessica Yarbro, and David C. Funder, "How Are Curious People Viewed and How Do They Behave in Social

Situations? From the Perspectives of Self, Friends, Parents, and Unacquainted Observers," *Journal of Personality* 81, no. 2 (February 5, 2013): 142–54, https://doi.org/10.1111/j.1467-6494.2012.00796.x.

10. Todd B. Kashdan and John E. Roberts, "Affective Outcomes in Superficial and Intimate Interactions: Roles of Social Anxiety and Curiosity," *Journal of Research in Personality* 40, no. 2 (April 2006): 140–67, https://doi.org/10.1016/j.jrp.2004.10.005.
11. "Tone," Cambridge Dictionary, accessed April 18, 2022, https://dictionary.cambridge.org/us/dictionary/english/tone.
12. Phil McAleer, Alexander Todorov, and Pascal Belin, "How Do You Say 'Hello'? Personality Impressions from Brief Novel Voices," *PLOS ONE* 9, no. 3 (March 12, 2014), https://doi.org/10.1371/journal.pone.0090779.
13. Alex B. Van Zant and Jonah Berger, "How the Voice Persuades," *Journal of Personality and Social Psychology* 118, no. 4 (April 2020): 661–82, https://doi.org/10.1037/pspi0000193.
14. Michael W. Kraus, "Voice-Only Communication Enhances Empathic Accuracy," *American Psychologist* 72, no. 7 (October 2017): 644–54, https://doi.org/10.1037/amp0000147.
15. Md Nasir, Wei Xia, Bo Xiao, Brian Baucom, Shrikanth S. Narayanan, and Panayiotis G. Georgiou, "Still Together?: The Role of Acoustic Features in Predicting Marital Outcome," *Interspeech 2015*, September 6, 2015, 2499–503, https://doi.org/10.21437/interspeech.2015-539; Md Nasir, Brian Robert Baucom, Panayiotis Georgiou, and Shrikanth Narayanan, "Predicting Couple Therapy Outcomes Based on Speech Acoustic Features," *PLOS ONE* 12, no. 9 (September 21, 2017), https://doi.org/10.1371/journal.pone.0185123.
16. Xin (Shane) Wang, Shijie Lu, X. I. Li, Mansur Khamitov, and Neil Bendle, "Audio Mining: The Role of Vocal Tone in Persuasion," *Journal of Consumer Research* 48, no. 2 (February 23, 2021): 189–211.
17. Voss, *Never Split*, 31–33.
18. Andrew Huberman, "How to Succeed at Hard Conversations," YouTube, posted October 2, 2023, https://www.youtube.com/watch?v=q8CHXefn7B4.
19. McAleer et al., Personality Impressions from Brief Novel Voices," *PLoS ONE* 9, no. 3 (March 12, 2014), https://doi.org/10.1371/journal.pone.0090779.
20. Wang et al., "Audio Mining."
21. Joe Navarro with Marvin Karlins, *What Every Body Is Saying: An Ex-FBI Agent's Guide to Speed Reading People* (HarperCollins, 2008), 2, 4.
22. Edward T. Hall, *The Hidden Dimension* (Anchor, 1990); Mark L. Knapp, Judith A. Hall, and Terrence G. Horgan, *Nonverbal Communication in Human Interaction*, 9th ed. (Kendall Hunt Publishing Company, 2021).
23. Carol Kinsey Gorman, "Great Leaders Talk with Their Hands," *Forbes*, published

September 21, 2010, updated June 19, 2013, https://www.forbes.com/2010/09/21/body-language-hands-gestures-forbes-woman-leadership-communication.html.

24. Navarro, *What Every Body*, 147; Joe Navarro, "Ex-FBI Agent Joe Navarro on the Most Powerful Behavior to Display Confidence," 21 Studios, YouTube, August 31, 2018, https://www.youtube.com/watch?v=ul62bMCP2Ec.
25. Linda Talley and Samuel Temple, "Silent Hands: A Leader's Ability to Create Nonverbal Immediacy," *Journal of Social, Behavioral, and Health Sciences* 12, no. 1 (2018): 129, 130–32, https://doi.org/10.5590/JSBHS.2018.12.1.09.
26. Navarro, *What Every Body*, 101.
27. Navarro, *What Every Body*, 111.
28. Navarro, *What Every Body*, 175.
29. Navarro, *What Every Body*, 176.
30. Paul Hömke, Stephen C. Levinson, Alexandra K. Emmendorfer, and Judith Holler, "Eyebrow Movements as Signals of Communicative Problems in Human Face-to-Face Interaction," *Royal Society Open Science* 12, no. 3 (2025), https://doi.org/10.1098/rsos.241632.
31. Haidt, *Righteous Mind*, 273. Emphasis added.
32. Kahneman, *Thinking*, 91.
33. Jana Nikitin and Alexandra M. Freund, "The Motivational Power of the Happy Face," *Brain Sciences* 9, no. 1 (January 7, 2019): 6, https://doi.org/10.3390/brainsci9010006.
34. Tara L. Kraft and Sarah D. Pressman, "Grin and Bear It," *Psychological Science* 23, no. 11 (September 24, 2012): 1372–78, https://doi.org/10.1177/0956797612445312.
35. Laura Mieth, Raoul Bell, and Axel Buchner, "Facial Likability and Smiling Enhance Cooperation, but Have No Direct Effect on Moralistic Punishment," *Experimental Psychology* 63, no. 5 (September 2016): 263–77, https://doi.org/10.1027/1618-3169/a000338.
36. Damasio, *Descartes' Error*, 142.
37. Rebecca Joy Stanborough, "What Is a Duchenne Smile and How Can It Influence Other People?" Healthline, June 29, 2019, https://www.healthline.com/health/duchenne-smile.
38. Yevgen Bogodistov and Florian Dost, "Proximity Begins with a Smile, but Which One? Associating Non-Duchenne Smiles with Higher Psychological Distance," *Frontiers in Psychology* 8 (August 9, 2017), https://doi.org/10.3389/fpsyg.2017.01374.
39. Navarro, *What Every Body*, 88.
40. Zloteanu Mircea tr: Mircea Zloteanu, Eva G. Krumhuber, and Daniel C. Richardson, "Sitting in Judgment: How Body Posture Influences Deception Detection and Gazing Behavior," *Behavioral Sciences* 11, no. 6 (2021): 85, https://doi.org/10.3390/bs11060085.
41. Navarro, *What Every Body*, 192.

42. Ellie Lisitsa, "The Research: Predicting Divorce from an Oral History Interview," The Gottman Institute, September 23, 2024, https://www.gottman.com/blog/the-research-predicting-divorce-from-an-oral-history-interview/; for the original study: John M. Gottman and Robert W. Levenson, "Marital Processes Predictive of Later Dissolution: Behavior, Physiology, and Health," *Journal of Personality and Social Psychology* 63, no. 2 (1992): 221–33, https://doi.org/10.1037/0022-3514.63.2.221.
43. Tara Parker-Pope, "Can Eye-Rolling Ruin a Marriage? Researchers Study Divorce Risk," *The Wall Street Journal*, August 6, 2002, https://www.wsj.com/articles/SB1028578553586958760; Eva Van Prooyen, "This One Thing Is the Biggest Predictor of Divorce," The Gottman Institute, June 26, 2024, https://www.gottman.com/blog/this-one-thing-is-the-biggest-predictor-of-divorce/; Ellie Lisitsa, "The Four Horsemen: Contempt," The Gottman Institute, October 10, 2025, https://www.gottman.com/blog/the-four-horsemen-contempt/.
44. Allan Paivio and Kalman Csapo, "Picture Superiority in Free Recall: Imagery or Dual Coding?," *Cognitive Psychology* 5, no. 2 (1973): 176–206.
45. Kiwon Seo, "Meta-Analysis on Visual Persuasion: Does Adding Images to Texts Influence Persuasion?," *Athens Journal of Mass Media and Communications* 6 (2020):177–90.

CHAPTER 9

1. Milton Friedman, "I, Pencil," posted July 31, 2012, by Free to Choose Network, https://www.youtube.com/watch?v=67tHtpac5ws.
2. Daniel M. Oppenheimer, "Consequences of Erudite Vernacular Utilized Irrespective of Necessity: Problems with Using Long Words Needlessly," *Applied Cognitive Psychology* 20, no. 2 (2006): 153, https://doi.org/10.1002/acp.1178.
3. Heath and Heath, *Made to Stick*, 20.
4. This seems to be an attempt at paraphrasing something he said in a 1933 lecture: "It can scarcely be denied that the supreme goal of all theory is to make the irreducible basic elements as simple and as few as possible without having to surrender the adequate representation of a single datum of experience." Andrew Robinson, "Did Einstein Really Say That?," *Nature*, April 30, 2018, https://www.nature.com/articles/d41586-018-05004-4.
5. Gary Keller and Jay Papasan, *The ONE Thing: The Surprisingly Simple Truth Behind Extraordinary Results* (Bard Press, 2013) 106. Throughout the book the authors write the phrase as "ONE Thing." I follow their practice.
6. Keller and Papasan, *ONE Thing*, 115–116.
7. Winston Churchill, "We Shall Fight on the Beaches," International Churchill Society, accessed August 12, 2025, https://winstonchurchill.org/resources/speeches/1940-the-finest-hour/we-shall-fight-on-the-beaches/.
8. Orwell, "Politics and the English Language," 363.

Index

INDEX

INDEX

INDEX

INDEX

INDEX

INDEX

INDEX

About the Author

MNPhotoStudios

Persuasion expert **Joshua Bandoch** has spent over a decade uncovering the secrets of persuasion. His proven approach is grounded in extensive neuroscience and psychology research and practical experience writing hundreds of speeches for and consulting with senior officials, executives, and professionals in dozens of industries as well as his own speaking, including his TEDx talk on persuasion. Bandoch uses and refines these persuasion techniques on a daily basis as a think tank leader, where he crafts and communicates policies on issues like poverty, social mobility, education, and the economy to politically diverse audiences, including elected officials, local and national media, and grassroots activists.